[redacted]



# IMPRISONMENT: THE LEGAL STATUS AND RIGHTS OF PRISONERS

[redacted]

AUSTRALIA AND NEW ZEALAND
The Law Book Company Ltd
Sydney: Melbourne: Perth

CANADA AND U.S.A.
The Carswell Company Ltd.
Agincourt, Ontario

INDIA
N.M. Tripathi Private Ltd.
Bombay
*and*
Eastern Law House Private Ltd.
Calcutta and Delhi
M.P.P. House
Bangalore

ISRAEL
Steimatzky's Agency Ltd.
Jerusalem: Tel Aviv: Haifa

# IMPRISONMENT: THE LEGAL STATUS AND RIGHTS OF PRISONERS

G. D. TREVERTON-JONES
M.A. (OXON)
*of the Inner Temple, Barrister*

LONDON
SWEET & MAXWELL
1989

Published in 1989 by
Sweet & Maxwell Limited of
11 New Fetter Lane, London
Computerset by
CCI Technical Services Limited
Hitchin, Herts.
Printed in Scotland

British Library Cataloguing in
Publications Data

Treverton-Jones, G.D.
Imprisonment: The Legal Status and
Rights of Prisoners
1 England. Imprisonment. Law
I Title
344.205.773

ISBN 0-421-32230-6

# PREFACE

"The mood and temper of the public with regard to the treatment of crime and criminals is one of the most unfailing tests of the civilisation of any country." W.S. Churchill.

Prisons have existed in England for over a thousand years. Imprisonment is the most serious form of punishment still regularly available. Yet until 1978 judicial intervention in prison life was virtually non–existent. The authorities administered prisons under a series of Prison Acts and Rules, with the courts declining to interfere.

All this changed with the rash of cases produced by the Hull prison riot of the late summer of 1976. Of greatest importance was the Court of Appeal decision in *ex p. St. Germain*. Henceforth, disciplinary hearings by Boards of Visitors would be subject to judicial review. Ten years later the House of Lords held that the same applied to disciplinary decisions by prison governors. The speed of change had by then quickened, with the Divisional Court decision in *ex p. Tarrant* that Boards of Visitors could permit legal representation at hearings. Meanwhile, both English and European judges were emphasising the importance of unfettered access by prisoners to legal advice and to the courts. As a result, the last decade has seen a vast increase in litigation by aggrieved prisoners.

This book attempts to describe these and other developments, and to summarise the law as it is, not as it should be. It is regrettable and a little absurd that prisoners complaining of ill–treatment should be forced to seek to rely upon a 300 year old statute, the Bill of Rights. Detailed consideration by the House of Lords of the precise status of and rights conferred by the Prison Rules is long overdue. The Rules themselves are to be brought more into line with their European equivalents. Pressure for changes in the disciplinary system will continue, despite the Government's loss of enthusiasm for the recommendations of the Prior Committee. Problems caused by overcrowding, staffing difficulties, lengthening sentences, and an increasingly aware prison population, will ensure that prisoners' rights remain fertile ground for important judicial decisions.

Many people over many years have helped in the writing of this book, both consciously and unconsciously. To the latter category belong Guy and Helen Hordern, Neil Johnson, Gunda Sjoberg, David French and Leonard Deas. In the former, Geoffrey Nice made initial introductions and suggestions; Peter Birts (twice), Caroline Jenkins, and Neil Johnson read the manuscript, each making invaluable suggestions from his or her own standpoint, as lawyer, writer, and prison governor, respectively. Lesley Shallcross provided idyllic Cotswold surroundings for some of the later work. Claire Jenkins and Nigel Pleming proved to be mines of useful information. The staff at Sweet and Maxwell watched with amused tolerance as deadlines drifted by, without delivery of the manuscript. Jenny Lemkey laboured skilfully and enthusiastically over the indexes. To all, my heartfelt thanks, with the usual proviso in books of this sort, that errors and omissions remain my responsibility alone.

The law is stated as at September 1, 1988, although two subsequent decisions can be briefly mentioned here. The House of Lords allowed the Home Secretary's appeal in *ex p. Read*, *The Times*, November 5, 1988 (see pp. 144–147), holding that the Home Secretary was empowered only to reduce the foreign sentence to the English maximum for the equivalent offence. In *R* v. *Home Secretary ex p. Benson*, *The Times*, November 21, 1988, the Divisional Court showed again, as in *ex p. Handscomb* (see pp. 152, 160), that it was prepared to scrutinise the Home Secretary's exercise of discretion in dealing with the release of a life sentence prisoner. Finally, *Weeks* v. *United Kingdom* is now reported at (1988) E.H.R.R. 293.

G. D. Treverton-Jones<br>Farrar's Building<br>The Temple.

## A NOTE ON THE CRIMINAL JUSTICE ACT 1988

Section 123 of the Criminal Justice Act, which came into force on October 1, 1988, has abolished the distinction between youth custody sentences and detention centre orders. These are replaced by a sentence of detention in a young offender institution. The preconditions for passing such a sentence are much the same as those which applied to its two predecessors. The relevant ages are 14–20 inclusive for males, and 15–20 inclusive for females. The maximum term for such a sentence is the maximum term of imprisonment which could be imposed for the offence, subject to the following:

(i) The maximum aggregate term for an offender under 15 is 4 months.
(ii) The maximum aggregate term for an offender aged 15 or 16 is 12 months.

The normal minimum term is 21 days, or four months and a day in the case of a female aged 15 or 16.

An offender sentenced to detention in a young offender institution must be detained in such an institution unless the Home Secretary directs that he shall be held in a prison or remand centre: if the offender is under 17 at the time of such direction, detention in the prison or remand centre can be for a temporary purpose only.

The treatment of those subject to the new sentence is regulated by the Young Offender Institution Rules (S.I. 1988 No. 1422), which also came into force on October 1, 1988. The amendments made by the Prison (Amendment) No. 3 Rules (S.I. 1988 No. 1421) have been incorporated in the Rules at Appendix 1.

## CONTENTS

CONTENTS

# TABLE OF CASES

# TABLE OF STATUTES

*Chapter 1*

# HISTORY AND STRUCTURE OF THE PRISON SYSTEM



## History of the Use of Imprisonment

Imprisonment is as old as civilisation itself, although the reasons for its use have varied through the ages. The first written evidence of imprisonment in Britain dates from the ninth century. In its early days its purpose was to remove the king's enemies from circulation and mischief, rather than to punish conventional law breakers. For the latter there was a wide range of corporal punishments, such as branding, whipping, and execution. By the eleventh century however, sheriff's prisons had started to develop, as had the practice of imprisonment pending trial.

In mediaeval Britain there was no form of central control or organisation of prisons. Sheriffs, local corporations, individual franchise holders, and the Church all operated and maintained gaols. The day-to-day running of these institutions was delegated to the gaoler who either bought his position or ran the gaol on a profit-sharing basis with its owner or franchise holder. There were thus obvious opportunities for profiteering and ill-treating of prisoners. These opportunities were often taken: many prisoners died of starvation, thirst and disease.

The political and religious upheavals of the sixteenth and seventeenth centuries led to a large increase in the numbers held in gaols. Those who offended against the state were usually sent to the Tower of London, but conventional crime increased too, as did the mobility of the population. Houses of Correction sprang up as workhouses for the able-bodied and unemployed, although they had not necessarily committed any offence. The Houses of Correction imposed compulsory labour and rigid discipline, and were prisons to all intents and purposes.[1] During the seventeenth century the system of transportation to the colonies commenced, thus relieving pressure upon prison accommodation, and providing an effective alternative to imprisonment.

Two particular problems at about this time are worthy of brief note. First, prisoners held on remand were subjected to unacceptably long delays before their trial. The Habeas Corpus Act of 1679 helped to alleviate this hardship. Secondly, and in human terms even more unacceptable, a large number of prisoners were debtors, many of whom were in gaol for debts of small sums. However, because prisoners were required to pay for their board and lodging, and because many gaolers made extortionate demands, imprisonment often achieved the opposite of its purpose, and the prisoner fell further into debt. This illogical situation led to some limited legislative intervention during the first half of the eighteenth century.

From around the second half of the seventeenth century the speed of change in the prison system quickened. Humanitarian interest in the plight of prisoners grew, and experiments in penal methods were made. From 1773 John Howard, high sheriff of Bedfordshire, carried out an extensive survey of prisons in Western Europe. He saw at first hand the appalling conditions in which prisoners were held, and the effect of a privately operated, profit-making prison system. Reforms were made by followers of Howard, particularly by Sir George Paul in Gloucestershire, who introduced visits to prisoners by the governor, warders, a doctor and a chaplain. Other prison reformers helped to improve the conditions of prisoners, most notably Elizabeth Fry, whose work at Newgate prison from 1816 lasted for nearly 30 years.

The American War of Independence between 1776 and 1783 caused a temporary end to transportation, and a corresponding

[1] The distinction between the two was not formally abolished until the Prison Act 1865, although for practical purposes the distinction had largely disappeared in the seventeenth century.

increase in the number of prisoners who had to be accommodated in Britain. A 1776 Act substituted sentences of hard labour of three to 10 years for criminals who would formerly have been transported to America. Where were these men to be held? The justices of Middlesex appointed Duncan Campbell to operate the system of hard labour, and he acquired two old ships in which to house the prisoners. Other hulks were acquired later. Conditions aboard these boats were generally miserable. During the day the prisoners would work in chain gangs to raise gravel from the Thames, and at night they would return to the hulks. At the height of their use, in the late 1820s, nearly 500 prisoners were held aboard the hulks; 30 years later this part of the prison "system" had come to an end.

Although the American War of Independence led to the loss of the American colonies as a receptacle for British prisoners, Captain Cook's voyages to Australia opened up an alternative. The first convict ships set sail for Australia in 1787. At the end of the eighteenth century there were thus three means of punishment for the most serious offenders; execution, transportation, or imprisonment in a local prison.

**The move towards centralisation**

The 1791 Gaols Act legislated for all prisons in England for the first time. This Act required justices to inspect, maintain and manage prisons, and marked the first step towards a unified national prison system, although it was nearly a century before such a system evolved. Further progress was made in 1815 with the abolition of prison fees, and in 1818, when, for the first time, annual returns had to be made to the Home Secretary. Next, after the appointment of Robert Peel as Home Secretary, came the Prison Act of 1823. This represented the first example of conscious penal reform by Parliament. It provided for the inspection of prisons by justices, and regular reporting by them to the Home Office. Unfortunately, the Act applied to only a minority of institutions; 150 gaols in the boroughs were excluded.

In 1816 the government started to construct a new prison at Millbank. This was finally completed five years later at vast expense. It marked the beginning of a split prison system: the "central service" was to consist of Millbank, the prison hulks, and later, a large number of new "convict prisons," built around the middle of the nineteenth century. This part of the prison system was administered by a Board of Directors. Meanwhile, the "local service" remained in existence, consisting of local prisons controlled by local justices. The latter were required to make rules for the management of these prisons.

The 1823 Act was unsuccessful in effecting the uniformity which Parliament desired, but it had at least pointed the way, and another Prison Act of 1835 continued this process. The twin objects of this Act were to achieve greater uniformity in prison administration, and to appoint prison inspectors. Five such inspectors were appointed initially. They published reports, an important weapon for them as they had no jurisdiction to impose their recommendations upon local justices. The 1830s and 1840s saw increasing government control over the design of new prisons and the renovation of old ones.

In 1842 a new convict prison opened at Pentonville. The regime here and at Millbank was based upon the separation of prisoners from each other: American experiments in penal reform had caused great interest in England, particularly those involving the principles of separation and seclusion, and, in some instances, a rule of complete silence. For instance, in later years, Pentonville was used to hold convicts who were awaiting transportation, and to "cure" these prisoners of their criminality before the journey: the method adopted was to place prisoners in solitary confinement for many months.

Meanwhile the search for uniformity continued. The Prison Act 1865 resulted from the recommendations of an important House of Lords select committee. It made further inroads into local authority autonomy over prisons, empowering the Home Secretary to close inadequate prisons. It established a detailed code of rules, obliging the gaoler to visit his prison daily, to see every prisoner, and to make nocturnal visits at least once a week.

During the mid-nineteenth century opinion swung against transportation, which was regarded as expensive, an inducement to crime, and a disincentive to voluntary emigration. By the end of the 1850s it had virtually ceased, as had the hulk system. These changes led to the construction of the large number of new prisons built in the 1840s, and the 1865 Act required local authorities to erect separate cells for all prisoners.

**1877 and after: the modern system**

In 1864 a Conservative government was returned to office, committed to reducing local rates. One method of doing this would be to remove the control of local prisons from the hands of the local authorities. The most radical penal reform of the century was thus inspired by a simple election promise. The 1877 Prison Act transferred every aspect of prison administration to the Home Secretary. Actual administration was delegated to a new body, the Prison Commission. The existing inspectorate was to continue, but both the commissioners and the inspectors were government appointees. Local prisons were placed under central government for the first time, and the role of the justices was relegated to visiting and inspecting the prisons within their jurisdiction. Another new body, the Visiting Committee, was to be appointed by Quarter Sessions or Benches of Magistrates. The immediate result of this legislation was a drastic reduction in the number of local prisons, and although local authorities were entitled to buy discontinued local prisons, few actually did so.

The first Chairman of the Prison Commissioners was Sir Edmund DuCane, who had been the Chairman of the Board of Directors of the convict prisons since 1869. The two bodies merged effectively, although formal merger did not take place until 1898. The first 20 years of the newly centralised system were dominated by DuCane, who can be said to have created the modern prison service, basing the staff structure upon military lines. However, his reforms, while achieving a measure of uniformity, also caused austerity and misery, and when the Gladstone committee commenced its deliberations, the time was ripe for a radical reappraisal of the aims and conditions of imprisonment.

The Gladstone committee report of 1895 was another important influence upon subsequent penal developments and the approach to imprisonment. Until the report, the prime task of the prison system had been seen as the deterrence from crime, and the control of inmates. The committee however started "from the principle that prison treatment should have as its primary and concurrent objects deterrence and reformation." It recommended reconsideration of the separate and silent systems in prison, and its influence can be seen in many of the reforms of the twentieth century.

DuCane retired at the time that the committee's report was published, being succeeded by the more liberal Sir Evelyn Ruggles-Brise, who held the post until 1921. Another major piece of legislation, the Prison Act 1898, established boards of visitors for the convict prisons, and enabled the Home Secretary to make Rules for all categories of prison. After the retirement of Ruggles-Brise, the most influential prison commissioner (though never the chairman) was Alexander Paterson, appointed in 1922. He was responsible for many reforms in prison and borstal conditions. By the Criminal Justice Act 1948 sentences of penal servitude and hard labour were abolished, leaving a single streamlined sentence of imprisonment. The 1960s saw the abolition of corporal and capital punishment, and the rash of prison escapes which led to the Mountbatten Report. Administratively, the Prison Commissioners were replaced by the prison department of the Home Office, and visiting committees were rendered obsolete by the enactment of the Courts Act 1971.

The post-war years witnessed a vast proliferation in non-custodial alternatives to imprisonment, together with attempts to curtail the actual time spent in custody by those sentenced to terms of imprisonment, most notably by the introduction of parole in 1968. In the face of this, one of the ironies of the age has been the remorseless increase in the prison population. The implications of this fall outside the scope of this book.

## Structure of the Prison System

### Sources of law

The legislative base upon which the prison system of England and Wales is constructed is the Prison Act 1952, which repealed and consolidated a number of earlier enactments.[2] The Act contains a broad range of provisions dealing with most aspects of prison administration, including the personnel of the prison service, and the confinement and treatment of prisoners. Section 47 empowers the Home Secretary to make rules for the regulation and management of penal institutions and "for the classification, treatment, employment, discipline and control of prisoners," whilst by section 16 he is empowered to make regulations as to the measuring and photographing of prisoners. The exercise of most of these powers is effected by statutory instrument, which is subject to annulment by resolution of either House of Parliament. Further provisions dealing with the treatment and supervision of prisoners are to be found in the Criminal Justice Acts of 1961, 1967, 1972 and 1982, and the Repatriation of Prisoners Act 1984.

The principal rules made under the Act are the Prison Rules 1964; these have been the subject of a number of amendments, sometimes following adverse decisions by European judicial

[2] Principally the Prison Acts of 1865, 1877, 1894 and 1898.

bodies. The Prison Act requires that the rules made thereunder must make provision for ensuring that a prisoner charged with an offence under the rules has a proper opportunity to present his case, and must also provide for the special treatment of certain categories of prisoner. The 1964 Rules regulate all of the most important facets of prison life.

In addition to the Act and any rules made thereunder, there are a large number of standing orders formulated by the Prison Department of the Home Office, which provide instructions and guidance for those involved in prison administration. These exist to ensure so far as possible that consistency and uniformity are maintained throughout the system, together with compliance with the latest judicial decisions. The standing orders have no legislative force, although they have on occasion been held to be in breach of the Convention for the Protection of Human Rights and Fundamental Freedoms. They are not generally available outside the prison service.

**The Home Secretary**

Since the dissolution of the Prison Commissioners, the Home Secretary has been responsible for the superintendence of prisons, the making of contracts, and the other acts necessary for the maintenance of prisons and prisoners. In particular, he has the authority to make the rules and regulations and to appoint the personnel of the prison service. By section 5 of the Prison Act 1952 (and under the Prison Commissioners Dissolution Order 1963) he must make an annual report on every prison, which is then laid before Parliament. The report must contain statements as to accommodation, numbers, work and punishment. The Home Secretary has direct ministerial responsibility for every aspect of the work of the prison service, for, unlike many national civilian services, the prison service is directly administered as part of a Government Department. He also acts as a *de facto* "Court of Appeal" against decisions of governors.[3]

**The Prison Department of the Home Office**

The Department as a whole administers the prison system, and the Prisons Board within it formulates policy and takes the major decisions. The latter is composed of 12 members under the chairmanship of the Director General of the Prison Service, who is a deputy under-secretary, England and Wales are divided into four

[3] See p. 138–9, *infra*.

regions for administrative purposes (North, Midlands, South East, South West): each has a regional director who is one of the 12 members of the Prisons Board. Their prime function is to ensure the efficient running of the penal establishments in their area.

**Boards of Visitors**

Boards of Visitors were established for non-local prisons in 1898. At that time local prisons already had visiting committees, elected by the magistrates of Quarter Sessions. After Quarter Sessions were abolished in 1971, Boards of Visitors were appointed for local prisons. By section 6 of the Prison Act 1952 a Board of Visitors for each prison must be appointed by the Home Secretary. There are over 100 such Boards. The Act requires Board members to pay frequent visits to the prison and to hear prisoners' complaints. Rule 96(1) of the Prison Rules 1964 requires the Board to arrange a rota whereby one of its members visits the prison between meetings of the Board. The Board itself must meet at least eight times per year at the prison. The Rules require meetings once a month, but they also permit the Board to resolve to meet less frequently.

The size of each Board is a matter for the Home Secretary. At least two of its members must be magistrates. Board members usually hold office for three years. Its quorum may be fixed at a minimum of three members for the regular meetings described above, though different provisions apply to disciplinary adjudications.

At the end of each year the Board is required to make a report to the Home Secretary concerning the state of the prison and its administration, including any advice which it considers appropriate.

**Functions of the Board**

The functions of the Board are set out in Rules 92 to 97 of the Prison Rules 1964 as amended, although additional individual ones are found elsewhere in the Rules. They cover three main areas:

(i) *Visits and inspections*

The frequency of visits to the prison is set out above. The Rules provide that the members of the Board should arrange for prisoners' food to be inspected; should inquire into any report made to them (irrespective of its source) that a prisoner's health may be injuriously affected by prison conditions; and may permit prisoners additional letters or visits. This list is not exhaustive, but demonstrates the wide area of influence which the Board can have upon the internal administration of a prison.

Essentially, the Board can be seen as an independent body concerned to ensure the smooth and humane running of a penal establishment. To this end the Rules provide that members of the Board have free access to every part of the prison, to all prison records, and to every prisoner. The prisoner may be interviewed by a Board member out of the sight and hearing of any prison officer.

(ii) *Prisoners' complaints*

Requests by prisoners to see a member of the Board of Visitors must be recorded, and it is the prison governor's responsibility to ensure that the member is told of the request upon his next visit to the prison. The member is required by Rule 95 to hear any complaint which the prisoner wishes to make.

(iii) *Disciplinary hearings and adjudications*

In relation to the most serious disciplinary offences the prison governor is required by Rule 52(1) to refer the case to the Board of Visitors unless the Home Secretary otherwise directs. The Board then acts as the disciplinary tribunal, hearing and adjudicating upon the case against the prisoner, and awarding punishment in the event of the charge being proved.

It follows from the above that a Board of Visitors has two contrasting functions. As well as supervising the proper running of the establishment, it sits as the adjudicating authority in serious offences against discipline. This, it is submitted, is plainly unsatisfactory, establishing the Board in the prisoner's eyes as part of the administration of the prison, rather than as a truly independent body. Concern about the dual roles of the Boards led to an independent committee being set up by three organisations.[4] The report which emerged, the Jellicoe Report (1975), concluded that it was "doubtful whether justice was seen to be done" by Boards of Visitors.[5] The Home Secretary disagreed, and

[4] The Howard League for Penal Reform, Justice, and National Association for the Fare and Resettlement of Offenders.

[5] See Chapters 3, 4, 6 and 7.

in due course the Court of Appeal in the *Hull Prison* case emphasised the independence and impartiality of the Boards.[6]

However, one of the complaints made by the applicant Campbell in *Campbell and Fell* v. *United Kingdom*[7] was that Boards of Visitors were not "independent and impartial tribunals" as required by Article 6 of the European Convention. The European Commission in its report upheld this complaint, reasoning as follows. Members of the Board were appointed by the minister in charge of prison administration. The Board's watchdog function brought it into day-to-day contact with prison officials in such a way as to identify it with the prison administration. The European Court reversed this finding, concluding that the method of appointment did not undermine the Board's independence from the executive, and that the combination of the two roles did not affect this. In both capacities it was there to "hold the ring" between the parties. The perception by prisoners of the Boards of Visitors being closely associated with the executive "which is probably unavoidable in a custodial setting," although of greater weight, was insufficient to establish lack of independence.[8]

The European Commission's report in *Campbell and Fell*, and serious disturbances in British prisons during 1983, had led to the setting up of a Home Office committee in May 1984 to investigate and report upon prison disciplinary offences and the arrangements for their investigation, adjudication and punishment. The Committee's Report[9] was presented to Parliament in October 1985 and contained 100 recommendations. The most important was the proposal to abolish Boards of Visitors, and to replace them with Prison Disciplinary Tribunals, each consisting of a legally qualified chairman and two lay members. This recommendation was subsequently laid to rest by the Government, and the Boards obtained another reprieve, even though criticism of their dual role is manifestly well founded.[10]

[6] *R.* v. *Board of Visitors, Hull Prison ex p. St. Germain* [1979] Q.B. 425; [1979] 2 W.L.R. 42; [1979] 1 All E.R. 701.

[7] (1984) 7 E.H.R.R. 165 (European Court); (1982) 5 E.H.R.R. 207 (European Commission).

[8] See too *R.* v. *Board of Visitors of Frankland Prison, ex p. Lewis* [1986] 1 W.L.R. 130, [1986] 1 All ER 272.

[9] The Prior Committee Report on the Prison Disciplinary System, Cmnd. 9641, (1985).

[10] The boards themselves have endorsed the criticism.

**The prison governor**

By section 7 of the Prison Act 1952, every prison must have a governor who is appointed by and answerable to the Home Secretary. The governor is responsible for the daily maintenance of security, good order and discipline within the prison, the regime of the prison, the co-ordination of work by all members of staff, and the treatment and training of prisoners. Although Lord Justice Lawton has described the prison governor as "nothing more than a manager,"[11] this description is over-simplified. The governor, in addition to his managerial functions, has important quasi-judicial functions to perform in conducting disciplinary hearings. In practical terms the governor is accountable to his regional director: the latter is accountable to the deputy director general, the professional head of the prison service.

## THE EUROPEAN DIMENSION

(i) *Background*

Following the horrors and atrocities of the Second World War, a new attempt was made to ensure that individual human rights were protected by international, enforceable provisions. In December 1948 a Universal Declaration of Human Rights was adopted by the General Assembly of the United Nations. This laid down the standards to be observed by nations, but established no machinery for enforcing them. In May 1949 the Council of Europe was established, its aims being to safeguard the ideals and principles common to its members, particularly "the maintenance and further realisation of human rights and fundamental freedoms."

The Council of Europe drafted the European Convention on Human Rights, which was signed in Rome in November 1950, and which came into force on September 3, 1953. It is a treaty under which the signatory states accept certain duties, consisting mainly in recognising that individuals have certain rights. For the first time, an international treaty afforded the right of individual action to citizens who claimed that the rights safeguarded by the treaty had been violated. All 21 members of the Council of Europe (including the United Kingdom) are now parties to the Convention.

11 *R.* v. *Deputy Governor of Camp Hill Prison, ex p. King* [1985] Q.B. 735, C.A.; [1985] 2 W.L.R. 36; [1984] 3 All E.R. 897.

The Convention is composed of statements of the rights and freedoms which the contracting parties "shall secure to everyone within their jurisdiction." It provides that the protection of human rights asserted by it should be effected by three bodies; the Commission, the European Court of Human Rights, and the Council of Ministers.

Although the United Kingdom has recognised the right of individual petition since 1965, it has not yet incorporated the Convention into domestic law.[12] As a party to it, the United Kingdom undertakes that its law will not be inconsistent with the Convention. To the extent that the Government is found to be in violation of the Convention, it is obliged to take steps to bring its law into conformity with the requirements of the Convention.

(ii) *The machinery: (a) the European Commission*

Complaints of violations of the provisions of the European Convention are made to the Commission, the right of an individual to make such a complaint being conferred by Article 25 of the Convention. The Commission's first task is to decide whether the application is admissible, and in practice rejects the vast majority (over 90 per cent.) of applications as being inadmissible. Its decision on the question of admissibility is final. The most important preconditions of admissibility are as follows:

(a) All domestic remedies must have been exhausted. In the case of applications by prisoners, this requirement includes petitioning the Home Secretary.
(b) The application must be lodged within six months of the final domestic decision.
(c) The complaint must not be the same as one already examined by the Commission or previously submitted to another international body.
(d) The complaint must be covered by the scope of the Convention.

Once an application is received as admissible the Commission goes on to establish the facts and to try to secure a friendly settlement between the state and the applicant. When a settlement is reached, the proceedings are ended and the Commission publishes a Report. If no settlement emerges (as has invariably been the case with complaints by prisoners against the United Kingdom), the Commission draws up a report stating its opinion.

[12] There have been attempts to do so by private members' bills: all have failed.

This is reached by majority vote, and is sent to the Committee of Ministers. The latter body decides whether there has been a breach of the Convention.

The Commission is composed of jurists and lawyers, and its membership is equal to the number of states that have ratified the Convention. No two members may be nationals of the same state. They are elected by the Committee of Ministers, hold office for six years and may be re-elected. They are independent of their state of origin.

(iii) *The machinery: (b) the European Court*

Either the Commission or the government concerned in the application may refer the matter to the European Court within three months of the transmission of the Commission's report, provided that the state concerned has accepted the compulsory jurisdiction of the Court, or has accepted it for the particular case in question. The Court considers the Commission's report, together with the oral and written submissions of the state. The Court's judgment is final, and is pronounced in open court. It has the power to award compensation to the injured party.

Every member state of the Council of Europe has one judge in the Court. Judges are elected by the Parliamentary Assembly, hold office for nine years, and may be re-elected. As with the members of the Commission, they are independent of their state of origin. Cases are normally dealt with by a chamber of seven judges, but will be referred for hearing by the full court if a serious question of the interpretation of the Convention is involved.

(iv) *The machinery: (c) the Committee of Ministers*

Where a case is *not* referred to the Court, the Committee of Ministers decides whether or not there was a breach of the Convention. The Committee's decision is final and binding, and it also decides whether to publish the Commission's report. The Committee is composed of the foreign ministers of member states or their deputies.

There are other international provisions. The European Standard Minimum Rules for the Treatment of Prisoners were adopted by the Council of Europe in 1973, after an United Nations resolution in 1957. These Rules have been the subject of recent revision, and at the time of writing the English Prison Rules are being amended to bring them into closer conformity with the European Rules. The European Rules have no binding force under the Convention, but are intended to act as guidelines to the bodies referred to above. The International Covenant of Civil and Political Rights was drawn up in 1966 under the auspices of the United Nations, and contains rights similar to those contained in the European Convention. The United Kingdom has ratified this Covenant, but has not accepted the right of individual petition. Finally, the Body of Principles for the Protection of all Persons under any Form of Detention or Imprisonment has been adopted within the United Nations.

### Effect of the European Convention in English law

The Convention, being a treaty obligation, has no direct binding effect in domestic law. It has, nevertheless, played a significant part in the outcome of cases, and has been considered in some detail by the English courts. Its status was summarised by Lord Denning M.R.[13] in the following terms:

> "What is the position of the convention in our English law? . . . The court can and should take the convention into account whenever interpreting a statute which affects the rights and liberties of the individual. It is to be assumed that the Crown, in taking its part in legislation, would do nothing which is in conflict with treaties . . ."
>
> "If an Act of Parliament contained any provisions contrary to the convention, the Act of Parliament must prevail."
>
> "I should repeat that whenever anyone is considering a problem concerning human rights we should seek to solve it in the light of the convention and in conformity with it."

## CATEGORIES OF ADULT PENAL ESTABLISHMENTS

Within the penal system there is a wide range of institutions, of which the most important are set out below. It should be noted that more than one category of prison can be contained within the same establishment. The most striking example is that of Wormwood Scrubs Prison, which houses a local prison, a long term training prison, facilities for category 'A' prisoners (*i.e.* those of a maximum security establishment), and a remand centre.

13 R. v. *Home Secretary, ex p. Bhajan Singh* [1976] Q.B. 198; [1975] 3 W.L.R. 225, [1975] 2 All E.R. 1081.

(i) *Local and training prisons*

Every adult prison other than remand centres falls into one of these two basic categories. Upon conviction, the prisoner is received into a local prison, usually sited in a large or medium-sized town, and often constructed in the nineteenth century, which serves the local network of courts. At local prisons the categorisation and medical examination and treatment of prisoners is effected.

The great majority of sentences should be served in training prisons, which may be open or closed establishments. In 1987 there were 27 adult male local prisons, and 48 male training prisons, of which 38 were closed, and 10 open. The general policy of the Prison Department is to try to ensure that prisoners are sent to training prisons within their home area. The prisons themselves are usually more modern than local prisons, with better facilities.

(ii) *Dispersal prisons: category 'A' prisoners*

Approximately 1 per cent. of all prisoners belong to category 'A', *i.e.* those whose escape would be highly dangerous to the police, the public, or the security of the state. Those prisoners are dispersed among the population of seven prisons and are held in conditions of maximum security.

(iii) *Open prisons*

An open prison is designed with no physical barriers to prevent inmates from escaping. Obviously, therefore, open prisons are suitable only for those who present a minimal security risk, and are unlikely to abuse the freedom which they obtain, or the trust which is placed in them. Moreover, due to concern amongst members of a community in which an open prison is to be sited, the Prison Department is often requested at planning application hearings to undertake to restrict the type of prisoner (*e.g.* to exclude violent and sexual offenders) to be held in such an institution.

(iv) *Women's prisons*

There is a surprisingly large discrepancy between the numbers of men and women in prison. The daily average prison population in 1986 was 46,770 of whom only 1,607 were women. Whereas there are over 60 closed penal establishments for males, there are only five such institutions for females.

(v) *Industrial prison*

Coldingley prison in Surrey, opened in 1969, is Britain's only industrial prison, in which the regime and conditions are intended so far as possible to be comparable to those in industry outside.

(vi) *Psychiatric prison*

Grendon Underwood prison, near Aylesbury, was opened in 1962 as Britain's first psychiatric prison, and exists to treat those prisoners with psychiatric or personality disorders who are nonetheless serving conventional prison sentences. Its regime and conditions differ markedly from any other institution in the country.

(vii) *Special hospitals*

Technically these are not part of the penal system, and are therefore beyond the scope of this book. There are a number of secure special hospitals for those persons who have been made the subject of various orders under the mental health legislation, or have been transferred to such hospitals by the Secretary of State.

*Chapter 2*

# THE SENTENCE OF THE COURT



## TYPES OF SENTENCE

### Suspended sentences

Power to suspend sentences of imprisonment was introduced by the Criminal Justice Act 1967, and is now contained in the Powers of Criminal Courts Act 1973. Section 22(1) of the latter Act provides that a court may suspend any sentence of imprisonment of up to two years, by ordering that unless within a stated period of between one and two years the offender commits another imprisonable offence, the sentence shall not take effect. Subsection 2 gives effect to judicial decisions which followed the passing of the 1967 Act by providing that suspended sentences should be imposed only where an immediate prison sentence would have been appropriate in the absence of a power to suspend.

If the offender commits an imprisonable offence during the operational period of a suspended sentence, the Court before which he is so convicted may deal with him in one of the following ways:

(i) It may order the suspended sentence to take effect with the original prison term unaltered.
(ii) It may order the sentence to take effect, but substitute a shorter term for that originally imposed.
(iii) It may "re-suspend" the original sentence for up to two years from the date of the re-suspension.
(iv) It may make no order, in which case the suspended sentence continues in operation if the operational period has not expired.

The normal approach of the courts, as required by section 23 of the 1973 Act, is to make the first of these four orders, with a direction that the implemented sentence run consecutively to any custodial sentence imposed for the second offence. The court should do this, "unless the court is of opinion that it would be unjust to do so in view of all the circumstances, including the facts of the subsequent offence, and where it is of that opinion the court should state its reasons." (section 23(1) of the 1973 Act as amended by section 31 of the Criminal Justice Act 1982.)

**Partially suspended sentences**

Partially suspended sentences had a painful birth, and an unhappy childhood. Contained in section 47 of the Criminal Law Act 1977, but not actually introduced until March 1982, the relevant provisions underwent significant amendments in the Criminal Justice Act 1982. Section 47 as so amended provides that sentences of between three months' and two years' imprisonment may be partly served in prison, with the remaining portion held in suspense after release. The part to be served in prison must be at least 28 days, and the minimum period to be suspended is one quarter of the total term. Therefore, in respect of any prison sentence of between three months and two years, all but 28 days of the total term may be suspended. Partially suspended sentences should only be imposed where total suspension appears inappropriate.

If, following release from prison but during the period held in suspense, the offender commits an imprisonable offence, the court may restore the period held in suspense and order that it be served. On the other hand, if it is of the opinion that it would be unjust to restore the whole period, it may restore a lesser portion or make no order. If the court restores all or part of the sentence, it may direct that it take effect immediately or upon the expiration of another term of imprisonment.

**Extended Sentences**

*History*

The problem of how best to deal with persistent offenders is one which confronts any sentencing system. The solution adopted by Parliament in the first years of the twentieth century was that of preventive detention, introduced by the Prevention of Crimes Act 1908, which itself incorporated the recommendations of the Gladstone Committee made over a decade earlier. The primary purpose of the new sentence was the protection of the public rather than the punishment of the individual offender. Thus although sentences of preventive detention were often very lengthy, they were served in conditions which were rather better than those of prisoners serving conventional sentences. A similar type of sentence, corrective training, was introduced by the Criminal Justice Act 1948, and was designed to deal with somewhat younger offenders (*i.e.* those between 21 and 30 years of age) who were in danger of becoming recidivists. As its name implies, the sentence had training as its prime object. That training element was the justification for imposing a longer sentence than would normally have been applicable.

Neither preventive detention nor corrective training proved effective, and both were unpopular with sentencing authorities. The wrong types of criminal, nuisances rather than menaces, tended to be sentenced to preventive detention, whereas any real difference in regime between corrective training and conventional prison sentences steadily disappeared.

*Introduction and purpose of extended sentences*

Both preventive detention and corrective training were abolished by the Criminal Justice Act 1967, and were replaced by the extended sentence. Again, the object of new sentence was to enable the Court to impose a longer term than the offence itself would have attracted, in order to protect the public from the activities of persistent offenders. At the same time the new sentence was intended to be shorter than the term of preventive detention which would have been imposed. Section 37 of the 1967 Act, which introduced the new sentence, was substantially re-enacted in section 28 of the Powers of Criminal Courts Act 1973.

The extended sentence provisions are capable of coming into effect where an offender is convicted on indictment of an offence punishable with a prison sentence of two years or more. Before the Court can pass an extended sentence it must be satisfied that by reason of the offender's previous conduct and of the likelihood of his committing further offences, it is expedient to protect the public from him for a substantial time. The following are the remaining conditions which must be satisfied:

(a) The offence must have been committed within three years of

(i) A previous conviction for an offence punishable on

indictment with a prison sentence of two years or more:
*or*

(ii) The final release (including release on licence) from serving a prison sentence, preventive detention or corrective training for such an offence; and

(b) Since the age of 21, the offender must have been convicted on indictment on at least three occasions of offences punishable on indictment with imprisonment for two years or more; and

(c) The total length of those sentences was at least five years, and on at least one occasion a sentence of preventive detention was imposed *or* on at least two of those occasions sentences of imprisonment or corrective training were imposed *and* either one was a sentence of at least three years' imprisonment for one offence, or two were sentences of at least two years' imprisonment for one offence.

(d) No account is to be taken of any previous conviction or sentence unless notice has been given to the offender at least three days in advance that it is intended to prove such conviction. Finally, where an extended sentence is imposed, the Court must issue a certificate to this effect.

The extended term which may be imposed by the Court may exceed the statutory maximum for the offence if that maximum is less than 10 years, but may not exceed 10 years if the maximum is less than 10 years, nor may it exceed five years if the maximum is less than five years. In *D.P.P.* v. *Ottewell*[1] the House of Lords held that an extended term may be imposed notwithstanding that the term so imposed is less than the statutory maximum for the offence.

The extended sentence has proved little more effective or popular than its predecessors. It is imposed upon only about 20 of 80,000 Crown Court defendants annually.

*Release*

Remission as such is not available to prisoners serving extended sentences. They are eligible to be considered for release on licence in the normal way after one third of their sentence. The likelihood of their being granted parole at a relatively early stage of their sentence must be very remote: passing an extended

[1] [1970] A.C. 642; [1968] 3 W.L.R. 621; [1968] 3 All E.R. 153.

sentence reflects the view of the trial judge that the public requires long-term protection from the offender. By section 60(3) and (5A) of the Criminal Justice Act 1967, the Secretary of State may direct that a prisoner serving an extended sentence be released on licence in lieu of remission. This licence remains in force until the expiration of the sentence. Thus, whereas other prisoners can look forward with confidence to release after the expiry of two-thirds of their sentences provided that no remission has been forfeited, those serving extended sentences can have no such expectation. Their release remains throughout a matter of executive discretion. Likewise, if the Secretary of State orders the early release of a prisoner serving an extended sentence under the provisions of the Criminal Justice Act 1982, such release is on licence, and does not denote the expiry of the sentence.

**Life Sentences**

A life sentence may be either the mandatory, or the maximum, sentence available for a given offence. By s.1(1) of the Murder (Abolition of Death Penalty) Act 1965, a person convicted of murder must be sentenced to life imprisonment (unless under 18 years of age at the time of the offence). Section 1(2) of the Act introduced the provision whereby the judge sentencing a murderer may declare the minimum period which in his view should elapse before release on licence. There are a number of offences for which a sentence of life imprisonment is the prescribed maximum.

As for the release of prisoners serving sentences of life imprisonment, see Chapter 8.

**Death Penalty**

Since the Murder (Abolition of Death Penalty) Act 1965, came into force, there are only two offences for which capital punishment remains. These are high treason and piracy with violence. The sentence has not actually been carried out since 1964. Although there remain various provisions in the Prison Rules 1964 concerning the treatment of and regime for prisoners facing the death penalty it is not proposed to consider them.

## CALCULATING THE LENGTH OF A SENTENCE

Save for that of life imprisonment, all prison sentences imposed by the Courts are of determinate length, and must not exceed the maximum period prescribed for the offence by the relevant statute except in the case of extended sentences. Of cardinal importance to the prisoner is the total period of imprisonment to which he has been sentenced, and the actual time which he can expect to serve. Consecutive sentences are added together, whereas in the case of sentences ordered to run concurrently the longest individual sentence will constitute the sentence of the Court. Usually the Judge will inform the offender of the total period whilst passing sentence upon him.

The total period in practice falls to be reduced as follows:

(i) The effect of section 67(1) of the Criminal Justice Act 1967 was to provide that the duration of any sentence of imprisonment must be treated as reduced by *time spent in custody on remand* in connection with the offence for which the term of imprisonment was passed. This was extended by section 49 of the Police and Criminal Evidence Act 1984, which amends section 67 of the 1967 Act by providing that time spent in *police detention* in respect of the relevant offence shall also be taken into account for the purpose of reducing the length of the sentence. That provision came into force on January 1, 1986, and applies only to periods spent in police detention after that date. "Police detention" is defined as meaning detention for the purposes of the 1984 Act, and detention under section 12 of the Prevention of Terrorism (Temporary Provisions) Act 1984.

(ii) Section 67(1) of the 1967 Act also provides that where an offender was previously subject to a probation order, a community service order, a conditional discharge, or a suspended sentence in respect of the relevant offence, any period spent in custody on remand (and now, by virtue of the 1984 Act, in police detention) before the order was made or suspended sentence passed shall be disregarded, and the sentence shall not fall to be reduced in the manner outlined at (i) above.

(iii) Offenders who receive *partially suspended sentences* are entitled to reduction as aforesaid in respect of that part of the sentence required to be served in prison.

(iv) the provisions summarised at (i) above apply to *sentences of youth custody and to detention centre orders*. Prior to the changes wrought by the Criminal Justice Act 1982, those sentenced to Borstal training and detention centre orders had not been entitled to any reduction in their sentences in respect of time spent in custody on remand, an unjust and anomolous situation.

(v) If a prisoner would normally be *due for release on a Saturday* (unless the sentence was for five days or less), *Sunday, Christmas Day, Good Friday, or a bank holiday* within the meaning of the Bank Holidays Act 1871, he must be released "on the next preceding day which is not one of those days": section 24(2) Prison Act 1952.

(vi) Where a person has been committed to prison for *non-payment of certain sums* ordered to be paid by the Crown Court or Magistrates' Court, he can secure immediate release from custody by payment in full of any amount outstanding, or reduction of the term to be served by part payment.

(vii) Time spent in custody will be further reduced by the granting of *remission or parole*, which are fully discussed elsewhere.

In contrast to the above, time spent in custody abroad pending extradition cannot be credited against any sentence imposed by the English Courts. However, in *R.* v. *Bennett*[2] the Court of Appeal observed that justice required that a term imposed by an English Court in such circumstances should reflect the fact of time spent in custody abroad, and reduced a sentence of three years' imprisonment by six months, as the appellant had spent six months on remand abroad.

Time during which an appellant is in custody pending the determination of his appeal is to be reckoned as part of the relevant sentence by section 29 of the Criminal Appeal Act 1968, unless the Court of Appeal directs otherwise. The Court has tended to exercise very sparingly its power to order that time spent in custody after conviction pending an application for leave to appeal should not count as part of the prisoner's sentence. Periodically the Court has issued warnings that it will exercise such power in respect of frivolous appeals. The power is exercisable not only by the full Court, but by the single judge who first considers the application.[3]

[2] (1975) Crim.L.R. 654.

[3] *R.* v. *Howitt* (1975) 61 Crim.App.R. 327 C.A.; (1975) Crim.L.R. 588, C.A. See also p. 98 *infra*, and *Monnell and Morris* v. *United Kingdom* (1988) 10 E.H.R.R. 205.

Where a prisoner is released under the provisions of section 28 of the Prison Act 1952, on grounds of ill health, the sentence does not run during the period of such release: the day of release counts towards the sentence, whilst the day of reception back into prison does not. During any other period of temporary release a sentence of imprisonment will continue to run normally.

*Chapter 3*

# PRISONERS' RIGHTS: A GENERAL SURVEY



The search for prisoners' rights is an elusive one. The words of Lord Wilberforce in *Raymond* v. *Honey*[1] that a convicted prisoner retains all civil rights not taken away expressly or by necessary implication, do not identify the rights to which he was referring. The United Kingdom has no written constitution, and has not yet incorporated the European Convention into its domestic law. The Bill of Rights is 300 years old, and its makers were looking backwards at Stuart excesses rather than seeking to declare universal human rights.

It has long been recognised that those in positions of authority in prisons are subject to the ordinary law of the land. Any suggestion to the contrary would be regarded as ridiculous, and as conferring a licence to ill treat prisoners. Thus in *R.* v. *Huggins*,[2] in which a gaoler and warder were charged with the murder of a prisoner who had been held in unhealthy conditions, and who had died as a result, Raymond C.J. said:

> "The duty of a gaoler is not to punish but to confine a party . . . In this case (the warder) exceeded that duty; he has been guilty of a breach of that trust which the law reposed in him, and is answerable for all the consequences of it."

[1] [1983] 1 A.C. 1; [1982] 2 W.L.R. 465; [1982] 1 All E.R. 756.
[2] (1730) 17 State Tr 309; 2 Stra. 883.

So too in *Osborne* v. *Angle*,[3] where a prisoner complained that he had been transferred to a strongroom of the prison in excess of the gaoler's authority, Tindal C.J., whilst holding that the action was lawful, said:

> "I am not sorry that this question has been brought under the consideration of this Court, because it is our duty, and it would afford us much satisfaction, to interpose if it were made to appear to us that a greater degree of severity and coercion had been exerted against a prisoner than the circumstances of the case called for."

**Ill-treatment of prisoners: the Bill of Rights 1688**

Where a prisoner complains of ill-treatment consisting of an identifiable criminal offence such as assault, or tort such as trespass to the person or false imprisonment, the matter can be raised directly by a criminal prosecution or private law action for damages, a declaration, and/or an injunction. Much more difficult is the position where the prisoner complains not of direct unlawful action by an identifiable member of the prison staff, but of the general conditions in which he is being held. Upon what basis can he found such a complaint?

The Bill of Rights 1688 prohibited the infliction of "cruell and unusuall" punishments, and has long been seen as being of fundamental importance in English constitutional law. In recent years it has been successfully invoked in attempts to declare taxation unlawful.[4] It has also been relied upon by prisoners seeking to attack the conditions of their imprisonment.

In the *Control Unit* case[5] the Court was asked to declare the Control Unit regime to be unlawful as constituting a cruel *or* unusual punishment in contravention of the Bill of Rights. Tudor Evans J. held that the words "cruel and unusual" should be interpreted conjunctively rather disjunctively, rendering it necessary for the Plaintiff to establish that the punishment was both cruel *and* unusual. On the facts, the judge found that it was neither.

The applicant in *R.* v. *Home Secretary ex p. Herbage (No. 2)*[6] also contended that the conditions in which he was held amounted to

3 (1835) 2 Scott 500.

4 *Att.-Gen.* v. *Wilts United Dairies* (1921) 37 T.L.R. 884, *Congreve* v. *Home Office* [1976] Q.B. 629; [1976] 2 W.L.R. 291; [1976] 1 All E.R. 697.

5 *Williams* v. *Home Office* (No.2) [1981] 1 All E.R. 1211.

6 [1987] Q.B. 1077; [1987] 2 W.L.R. 226; [1987] 1 All E.R. 324.

a breach of the Bill of Rights. He was held in Pentonville Prison awaiting an extradition warrant in favour of the United States. He was grossly obese and unable to walk upstairs. He was held on the ground floor of the hospital wing of the prison, accommodation usually reserved for mentally disturbed prisoners. Prisoners who needed hospitalisation, but who were not mentally disturbed, were held on the first floor. As there were no lifts in the wing, the applicant could not be accommodated on the first floor. His complaints were that he was consistently subjected throughout the night to shouting and screaming from the mentally disturbed prisoners around him, and that he was unable to sleep. He was granted leave to apply for judicial review, and later obtained an order for discovery of certain documents. On the Home Secretary's appeal against this latter order, it was contended on the Home Secretary's behalf that leave to apply for judicial review should not have been granted in the first place. The Court of Appeal held that it was not open to the Home Secretary to raise such a point on an appeal against an order for discovery. As to the potential merits of the case, Purchas L.J. expressed himself in unambiguous language:

> "Counsel for the applicant emphasised that the case against the Governor, however, was not based merely upon breaches of the 1964 Rules, but on an alleged breach of the provision of the Bill of Rights, namely that the applicant was entitled not to be inflicted with 'cruell and unusuall punishments.' This is a fundamental right which, in my judgment, goes far beyond the ambit of the 1964 Rules. For my part, if it were established that a prison Governor was guilty of such conduct, it would be an affront to commonsense that the Court should not be able to afford relief under Order 53."

And, later:

> "If it were to be established that medical opinion supported the contention that the applicant's detention was inflicting a 'cruell and unusual' punishment on him, then in my judgment the Court has power, and ought, to intervene."[7]

**Ill-treatment of prisoners: "A minimum standard of conditions"**

A similar attack upon the conditions of imprisonment was made in *R.* v. *Metropolitan Police Commissioner ex p. Nahar*,[8] in

[7] [1987] Q.B. 1077 at pp 1095, 1096.
[8] *The Times* May 28, 1983.

which the applicants sought writs of habeas corpus based upon the conditions in which they were being held as remand prisoners. They were being held in magistrates' court cells due to overcrowding in prisons. Their claim failed, but Stephen Brown J. accepted that there must be some minimum standard below which detention would become unlawful. He did not find the terms of Article 3 of the European Convention, which states that "no-one shall be subjected to torture or to inhuman or degrading treatment or punishment" of assistance in defining that minimum standard.

**The tort of false imprisonment**

The tort of false imprisonment consists of the complete deprivation of liberty for any time, however short, without lawful cause.[9] A number of nineteenth century authorities established that although imprisonment in one prison or part of a prison may be lawful, it becomes unlawful if the prisoner is confined in the wrong place. For instance in *Osborne* v. *Milman*,[10] the Plaintiff was committed to prison for having practised as a solicitor when not qualified to do so. He was placed on the "criminal side" of Holloway Prison, and treated as a convicted criminal not sentenced to hard labour. He sued for false imprisonment, claiming that he had not been convicted of any criminal offence, and that his detention on the criminal side was unlawful. He succeeded at first instance, although the decision was reversed on another point on appeal.[11]

In view of the vast changes in the system of imprisonment since the nineteenth century, the decisions dealing with "imprisonment in the wrong place" are now of little more than academic importance. The decisions themselves have been interpreted restrictively in later cases such as *Arbon* v. *Anderson*[12] and the *Control Unit* case.[13] The modern position is governed by section 12(1) of the Prison Act 1952 which provides that a "prisoner whether sentenced to imprisonment or committed to prison on remand or pending trial or otherwise, may be lawfully confined in any prison." The section will provide a complete defence to most actions for false imprisonment brought by prisoners against prison authorities. However, in the *Control Unit* case, fully dis-

[9] Clerk & Lindsell on Torts 15th ed., Ch. 14.
[10] (1886) 17 Q.B.D. 514.
[11] (1887) 18 Q.B.D. 471.
[12] [1943] K.B. 252; [1943] 1 All E.R. 154.
[13] *Williams* v. *Home Office (No.2)* [1981] 1 All E.R. 1211.

cussed elsewhere,[14] it was contended for the Plaintiff that section 12 only operated as a defence to an action based upon the location or place of imprisonment, and was not concerned with tortious acts done to a prisoner inside the prison. Tudor Evans J. reviewed a number of the older authorities, and concluded that there was no authority in modern law to support the proposition that although a detention can be lawful, it becomes unlawful if its nature (*i.e.* conditions) changes.

> "In my judgment the sentence of the Court and the provisions of Section 12(1) always afford a defence to an action for false imprisonment. The sentence justifies the fact of imprisonment and the subsection justifies the confinement of a prisoner in any prison. How then can it be unjustifiable and unlawful to confine him there? . . . The sentence of the Court and the provisions of section 12(1) provide a defence to this action, subject to the argument based upon the Bill of Rights and natural justice."

In a later passage the judge said:

> "Counsel for the Plaintiff submits that in this case there was an imprisonment within an imprisonment, that is to say a tortious imprisonment within the currency of a lawful imprisonment. I find the concept hard to apply." . . . "I find it difficult to see how the concept of false imprisonment has any application in a case such as this . . ."[15]

This reasoning was accepted and followed by Mann J. in *R.* v. *Board of Visitors of Gartree Prison ex p. Sears.*[16]

> "The distinction drawn between place and conditions is, in my view, a sound and decisive one. If a person is imprisoned in a place where he is lawfully so imprisoned, then it does not seem to be that a variation in conditions of confinement can constitute the tort of false imprisonment at common law."

However, merely because section 12 justifies the fact of imprisonment, it cannot be used to justify all that happens once the prisoner has been physically incarcerated. It is submitted that the prisoner should be entitled to a remedy if he is held in conditions

[14] *Infra* pp. 103–106.
[15] [1981] 1 All E.R. 1211 at pp. 1241, 1242.
[16] *The Times*, March 20, 1985.

which fall below what could be described as the minimum standard of acceptability. It may be that the Courts would be more sympathetic to such an argument in the context of a public law application rather than a private law action. As will be seen below, although a breach of the Prison Rules 1964 gives no right to damages at the suit of the aggrieved prisoner, such a breach may well give rise to a remedy in public law.

**The Prison Act 1952 and Prison Rules 1964: legally enforceable rights?**

One of the most vexed questions in the law concerning prisons and prisoners is the extent to which the 1952 Act, and more particularly the 1964 Rules made thereunder, confer legally enforceable rights. Both the Act and the Rules appear at first sight to confer rights upon prisoners. The Act contains the following provisions:

(i) *Accommodation*

Section 14—the Home Secretary is under a duty to satisfy himself that sufficient accommodation is provided for all prisoners in every prison, and each cell must be formally certified as adequate.

(ii) *Segregation and special treatment*

Sections 15 and 47(4)—these sections require the segregation of men from women, and the making of special rules for the treatment of certain categories of prisoner.

(iii) *Painful tests*

Section 17—the prison medical officer cannot apply any painful test to a prisoner without the permission of the Board of Visitors.

(iv) *Calculation of sentence*

Section 24—this section regulates the calculation of the length of a sentence, and requires release in certain circumstances.

(v) *Discipline*

Section 47(2)—Rules made under the section must make provision for ensuring that a prisoner charged with a disciplinary offence has a proper opportunity of presenting his case.

The 1964 Rules confer a wide range of apparent rights upon prisoners, in respect of virtually every aspect of prison life. A cursory reading of the rules would indicate that the prisoner had various entitlements regarding information (rule 7), exemption from work on religious festivals (rule 15), visits from ministers of religion (rule 12), the availability of religious books (rule 16), the adequacy of food (rule 21), and bedding (rule 24) and toilet articles (rule 26), exercise (rule 27), fitness for work (rule 28), and a swift and fair disciplinary system (rules 48 and 49). Most noticeably, rule 34(2) provides that a convicted prisoner "shall be entitled" to certain minimum facilities for visits and correspondence. The rules make separate and elaborate provision for female and unconvicted prisoners.

What though, if the authorities fail to deal with the prisoner according to their apparent duties under the Act and Rules? The leading modern authority is *Arbon* v. *Anderson*,[17] in which the Plaintiffs were detained in prison by virtue of orders made by the Home Secretary under the Defence (General) Regulations 1939, under which he also had the power to issue a command paper dealing with treatment in prison. The Plaintiffs complained that they had not been treated in accordance with the instructions contained in the Command Paper, and that the provisions of the Prison Rules 1933 had been breached.

Goddard L.J. heard the action as an additional judge of the King's Bench. He held that on the facts there had been no breach of the Prison Rules, but continued:

> "With regard to the Prison Rules, it would be enough to say that there were no breaches, but, in case a higher court should take a different view, I should say that, in my opinion, neither do these rules confer rights on prisoners which can be enforced by action. . . . The real question which falls to be determined is whether it is intended by the statute to confer an individual right. I am clearly of the opinion that neither the Prison Act 1898, nor the rules were intended to confer any such right."

In a subsequent passage, which has found echoes in later cases, the learned judge stated:

> " . . . it seems to me impossible to say that if (the prisoner) can prove some departure from the prison rules which caused him inconvenience or detriment he can maintain an action. It would be fatal to all discipline in prisons if governors and

[17] [1943] K.B. 252; [1943] 1 All E.R. 154.

> warders had to perform their duty always with the fear of an action before their eyes if they in any way deviated from the rules. The safeguards against abuse are appeals to the governor . . . and . . . to the Secretary of State, and those in my opinion, are the only remedies."

These dicta have been followed in several later cases[18] and received vigorous support from Lord Denning M.R. in *Becker* v. *Home Office*,[19] in which, in a celebrated passage, he said:

> "If the courts were to entertain actions by disgruntled prisoners the governor's life would be made intolerable. The discipline of the prison would be undermined. The Prison Rules are regulatory directions only. Even if they are not observed, they do not give rise to a cause of action."

Edmund Davies L.J., in rather less robust language, agreed that "a breach of these prison rules does not *per se* create any civil liability at the suit of a party who claims to have been damnified thereby."

Finally, in the *Control Unit* case,[20] in which Tudor Evans J. found that the provisions of Rule 43 of the Prison Rules 1964 had been breached, it had been accepted by counsel for the Plaintiff that there was "ample authority that a prisoner cannot rely upon a breach of the rules to establish or support a cause of action."[21] In dismissing the Plaintiff's appeal (as the Court of Appeal had been invited to by counsel for the Plaintiff) both Cumming-Bruce and Brightman L.J.J. agreed that the question whether rule 43 of the Prison Rules 1964 gave a right to a cause of action was an arguable point for the House of Lords. Leave to appeal to the House of Lords was, however, refused for technical reasons.[22]

Subject to consideration of the point by the House of Lords it is now clear that a breach of the Prison Rules 1964 cannot give rise *per se* to a claim for damages at the suit of an aggrieved prisoner. It is equally clear that such a breach can give rise to a remedy in public law. The Courts have been prepared to construe the meaning of the Rules on a number of occasions. In *Guilfoyle* v. *Home Office*[23] the Court of Appeal construed the meaning of the term

[18] e.g. *Silverman* v. *Prison Commissioners* (1955) Crim.L.R. 116; *Hinds* v. *Home Office*, *The Times*, January 17, 1962.

[19] [1972] 2 Q.B. 407; [1972] 2 W.L.R. 1193. [1972] 2 All E.R. 676.

[20] *Williams* v. *Home Office (No.2)* [1981] 1 All E.R. 1211.

[21] *Ibid.* at p. 1218.

[22] [1982] 2 All E.R. 564.

[23] [1981] Q.B. 309; [1981] 1 All E.R. 943; [1981] 2 W.L.R. 223.

"legal proceedings" in rule 37(A)(1) of the 1964 Rules, Sir John Megaw saying:

> "So we pass to a relatively dull and technical question of construction, the answer to which may in some degree affect the Plaintiff's legal rights."

In that case the Plaintiff had contended that he was entitled to the privilege conferred by the rule of not having his correspondence with his legal adviser read or stopped. Likewise, in *Raymond* v. *Honey*[24] Lord Bridge spoke of rule 37(1) as giving an "unfettered right of communication."[25] More strikingly, in *R.* v. *Board of Visitors, Dartmoor Prison ex p. Smith*[26] the Court of Appeal held that the requirement in Rule 48(1) that a disciplinary charge be laid "as soon as possible" was mandatory rather than directory, and that a charge which was not laid as soon as possible was nullified. It can be seen therefore that while a breach of a rule gives no private law right to damages, a decision taken in breach of a rule will be reviewed and if necessary quashed by the Courts.

**Particular rights of prisoners**

(i) *Safe premises*

The prison authorities owe a general duty of care to prisoners. One aspect of that duty is to take reasonable care to provide prisoners with premises which are reasonably safe. Although a prisoner may not be a "visitor" within the meaning of the Occupiers Liability Act 1957, the existence of a general duty is not in doubt, and in *Christofi* v. *Home Office*[27] a prisoner was awarded damages for injuries received as a result of a fall on a broken step.

(ii) *Safe place and system of work*

The duty of the prison authorities extends to providing the prisoner with a reasonably safe place and system of work. This is discussed at Chapter 5, pp. 64–65, *post*.

(iii) *Protection from other prisoners*

The possibility of physical attack by one prisoner upon another is one which exists in every penal establishment. The duty cast upon the prison authorities by the common law is to take reasonable care for the safety of those within the prison, whether they

24 [1983] 1 A.C. 1; [1982] 2 W.L.R. 465; [1982] 1 All E.R. 756.
25 *Ibid.* at p. 15.
26 [1987] Q.B. 106; [1986] 3 W.L.R. 61; [1986] 2 All E.R. 651.
27 *The Times*, July 31, 1975.

be staff or inmates. The leading case dealing with the discharge of this duty is *Ellis* v. *Home Office*.[28] The Plaintiff was assaulted and seriously injured by a fellow prisoner whilst on remand in the prison hospital wing. His assailant was thought to be mentally defective, but Devlin J. found that there was nothing in his previous record showing him to be likely to commit an act of violence. At the time of the attack, the one prison officer on duty in the wing was absent, and the cell doors were unlocked. Devlin J., finding that there was no reason for the prison authorities to anticipate any act of violence by the assailant, dismissed the Plaintiff's claim. The Court of Appeal unanimously dismissed the Plaintiff's appeal. The findings of fact made by the trial judge had effectively disposed of the claim, and Jenkins L.J. observed:

> " . . . the mere fact that the Plaintiff while in prison was attacked and injured by a fellow prisoner does not entitle him to succeed against the government department responsible for the management of the prison . . . he must show that the injury which he sustained was due to some breach of duty on the part of those responsible for the management of the prison."[29]

As there was no need for special vigilance by the authorities since nothing indicated the likelihood of an attack, the authorities had discharged the duty owed. To hold otherwise, would, in the opinion of the judge, have been to place too high a duty on the authorities.[30]

Some prisoners are particularly likely to be the subject of assault by fellow inmates. The Plaintiff in *Egerton* v. *Home Office*[31], as a sexual offender against young girls, fell into this category. He started his 12 year sentence as a rule 43 prisoner, but was taken off rule 43 at his own request. Within a few days he was seriously assaulted by fellow prisoners in the lavatory of the canvas shop where he was working. The prison officers on duty in the canvas shop were unaware of the Plaintiff's offences, or that he had just

[28] [1953] 2 Q.B. 135; [1953] 2 All E.R. 149; [1953] 3 W.L.R. 105.
[29] [1953] 2 Q.B. at p. 145.
[30] A similar result was reached by Milmo J. in *Anderson* v. *Home Office* The Times October 8, 1965, whereas in *D'Arcy* v. *Prison Commissioners* the Plaintiff succeeded in an action against the authorities following an attack by fellow prisoners: (1956) Crim.L.R. 56. See too *Porterfield* v. *Home Office, The Times* March 9, 1988.
[31] (1978) Crim.L.R. 494.

come off rule 43. His claim for damages for negligent supervision failed. May J. accepted that where a particular prisoner was potentially more at risk than others, then, to the extent that it was reasonable and practicable, he should be the subject of greater care and supervision. The prison officers supervising in the canvas shop should have been made aware that the Plaintiff had just come off rule 43, but the spontaneous attack upon him could not reasonably have been foreseen by an experienced prison officer, and the claim thus failed.

(iv) *Racial discrimination*

In *Alexander* v. *Home Office*[32] a West Indian prisoner alleged that he had been refused jobs in the prison on racial grounds. The Home Office argued that as a prisoner the applicant did not have the right to bring proceedings under the Race Relations Act 1976. The County Court judge held that the complaint fell within the scope of the Act, and that the court had jurisdiction to hear it. The applicant was subsequently awarded £50 as compensation after the allegation was found proved, and on appeal the award was increased to £500.[33]

(v) *Free access to the Courts, and a fair disciplinary system*

These are discussed at length at Chapters 6 and 7.

(vi) *Damages for personality change leading to imprisonment*

One of the strangest cases ever to come before the Courts was litigated in July 1984. The Plaintiff in *Meah* v. *McCreamer*[34] was a passenger in a vehicle which was involved in an accident. The Plaintiff sustained severe head injuries and brain damage, which caused a personality change. As a result he committed serious sexual assaults upon a number of women, for which he was sentenced to life imprisonment. Prior to the accident, although he had committed a number of criminal offences, he had manifested no violence towards women. Woolf J. held that since, but for the head injuries and subsequent personality change, the

[32] [1985] C.L.Y. para 1669. See too the Court of Appeal's decision on the measure of damages: [1988] 2 W.L.R. 1017 and [1988] 2 All E.R. 118.
[33] *Ibid.*
[34] [1985] 1 All E.R. 367.

Plaintiff would not have committed the offences for which he was serving a life sentence, he was entitled to substantial damages to compensate him for being in prison. He awarded the Plaintiff a total of £60,000 general damages, without specifying what proportion of that sum was specifically intended to compensate the Plaintiff for his imprisonment. The decision is a strange one, in that it does not seem to have been contended on behalf of the Defendant that the criminal offences, which were voluntary and for which the Plaintiff was legally responsible, broke the chain of causation between the accident and the imprisonment. It must be doubted whether any appellate Court would uphold the correctness of the decision.

*Chapter 4*

# CLASSIFICATION OF PRISONERS



The classification of prisoners into different categories is inevitable in any penal system. Each prisoner poses an individual security risk, and considerations of age, sex, the nature of the offence, the stage of the criminal process reached, and the mental state of the prisoner all combine to require various categories of prisoners. By section 47(4) of the Prison Act 1952, Rules made under that section must provide for the special treatment of certain prisoners, whilst the Prison Rules themselves provide that prisoners shall be classified having regard to their age, temperament and record, and with a view to facilitating training and maintaining good order.[1]

## Prisoners on Remand

There is an obvious and important distinction to be drawn between convicted prisoners and those held on remand pending

[1] Rule 3(1), Prison Rules 1964.

trial. The former are detained as punishment, whereas the latter, who are in law presumed innocent, are detained for safe custody and to ensure attendance at trial. Section 39 of the Prison Act 1877 set out the "clear difference" in treatment which unconvicted prisoners were entitled to receive, and required the Secretary of State to make special rules in respect of it. Such a requirement is now found in section 47(4)(*d*) of the Prison Act 1952.[1a]

Although there are no modern English authorities dealing specifically with the basis of treatment of remand prisoners in the United Kingdom,[2] persuasive dicta are to be found in the judgments of the South African Court of Appeal in *Whittaker* v. *Roos*, *Morant* v. *Roos*.[3] The Plaintiffs were held on remand having been unable to raise the required £1,000 bail deposit. Their complaints, were that they had been held in punishment cells and in solitary confinement, and had been denied other facilities, such as exercise, reading material, and access to legal advisers. Both succeeded in actions against the prison governor. Innes J. regarded the segregation in solitary confinement as illegal simply because it differentiated between the Plaintiffs and all other remand prisoners in the gaol. In a passage of wider application, which, it is submitted, sets out the correct legal position, he said[4]:

> "The fact that their liberty had been legally curtailed would afford no excuse for a further illegal encroachment upon it ... They were entitled to all their personal rights and personal dignity not temporarily taken away by law, or necessarily inconsistent with the circumstances in which they had been placed."

Solomon J. echoed that view[5]:

> " ... in my opinion any differential treatment of an awaiting trial prisoner under which he is subjected to harsher or more

1a As amended by s.42(1) and (3) and Schedule 4 of the Criminal Justice Act 1961.

2 Prison Act 1899, s.39, is worthy of mention however. It reads as follows "Whereas it is expedient that a clear difference shall be made between the treatment of persons unconvicted of crime and in law presumably innocent during the period of their detention in prison for safe custody only, and the treatment of prisoners who have been convicted of crime during the period of their detention in prison for the purpose of punishment and that, in order to secure the observance of such difference there shall be in force in every place in which prisoners are confined for safe custody only, special rules regulating their confinement in such manner as to make it as little as possible oppressive ..."

3 (1912) App.D. 92.

4 *Ibid.* at pp. 122–123.

5 *Ibid.* at p. 128.

severe treatment than the rest savours of punishment and is prima facie illegal. When such exceptional treatment is specifically provided for by any gaol regulation, or is required for the purpose of providing good order and discipline in the gaol it is of course justifiable."

As a result of the distinction referred to above, the Prison Rules provide that unconvicted prisoners should be kept out of contact with convicted prisoners so far as that can reasonably be done.[6] The most significant differences in regime are as follows:

(i) *Personal appearance*

An unconvicted prisoner may wear his own clothing, and arrange to receive sufficient clean clothing from outside prison.[7] He may wear his hair and beard as he wishes, unless the prison's medical officer directs otherwise on grounds of health or cleanliness.[8]

(ii) *Contact with the outside world*

An unconvicted prisoner may send and receive as many letters as he wishes, and may receive as many visits as he wishes, subject to any directions of the Secretary of State.[9]

(iii) *Work*

An unconvicted prisoner cannot be required to work by the prison authorities, but is entitled, if he so wishes, to work as if he were a convicted prisoner.[10]

In addition, special permission is required to measure or photograph an unconvicted prisoner: if he is so measured or photographed and is subsequently acquitted, all photographs fingerprints and records of measurements must immediately be destroyed or handed over to the prisoner.[11] This does not apply where such a prisoner has a previous criminal conviction.

There are also a number of means by which a remand prisoner may improve the conditions of his imprisonment at his own expense. He may have supplied to him books, newspapers, writing materials, and other means of occupation except those that appear objectionable to the Board of Visitors, or, pending

[6] Prison Rules 1964, S.I. 1964 No. 388 r. 3(2).
[7] *Ibid*. r. 20(1).
[8] *Ibid*. r. 26(2) proviso.
[9] *Ibid*. r. 34(1).
[10] *Ibid*. r. 28(5).
[11] Regulations dated June 20, 1896, S.R. & O. 1896 No. 762 regs. 4 & 5.

consideration by the Board, the Governor.[12] If the prisoner desires the attendance of a doctor or dentist, and pays the expense involved, such a visit will be permitted provided that the Governor is satisfied that there are reasonable grounds for the request.[13] Finally, and most strikingly, if the prisoner pays a sum fixed by the Home Secretary, he may be permitted by the governor or board of visitors to occupy a special cell, furnished at his own expense (if he so wishes), and to be relieved of the duty to clean his cell.[14] Most of the additional rights available to a remand prisoner upon payment are expressed to be subject to any directions of the Home Secretary. Until February 1988 remand prisoners could be supplied with food and drink (including alcohol): this ceased with effect from February 29, 1988.[15]

Remand prisoners are subject to the same scheme of discipline as convicted prisoners. They may be ordered to lose remission in the event of a conviction and sentence of imprisonment, and, by rules 51(4)(g) and (h) of the Prison Rules 1964 may, as a disciplinary award, forfeit the right to receive books, newspapers and writing materials, and to wear their own clothing if guilty of an actual or attempted escape. In addition such prisoners may be transferred from one prison to another by the exercise of executive discretion, and the courts will be reluctant to interfere.[16]

**Female prisoners and babies**

By section 15 of the Prison Act 1952, in a prison used both for men and women, separate buildings or parts of a building must be used for each respectively so as to prevent them seeing or communicating with each other. This is underlined by rule 9(1) of the Prison Rules 1964, under which female prisoners must be kept entirely separate from their male counterparts. In virtually all other respects the Rules apply to male and female prisoners alike. The only example of different treatment is that a female prisoner's hair may not be cut without her consent unless the prison medical officer certifies it to be necessary for the sake of

[12] *Ibid*. r. 41(1). See also *R.* v. *Bryson* (1848) 12 J.P. 585; 37 Digest (Repl.) 442.
[13] *Ibid*. r. 17(4).
[14] *Ibid*. r. 25. This provision is defunct. No such applications have been made or granted in recent years, and, so far as is known, no prison has accommodation available for the purpose: see the Handbook of the Association of Members of Boards of Visitors.
[15] 1988 S.I. No. 89.
[16] See *R.* v. *Home Secretary ex parte McAvoy* [1984] 1 W.L.R. 1408; [1984] 3 All E.R. 417, discussed at p. 140–142 *post*.

health or cleanliness.[17] The male prisoner, on the other hand, is required to have his hair cut as often as may be necessary for neatness.

Subject to any conditions he may think fit, the Home Secretary may permit a female prisoner to have her baby with her in prison, and in such a case everything necessary for the baby's care and maintenance shall be provided there.[18] In 1983 the Home Secretary issued a circular to all prison establishments for women and girls, laying down the criteria for admission to a mother and baby unit, and providing that the final decision should rest with the governor of the relevant establishment. In *R.* v. *Home Secretary ex p. Hickling*[19], the governor of an open prison became concerned at the behaviour of the applicant towards her baby, and ordered that the applicant be sent back to a youth custody centre. The baby was placed in the care of the local authority. The applicant's contentions that the governor had no power to take this course without reference to the Home Secretary, and that the governor had acted in breach of the principles of natural justice failed both at first instance and in the Court of Appeal: it was held to be unrealistic to suggest that the applicant's behaviour should be the subject of special consideration by the Home Secretary, since the governor was the best person to judge. The Home Secretary of State had laid down conditions which had to be fulfilled and it was right to allow the governor to decide whether those conditions were being kept.

## YOUNG PEOPLE IN CUSTODY

### Historical introduction

From the mid nineteenth century onwards there was a steady limitation upon the use of imprisonment for children and young offenders, together with increasing emphasis on separating such offenders from adults in the penal system. From 1838 an old military hospital at Parkhurst was used to hold those offenders aged under 18 who had been sentenced to transportation. Three principal penal institutions developed during the nineteenth and twentieth centuries for the purpose of punishing and educating young offenders and other delinquent children.

[17] rule 26(3) Prison Rules 1964.

[18] *Ibid.* Rule 9(3). Originally children under the age of three could remain with their mothers in open prisons, but the age limit has since been reduced to 18 months.

[19] *The Times*, November 7, 1985.

(i) *Approved schools and community homes*

The Youthful Offenders Act 1854 set up reformatory schools to which those under 16 years of age could be sent for between two and five years following a sentence of imprisonment. Three years later industrial schools were established, and were soon brought under Home Office control. These institutions were aimed at catering for young vagrants. Their use began to change, and under the Children Act 1908 children under 14 could be sent to industrial schools for reasons other than a conviction under the vagrancy legislation. The "sentence" began to resemble the modern care order, whilst reformatory schools were reserved for young offenders as such: under the 1908 Act those between 12 and 16 years of age could be sent to a reformatory school if convicted of an offence punishable with a sentence of imprisonment. These institutions were reorganised in the 1930s to become "schools approved by the Secretary of State" (the so-called "approved schools") for delinquent children between the ages of 10 and 17. The 1969 Children and Young Persons Act brought about a further major reorganisation in the welfare and detention of young persons, and led to the replacement of such sentences by care orders, the direction of the Department of Health of Social Security in these matters, and the introduction of community homes for delinquent and other disadvantaged children.

(ii) *Borstal*

The Gladstone Committee of the 1890s paid particular attention to the age group between 16 and 20, who were still being incarcerated in the mainstream prison system. The committee felt that such persons should be dealt with separately, and recommended a half-way house between prison and reformatory schools, set in a rural area, combining elements of punishment, education and reformation. So began an experiment in 1901 at a village in Kent that was to give its name to a system of punishment. The borstal system was set up nationally by the Prevention of Crimes Act 1908. Its most popular period proved to be the inter-war years, but after the Second World War a combination of factors led to its decline and eventual replacement by the sentence of youth custody.

(iii) *Detention centres*

Yet another form of custodial treatment for young offenders was introduced by section 18 of the Criminal Justice Act 1948, namely detention centres. These were designed to impose a "short sharp shock" upon offenders, and despite suggestions that they were to be abolished in the 1960s and 1970s, they have remained.

**The present system: (i) age categories for sentencing purposes**

There is an irrebuttable presumption that no child under the age of 10 can be guilty of any criminal offence. Between the ages of 10 and 21 there exist three categories for the purposes of criminal law and sentencing:

(a) "children" are those aged 10 or over but less than 14. This category is virtually immune from any custodial sentence.
(b) "young persons" are those aged 14 or over but less than 17. For the purposes of the criminal law all persons under the age of 17 are treated as "juveniles."
(c) "young adults" are those aged 17 or over but less than 21. The significance of this category in the sentencing process has largely evaporated with the changes in the law outlined below, but 17 remains the age at which offenders are automatically dealt with in the adult, as opposed to the juvenile, courts.

**The present system: (ii) reforms made by the Criminal Justice Act 1982**

Before the Criminal Justice Act 1982 came into force, there were three principal custodial sentences for those aged 14 or over and less than 21, namely:

(a) *Detention Centres*

Section 4 of the Criminal Justice Act 1961 gave the courts power to send those aged 14 or over but less than 21 to a detention centre for terms of between three and six months, save that magistrates were limited to a sentence of three months for those offenders under the age of 17.

(b) *Borstal training*

This sentence was available in respect of offenders who were aged 15 or over but less than 21. It was an indeterminate sentence of between six months and two years, release being determined by the Borstal authorities. In practice most trainees were released within a year.

(c) *Imprisonment*

Offenders who were aged 17 or over but less than 21 could be sentenced to a term of imprisonment in certain circumstances, but, subject to exceptions, the length of the sentence had to be of six months or less, or three years or more. This provision was introduced by section 3 of the Criminal Justice Act 1961, with the intention that constructing sufficient number of detention centres would mean the abolition of all sentences of imprisonment of less than three years. The centres were never built. Instead, there was considerable judicial and academic disquiet about a framework which prevented judges from passing sentences which they felt appropriate. Other unfair anomalies existed, in that no remission was available to Bortsal trainees. Periods spent in custody on remand, sometimes of long duration, did not count towards the sentence; this resulted in the absurdity of young people spending longer in custody than older offenders convicted of a similar offence.

The Criminal Justice Act 1982 abolished sentences of imprisonment for those under 21 and borstal training altogether, and replaced them with a single determinate sentence of youth custody. The Act also altered the length of detention centre sentences. The position at present can be summarised as follows:

(i) *Children and Young Persons Act 1933*

(a) Offenders convicted of murder who were under the age of 18 at the date of the offence must be sentenced to detention at Her Majesty's pleasure, and may be detained in such a place and under such conditions as the Secretary of State may direct: section 53(1).

(b) Where a child or young person is convicted of an offence punishable in the case of an adult with imprisonment for 14 years or more the Court may order the detention of the offender for any term within the maximum term available in the case of an adult. Again, such an offender may be detained in such a place and under such conditions as the Secretary of State may direct: section 53(2). These provisions remain unaffected by the 1982 Act.

(ii) *Detention centre orders*

For those offenders aged 14 or over and under 21, convicted of an offence which would be imprisonable in the case of a person aged 21 or over, the Court may make a detention centre order. The length of the sentence must normally be between 21 days and four months.

(iii) *Youth custody orders*

Where a person aged 15 or over, but less than 21 is convicted of an offence which would be imprisonable in the case of a person aged 21 or over, the Court may pass a sentence of youth custody. Such a sentence must not normally be of less than four months, whilst the maximum term corresponds with the maximum term of imprisonment for the offence or offences. Such sentences may be ordered to run consecutively to one another, but, curiously, there is no power to suspend a sentence of youth custody, either wholly or in part. For offenders aged less than 17 there is an effective maximum sentence of 12 months. The Act contains provision for the conversion of a sentence of youth custody into a sentence of imprisonment when the offender reaches 21 and in other circumstances.

(iv) *Custody for life*

Where a person under the age of 21 is convicted of murder or any other offence for which the sentence is fixed by law as life imprisonment, he must be sentenced to custody for life unless section 53(1) of the Children and Young Persons Act 1933 (*supra*) applies. Secondly, where a person aged 17 or over, but under 21 is convicted of an offence which might be punishable by life imprisonment in the case of a person over 21, the Court may impose a sentence of custody for life.

Following the enactment of the Criminal Justice Act 1982, the Youth Custody Rules 1983 and the Detention Centre Rules 1983 were laid before Parliament and came into force on May 24, 1983.[19a] Many of their provisions are identical or closely approximate to the provisions of the Prison Rules 1964 in their variously amended form. It is only where the 1983 Rules significantly add to or differ from the 1964 Rules as amended that such additions or differences will be summarised. It should also be noted that sentences of youth custody and detention centre orders now attract remission in a manner identical to sentences of imprisonment upon adult offenders.

**The treatment of those serving sentences of youth custody**

(i) *General Purpose*

Whereas the purpose of a prison sentence is stated in the

[19a] 1983 S.I. No. 569 (Detention Centres); 1983 S.I. No. 570 (Youth Custody Centres).

Prison Rules as being to encourage and assist prisoners to lead a good and useful life, the purpose of a sentence of youth custody is described altogether more elaborately in Rule 3 of the Youth Custody Centre Rules 1983:

> "The aims of a youth custody centre shall be to provide work training and instruction of a kind that will assist offenders to acquire or develop personal resources, interests and skills; to encourage offenders to exercise self-discipline and accept responsibility; to foster their links with the outside community; and to help them with their return to the community in cooperation with the services responsible for supervision."

(ii) *Regime activities, training courses, education and physical education*

By Rule 34 inmates must be occupied in "work, training courses, education and physical education" in accordance with the aims espoused in Rule 3. In all such activities regard shall be paid to individual assessment and personal development. An inmate may be required to participate in regime activities for a normal working week of no more than 40 hours and for no more than eight hours a day. Inmates may be paid for their work or participation in other activities at rates approved by the Home Secretary. Provision must be made for training courses and education by means of class teaching or private study within the normal working week, and these (together with work) must all be such as will foster an inmate's personal resources, interests and skills and fit him for his return to the community. If an inmate is of compulsory school age, arrangements must be made for his participation in education or vocational training courses for at least 15 hours a week within the normal working week. Other inmates who are backward or illiterate (irrespective of age) must have appropriate arrangements made for their education, if necessary within the normal working week.

Physical education must be provided for inmates for an average of at least two hours per week within the normal working week as well as evening and weekend physical recreation. In the case of inmates of compulsory school age, this is additional to the minimum of 15 hours per week of formal education. Physical education should be designed to foster an inmate's personal resources etc., and to encourage him to make good use of his leisure on release. Appropriate facilities must be provided for any inmate with a need for remedial physical activity.

(iii) *Discipline*

The disciplinary structure in youth custody centres is identical to that in adult establishments, save that powers of punishment are slightly different and more restricted. Both the offences and the procedures for dealing with them are identical, but the range of awards available is as follows:

(i) The Governor may make the following awards:
   (a) Caution.
   (b) Removal of privileges; removal from activities (other than work, training courses, education and physical education within the normal working week); extra work outside the normal working week; stoppage of earnings; and removal from the wing or living unit: all for a *maximum of 14 days*, although provisions exist for the stoppage of a proportion of the inmate's earnings for a longer period.
   (c) Confinement to the cell or room for a maximum of three days.
   (d) Forfeiture of remission for a maximum of 28 days.
(ii) The Board of Visitors or officer of the Secretary of State have the same range of awards available to them, but their powers are greater than that of the governor:
   (b) The maximum for this group of awards is 28 rather than 14 days.
   (c) The maximum for this award is seven days.
   (d) For offences of mutiny, incitement to mutiny, doing gross personal violence to an officer or to any other person, or assaulting an officer, the Board may order forfeiture of remission for a maximum of 180 days: for other offences referred to the Board by the governor, the appropriate maximum is 90 days.

The same provisions concerning suspension, remission and mitigation of awards apply to youth custody centres as apply to adult establishments.

(iv) *Female inmates*

The following specific provisions are made in respect of female inmates of youth custody centres:

(i) The Secretary of State may, subject to conditions, permit a female inmate to have her baby with her in a youth custody centre, and everything necessary for the baby's maintenance and care may be provided there.

(ii) In the case of a female inmate aged 21 or over who is serving a sentence of imprisonment, or who has been committed to prison for default, and who is detained in a youth custody care centre instead of a prison, reasonable facilities must be afforded if she wishes to improve her education, by class teaching or private study. Likewise, such a female must (if not engaged in outdoor work or detained in an open youth custody centre) be given exercise in the open air for not less than one hour in all, each day, weather permitting, although the Secretary of State may in special circumstances reduce this to half an hour per day.

(iii) In the case of a female inmate aged 21 or over who is serving a sentence of imprisonment, or who has been committed to prison for default, the governor has slightly increased disciplinary powers, in that he can order loss of privileges and stoppage of earnings for a maximum of 28 days, rather than the 14 days applicable in the case of conventional inmates (whether male or female). Likewise the Board of Visitors or officer of the Secretary of State have increased powers as follows:

(a) Loss of privileges for any period.
(b) Stoppage of earnings and confinement to cell or room carry a maximum of 56 days.
(c) Forfeiture of remission for a maximum of 180 days, except in the case of mutiny, incitement to mutiny, or doing gross personal violence to an officer, when there is no maximum period.

These provisions are designed to ensure that such females can be treated in a fashion identical to the way in which they could be treated in an adult establishment.

(v) *Supervision and after-care*

By section 15 of the Criminal Justice Act 1982, those released from sentences of youth custody or detention centre remain under the supervision of a probation officer or local authority social worker whilst under 22 years of age in the following circumstances:

(i) If granted neither remission nor parole, for a period of three months from the date of release.

(ii) If granted remission, for a period of three months from the date of release, or until the date upon which the sentence would otherwise have expired, whichever occurs the later.

(iii) If released on parole, the period of supervision begins at the expiration of the period of licence, and ends on the date upon which the offender would have been released had he been granted neither remission nor parole.

All of the above periods of supervision are subject to termination if the offender's 22nd birthday falls during that period. In the case of (ii) and (iii), there is also a maximum, by section 15(9), of 12 months' supervision.

**The treatment of those at detention centres**

The Detention Centre Rules 1983 are closely similar in form and content to the Youth Custody Rules 1983 summarised above. By rule 5 of the former, the Secretary of State must provide junior detention centres for offenders under the age of 17, and senior detention centres for those aged 17 or over. Normally an inmate will be detained at a detention centre appropriate to his age, unless the Secretary of State, taking into account the person's physical and mental development, otherwise directs.

The aims of detention centres are stated in the rules in similar terms to those of youth custody centres, save for the notable addition of the provision of "a disciplined daily routine." In keeping with the general aim of providing offenders with a "short, sharp shock," rule 38 states that provision may be made at a detention centre for parades, drill and inspection. This should be such "as will foster the inmate's personal resources and aptitudes."

Remission is available: for those aged under 17 on the date of their sentence, the maximum remission is one half of the sentence. As for privileges, these are dependent upon a system of grades, determined by the governor and altered from time to time by him in what he considers to be the best interest of the inmate concerned.

The following disciplinary awards are available:

(a) Caution.

(b) Reduction in grade.

(c) Removal from activity of the detention centre (other than work, education or physical education within the normal working week); extra work outside the normal working week; stoppage of earnings; removal from the wing or living unit; all for a maximum of 14 days if the award is made by the governor, or 28 days if imposed by a Board of Visitors.

(d) Confinement to the cell or room for a maximum of three days if the award is made by the governor, or seven days in the case of the Board of Visitors.

(e) Forfeiture of remission for a maximum of seven days if awarded by the governor. There is no limit upon this award if made by a Board of Visitors.

## APPELLANTS AND PRISONERS AWAITING SENTENCE

Prior to 1972, rules 57–62 of the Prison Rules 1964 made special provision for visits, correspondence and medical facilities for appellants and those awaiting sentence. With the introduction of rule 37(A) separate categorisation was rendered largely unnecessary. Appellants and those prisoners awaiting sentence are now treated identically to convicted prisoners, and have lost their privileged status as remand prisoners. The 1972 changes involved the abrogation of certain visiting privileges.

## POLITICAL PRISONERS

By rule 64 of the Prison Rules 1964, prisoners serving sentences on conviction of sedition, seditious conspiracy and seditious libel were afforded special treatment analogous to that afforded to remand prisoners. The offences were rarely charged, and the special status of such prisoners was abolished by the Prison (Amendment) Rules 1972. Similarly, between 1972 and 1976, a "special category" status for certain convicted prisoners in Northern Ireland existed, but was abolished in respect of those convicted after March 1, 1976.

## PRISONERS IMPRISONED FOR CONTEMPT

This group of prisoners must, by rule 63(2) of the Prison Rules 1964, be treated as a separate class, and has the same rights and privileges as unconvicted prisoners in respect of clothing, correspondence and visits. Although separately classified, such prisoners may be permitted to associate with any other class of prisoners if willing to do so. So long as their detention is for a stated period in excess of five days, they must be treated as serving an equivalent term of imprisonment for the purposes of eligibility for and calculation of remission.

## Civil Prisoners

By section 47(4)(d) of the Prison Act 1952 rules made under the section must provide for special treatment of civil prisoners, and by rule 63 of the Prison Rules 1964 they have the same rights and privileges as unconvicted prisoners in respect of clothing, correspondence and visits. The numbers of such prisoners are small, being restricted to maintenance defaulters, and those who have failed to pay taxes or rates. By rule 36 a person detained in prison in default of payment of a sum of money may communicate with, and be visited at any reasonable time of day by, any friend or relative to arrange for payment in order to secure his release from prison.

## Military Prisoners

The disciplinary provisions applicable to members of the armed forces are found in a number of statutes, principally the Army Act 1955, the Air Force Act 1955, and the Naval Discipline Act 1957, together with Queen's Regulations made under the royal prerogative, and the Armed Forces Act 1971. By section 53(1) of the Prison Act 1952, naval, military and air force prisons are excluded from the scope of the Act. If military prisoners are transferred to civil prisons they are to be treated as if confined under a like sentence of a civil court.[20] By section 46 of the Mental Health Act 1983, the Home Secretary may direct the detention in hospital of any serviceman ordered to be detained at Her Majesty's pleasure: such a direction has the effect of a restriction order without limit of time.[21]

[20] See Army Act 1955, s.125(1), Air Force Act 1955, s.125(1) and Naval Discipline Act 1957, s.83.

[21] See "Mentally Disordered Prisoners," p. 52–3.

## Mentally Disordered Prisoners

### Hospital orders

The Mental Health Act 1983 received the royal assent on May 9 of that year, substantially altering and replacing the 1959 Act of the same name, and consolidating other enactments. Insofar as it concerns offenders, it provides by section 37 that a criminal court may authorise the admission to and detention at a hospital specified in the order if satisfied on the oral or written evidence of two registered medical practitioners that the offender is suffering from mental illness, psychopathic disorder, severe mental impairment, or mental impairment, and that this mental disorder is of such a nature and degree that detention in hospital for treatment is appropriate. The court must also be satisfied that this is the most suitable method of disposing of the case.

Under section 41, the Crown Court can order restriction on discharge for a specified or unlimited period. The Act also provides for interim hospital orders for up to 12 weeks (but renewable thereafter for 28 days at a time, up to a total of six months detention). The court has power to order a remand to a hospital for reports upon the accused's mental condition, or for treatment. The detailed workings of hospital orders and the provisions for seeking discharge from such orders fall outside the scope of this book.

### Transfer from prison to hospital

Section 47 of the 1983 Act enables the Home Secretary to direct that a person serving a sentence of imprisonment or other detention be removed to and detained in a mental hospital (referred to under the Act as a "transfer direction"). Such a direction has the same effect as a hospital order made without restriction on discharge, under section 37. The Home Secretary has power where he thinks fit to direct that the offender be subject to section 41 restrictions, and such a direction ("restriction direction") is usually made. This restriction direction ceases to have effect on what would have been the patient's earliest date of release had he remained in prison.[22] Before making a transfer direction, the Home Secretary must be satisfied by reports from at least two registered medical practitioners that the prisoner is suffering from one of the four conditions set out in section 37 (see above), and that this mental disorder is of a nature or degree which makes

[22] Mental Health Act 1983, s.50(2)–(5).

it appropriate for him to be detained in a hospital for medical treatment.

The Home Secretary has similar powers to direct the transfer of remand prisoners and civil prisoners, where such persons are suffering from mental illness or severe mental impairment of a sort which requires urgent medical treatment. Such a transfer direction ceases to have effect in the case of a remand prisoner when the matter is finally dealt with by the appropriate court, but in the meantime the Home Secretary has power to direct the patient's return to prison.[23] Likewise, a transfer direction made in respect of a civil prisoner or a person detained under the Immigration Act 1971 ceases to have effect on the expiration of the period of detention that would have occurred had the removal to hospital not taken place.

## Transfer from hospital to prison

Section 50 of the 1983 Act provides that if the Home Secretary is informed[24] that a prisoner who has been transferred to hospital subject to a restriction direction no longer requires treatment, he may either direct that the patient be returned to prison to serve the remainder of his sentence, or release him from hospital on the same terms as those upon which he could have been released from prison.

## Mentally disordered offenders in prison

The only provision in the Prison Act 1952 or the 1964 Rules dealing with mentally disordered offenders is Rule 18, under which the prison's medical officer must report to the governor on the case of any prisoner whose health is likely to be injuriously affected by continued imprisonment or by prison conditions. The governor in turn must send this report, together with his own recommendations, to the Home Secretary without delay. Rule 18(2) and (3) requires the prison's medical officer to pay special attention to any prisoner whose mental condition appears to require it, and to inform the governor if he suspects any prisoner of having suicidal intentions.

[23] Mental Health Act 1983, s.51(2) and (3).
[24] By the responsible medical officer, any other medical practitioner, or the Mental Health Review Tribunal.

## *Chapter 5*

# THE DAILY REGIME IN PRISONS



The purpose of the training and treatment of convicted prisoners is stated in rule 1 of the Prison Rules 1964 to be "to encourage and assist them to lead a good and useful life." A large number of the rules concern aspects of everyday life in prisons, and it is the purpose of this chapter to summarise these and the decided cases arising out of them. It should be borne in mind that the present state of the law is that a breach of the rules by the authorities gives the prisoner no right to sue in private law for damages, although decisions arrived at by the prison authorities in breach of the provisions of a rule may in some circumstances be successfully challenged in judicial review proceedings.

## Reception

A prisoner may be lawfully confined in any prison, and the choice of the institution to which he is sent lies wholly in the hands of the prison authorities, acting under the direction of the Home

Office.[1] The prisoner is not liable to pay the cost of his conveyance to prison.[2]

On reception every prisoner is *searched* by an officer of the same sex "in as seemly a manner as is consistent with discovering anything concealed," although he may not be stripped and searched in the sight of another prisoner.[3] Prisoners may be *photographed* and *measured* on reception, and indeed subsequently, but copies of such photographs may not be given to persons unauthorised to see them.[4] Regulations dated June 20, 1896 govern the photographing of prisoners[4a]: they may be photographed full face and in profile, and the regulations provide for the clothes which may be worn on such occasions. *Finger-prints* may be taken, and descriptions of scars and other distinctive marks made. The prisoner's *religious denomination* is recorded. Finally, a personal record of every prisoner is prepared and maintained subject to the directions of the Home Secretary.[5]

On a more pleasant note, rule 26(2) of the Prison Rules 1964 provides that every prisoner shall be required to take a hot bath on reception. The rules require the prison authorities to provide every prisoner as soon as possible after reception, and in any event within 24 hours, with written information about the rules, earnings, privileges, methods of complaint, etc. By rule 7 the governor must also ensure that a prisoner has read, or had explained to him, the written information which the prison authorities are obliged to supply. A copy of the rules must be available to the prisoner on request.[6]

As for any property on the prisoner's person on reception into prison, that which he is not permitted to retain for his own use is taken into the governor's custody, and an inventory of such property must be kept. The prisoner must sign the inventory, after being given a proper opportunity to ensure its accuracy. Any cash which the prisoner has must be paid into an account

[1] s.12 Prison Act 1952.
[2] *Ibid.*, s.21.
[3] Prison Rules 1964, r. 39.
[4] *Ibid.*, r. 40(2).
[4a] 1896 SR&O. 1896 No. 762. See too S.54(3) Prison Act 1952
[5] *Ibid.*, r. 40(1).
[6] See generally the amendments made to rule 7 by (1983) S.I. No. 568: in practice prisoners are supplied with a booklet, "Information to Prisoners" supplemented by leaflets dealing with individual matters such as legal aid, bail, and appeals.

under the governor's control, and the prisoner must be credited with that amount in the books of the prison.[7]

## THE SECURITY CLASSIFICATION OF PRISONERS

Rule 3(1) of the Prison Rules 1964 provides for classification of prisoners in accordance with any directions of the Secretary of State having regard to their age, temperament and record, and with a view to maintaining good order, facilitating training, and encouraging and assisting them to lead a good and useful life.

Although there is no specific statutory basis for such a practice, prisoners are classified for security purposes into four categories:

(1) *Category A*
Those whose escape would be highly dangerous to the public, to the police, or to the security of the state.

(2) *Category B*
Those for whom the very highest conditions of security are not necessary but for whom escape must be made very difficult.

(3) *Category C*
Those who cannot be trusted in open conditions, but who do not have the ability or resources to make a determined escape attempt.

(4) *Category D*
Those who can reasonably be trusted to serve their sentences in open conditions.

In *R.* v. *Board of Visitors Hull Prison ex p. St. Germain* Waller L.J. said, *obiter*:

> "There are many administrative decisions which would not be capable of review and which would have as serious consequences to the prisoner as some findings of a board of visitors. . . . Prisoners may be categorised A, B or C and the consequences in conditions may be very different, for example the difference between a top-security prison and an open prison."[7a]

The correctness of this assertion is now open to question.

[7] Prison Rules 1964, r. 41(2) and (3).
[7a] [1979] Q.B. 425 at p. 466 [1979] 2 W.L.R. 42 at p. 71 [1979] 1 All E.R. 701 at p. 725.

Although the prisoner has no right or opportunity to make representations in respect of his security classification, it has been held that there is always a duty on the prison authorities in deciding that classification to act fairly;[8] and it is submitted that if a prisoner could produce evidence that the relevant prison authorities had acted unfairly or capriciously in determining his security classification, the courts would be prepared to review the decision. There is an analogy between this type of situation, and the wide power vested in the Home Secretary in respect of transfers of prisoners from one prison to another, a power which is subject to some limited judicial supervision.[9] Finally, the security classification of prisoners does not fall within the scope of any of the rights or freedoms guaranteed by the European Convention.[10]

## THE SYSTEM OF PRIVILEGES

By rule 4 of the Prison Rules 1964, there must be a system of privileges established at every prison. This must be approved by the Home Secretary and be appropriate to the classes of prisoners held there. The system must include arrangements under which money earned by prisoners may be spent by them in prison. Rule 22(2) expressly provides that no prisoner may be permitted to smoke or have tobacco save as a privilege and in accordance with any orders of the governor. Curiously, this provision appears to apply equally to unconvicted prisoners. Once granted, privileges can be taken away without explanation or reason being given; they may also be forfeited as a disciplinary sanction.

In the nineteenth century, under the "silent" system, talking was a privilege. In the late twentieth century, there are three ranges of privileges:

(i) The first range, available to all prisoners, consists of library and other books and other reading matter, educational classes and correspondence courses, canteen purchases from earnings, and the possession of tobacco and a radio.

(ii) The second range is at the governor's discretion and is dependent upon the accommodation and facilities available. It consists of association for meals and recreation,

[8] *Payne* v. *Home Office*, unreported, May 2, 1977, *per* Cantley J.

[9] As decided in *R.* v. *Home Secretary ex p. McAvoy* [1984] 3 A.E.R. 417; [1984] 1 W.L.R. 1408.

[10] *Brady* v. *U.K.* (1979) 3 E.H.R.R. 297 at p. 300, and App. No. /0117/82 v. *U.K.* (1985) 7 E.H.R.R. 140.

television and other forms of entertainment, and games, occupations and personal possessions in the prisoner's cell.

(iii) Prisoners serving longer sentences in training prisons become eligible for the third range of privileges after having served three years. These privileges include flowers and pot plants, bedspreads, table covers, etc. in the prisoner's cell.[11]

## ACCOMMODATION

### Cells and sleeping accommodation

By section 14(2) of the Prison Act 1952, no cell may be used for confining a prisoner unless its size, heating, lighting, ventilation and fittings have been certified as adequate for health and for communication with prison staff. The certificate is issued by an officer of the Secretary of State, not being an officer of the prison, and must identify the cell to which it relates. The cell itself must be conspicuously marked. The certificate may limit both the period of time for which a prisoner can be separately confined in the cell, and the number of hours per day during which a prisoner can be employed therein. The certificate may be withdrawn if the conditions in the cell no longer correspond to those certified. The Secretary of State must satisfy himself from time to time that sufficient accommodation is provided for all prisoners in every prison.[12]

No cell can be used as sleeping accommodation for a prisoner unless so certified under section 14 above. The certificate must specify the maximum number of prisoners who may sleep or are confined in the cell to which it relates: that number may only be exceeded with the leave of the Secretary of State.[13] Every prisoner is entitled to a separate bed and to bedding adequate for his warmth and health.[14]

It can be seen that the force of section 14 is greatly diminished by the discretion to exceed the proper maximum number of prisoners to a cell conferred by rule 23. The clear intention of

[11] See generally *Prisons and the Prisoner* 1977, H.M.S.O., in particular paragraphs 74 and 77.
[12] s.14 Prison Act 1952.
[13] rule 23 Prison Rules 1964.
[14] *Ibid.*, rule 24.

section 14 is that a prisoner's accommodation should be suitable and sufficient, and that the Secretary of State should satisfy himself of this. Yet the rule made under the powers conferred by the Act permits the Secretary of State to sanction overcrowding. It is an illogical and highly unsatisfactory position, compounded by the rejection by Tudor Evans J. in the *Control Unit* case[15] of the proposition that although detention is lawful, it may become unlawful if the conditions of imprisonment change. Some grounds for optimism for convicted prisoners are provided by the provisions of the Bill of Rights 1688, prohibiting the infliction of cruel and unusual punishments, and by the decisions in *ex p. Nahar* and *ex p. Herbage (No. 2)* summarised in Chapter 3.[16]

## FOOD AND DRINK

There are no detailed provisions in the Prison Rules as to the frequency of meals, or the quantity of food to be provided. However, by rule 21(4), such food must be wholesome, nutritious, well prepared and served, reasonably varied, and sufficient in quantity. To comply with these provisions, the rules require regular inspection of the food served, both before and after cooking, by the Prison's Medical Officer.[17] Moreover, by rule 95(2), as amended in 1971, the Board of Visitors must arrange for the food to be inspected by a member at frequent intervals.

No convicted prisoner can be given less food than ordinarily provided except by the authority of the medical officer,[18] and the former punishment of restricted diet (known to laymen as "bread and water") was abolished in 1974. Nor can a convicted prisoner be given food different to that ordinarily provided save by the authority of the medical officer, or by direction of the Secretary of State.

Convicted prisoners are not permitted to have alcohol except under the written order of the medical officer. The provisions in

[15] *Williams* v. *Home Office No. 2* [1981] 1 All E.R. 1211: for a full discussion of the case, see pp. 103–106 below.
[16] *Supra* pp. 26–28.
[17] rule 21(5) Prison Rules 1964.
[18] rule 21(2) and (3) Prison Rules 1964. In paragraph 58 of Prisons and the Prisoner (H.M.S.O. 1977) the Home Office state: "Arrangements are also made where necessary for prisoners to comply, within reason, with the terms of their faith in matters of dress and diet."

respect of unconvicted prisoners were substantially more flexible as regards both food and drink, until February 1988. Possession of tobacco is expressly stated to be a privilege by rule 22(2) of the Prison Rules.

## CLOTHING

Convicted prisoners must be supplied with clothing adequate for their warmth and health, including suitable protective clothing for use at work where necessary. A prisoner may be provided where necessary with suitable and adequate clothing on his release. Convicted prisoners are not entitled to wear clothing other than that supplied under the Prison Rules, except on the directions of the Home Secretary. However, when a prisoner is taken in custody to court, he must be permitted to wear his own clothing, or clothing different to that ordinarily provided under the rules.[19]

In *McFeeley* v. *United Kingdom*[20] the applicants had been sentenced to varying terms of imprisonment for terrorist offences in Northern Ireland. The so-called "special category" status for certain prisoners, under which they had been permitted to wear their own clothes, was phased out, and the applicants were required to submit to the ordinary prison regime. This led to a prolonged and widespread protest by a number of prisoners, who refused, *inter alia*, to wear prison clothing. The European Commission held that the Convention imposed no obligation upon the British Government to accept the applicants' demands not to wear prison clothing. Moreover:

> "The Commission does not consider there to be anything inherently or objectionable about the requirement to wear a uniform . . . "

## MEDICAL CARE

### Rights and duties of the prison medical officer

Every prison must have a medical officer, duly registered

[19] Prison Rules 1964, rr. 20 and 38(3). The standing orders require clothing to be "clean, aired and in a reasonable condition," with socks and underclothes being changed regularly and as frequently as practicable.
[20] (1980) 3 E.H.R.R. 161, at p. 196.

under the Medical Acts and appointed by the Home Secretary.[21] The medical officer is a prison officer within the meaning of the Prison Act 1952.[22] He has the care of the mental and physical health of all of the prisoners in the prison. He may consult with another medical practitioner if he so desires, and must do so before performing any serious operation if time permits. Every request made by a prisoner to see the medical officer must be recorded by the officer to whom the request is made, and promptly passed on to the medical officer.[23]

By rule 18 of the Prison Rules 1964, the medical officer must report to the governor on the case of any prisoner whose health is likely to be injuriously affected by continued imprisonment or conditions thereof, and must pay special attention to any prisoner whose mental condition appears to require it. Likewise, if the medical officer suspects the prisoner of having suicidal intentions, he must inform the governor and the prisoner must be placed under special observation.[24] The medical officer must regularly inspect prison food, both before and after cooking: if he finds any deficiency or defect, he must report it to the governor.[25] Finally, he must decide upon the fitness of every prisoner for exercise and physical training.[26]

A prison's medical officer also possesses a wide range of discretionary powers. He can authorise the provision of food other than that supplied to the rest of the prisoners; by written order he may permit a prisoner to take alcohol; he may exempt a prisoner from the requirement to shave daily; he may excuse the prisoner from activities such as exercise and work.[27] If the medical officer so advises on medical grounds, the governor must arrange the resumption of association for any prisoner removed from such association under rule 43.

Where a prisoner is a party to legal proceedings he may select a medical practitioner to examine him in connection with those

[21] Prison Act 1952, s.7(1), (5). In practice over half of the medical work in prisons is carried out by doctors from outside the full-time prison service, namely by part-time general practitioners and visiting specialists.

[22] See *Freeman* v. *Home Office* [1984] Q.B. 524; [1984] 2 W.L.R.; [1984] 1 All E.R. 1036 802 C.A.

[23] Prison Rules 1964, r. 17(1), (2), (3).

[24] *Ibid.*, r. 18(1)–(3).

[25] *Ibid.*, r. 21(5).

[26] *Ibid.*, r. 27(3).

[27] *Ibid.*, rr. 21(2), 22 (1), 26(2), 27(3).

proceedings, and the doctor must be afforded reasonable facilities to examine him. Such examination must be out of the hearing but may be in the sight of a prison officer.[28] This is the only provision in the rules which permits a convicted prisoner a medical examination by a doctor of his own choice.

Section 22(2)(b) of the Prison Act 1952 authorises the Home Secretary, if he is satisfied that a prisoner requires medical or surgical treatment, to direct that prisoner to be taken to a hospital or other suitable place for treatment. Under section 17 of the Act, the medical officer is prohibited from applying any painful tests to a prisoner for the purpose of detecting malingering or for any other purpose save with proper authority.

There is no specific provision, either in the Act or the rules, dealing with the prisoner's consent to medical treatment. This issue arose in *Freeman* v. *Home Office*.[29] In 1973 drugs had been administered to the plaintiff, who was serving a life sentence. Six years later he sued the Home Office in trespass to the person and negligence, alleging that the drugs had been administered without his consent. The claim in negligence was struck out as being statute barred, and so the case proceeded in trespass only. The plaintiff alleged that the drugs had not been for the relief of any recognised medical disorder, but were administered to control him as a disciplinary rather than medical measure, and that his consent was not "informed," in that he had not been told the nature of his illness, the nature of the treatment proposed, or the risks of that treatment. The judge at first instance rejected the plaintiff's evidence, holding that although the court must be alive to the risk that what might appear to be real consent was not in fact such, on the facts it could not be inferred that an assault had been committed. In the Court of Appeal it was held that since the doctrine of informed consent had no place in English law, the issue was a purely factual one, and had been resolved by the judge at first instance. The appeal was therefore dismissed.[30]

Where a governor has ordered a prisoner to be put under restraint, notice of such order must be given to the medical officer without delay. On receipt of the notice, the medical officer must

[28] *Ibid.*, r. 27(A)(3), as amended by (1972) S.I. No. 1860.

[29] [1984] Q.B. 524; [1984] 2 W.L.R. 802; [1984] 1 All E.R. 1036.

[30] At the time that the Court of Appeal decided *Freeman*, appeal to the House of Lords in *Sidaway* v. *Bethlehem Royal Hospital* [1985] A.C. 871 [1985] 2 W.L.R. 480; [1985] 1 All E.R. 643 was pending. In view of the restatement by their Lordships that the doctrine of informed consent had no place in English law, the decision in *Freeman* remains good law.

inform the governor whether he concurs in the order. The governor is then bound to give effect to any recommendation made by the medical officer.[31]

**Temporary removal and release due to ill health**

This is discussed in Chapter 8.

## HYGIENE

After taking a hot bath on reception into prison,[32] the prisoner must be provided with toilet articles necessary for health and cleanliness, which must be replaced as the need arises. Prisoners are required to wash at proper times, to bath at least once a week, to shave or be shaved daily, and to have their hair cut as often as is necessary for neatness. These provisions are subject to the discretion of the governor or medical officer, and differ in the cases of female and unconvicted prisoners.[33] There is no specific provision in either the principal Act or the rules imposing any duty upon the authorities to provide and maintain suitable sanitation: hence the practice of providing prisoners with chamber pots, and the "slopping out" of these each morning, has become a feature of life in many prisons, despite attracting widespread and deserved criticism.

## WORK

The prison authorities may require convicted prisoners to do useful work for a maximum of 10 hours per day (no minimum being prescribed), and where possible arrangements must be made to allow them to work outside their cells and in association with one another. The work must be of a kind authorised by the Home Secretary, and a prisoner cannot work in the service of another prisoner or of a prison officer or for the private benefit of another person without such authority. Prisoners may be paid for their work at rates approved by the Home Secretary either generally or in particular cases. The medical officer may excuse a prisoner from work on medical grounds, but otherwise, by rule

[31] rule 46, Prison Rules 1964.
[32] See p. 55 *ante*.
[33] Prison Rules 1964, r. 26. In practice adult prisoners are now allowed to wear their hair much as they wish.

47(17) of the Prison Rules, it is a disciplinary offence to refuse to work or to be idle, careless or negligent at work. Prisoners may not however be required to do work which is not of a class for which they have been passed fit by the medical officer.[34] Arrangements must be made so as not to require prisoners to do unnecessary work on their recognised days of religious observance.[35]

**The common law duty owed by the prison authorities**

Those responsible for the administration of a prison owe to those detained within it the common duty to take reasonable care for their safety. In the context of employment the authorities owe a duty to those prisoners engaged in work to provide them with a reasonably safe place and system of work. This was clearly recognised by Lord Goddard C.J. in *Pullen* v. *Prison Commissioners*.[36] The plaintiff, while in prison, was put to work on the manufacture of mats in the prison workshop. While on remand he had been examined and found fit for normal work. Four months after being released, he was found to be suffering from tuberculosis. The judge found that there was no negligence on the part of the prison authorities, and that there was nothing to alert the prison doctors to the fact that the Plaintiff might be a tuberculosis sufferer. He did, however, observe:

> "If I were satisfied that the prisoner was set to work in such conditions that his health was undermined by the conditions in which he was working, I think it might very well be that . . . he might have a cause of action: but I cannot find that here."

The plaintiff in *Ferguson* v. *Home Office*[37] was successful in his action for negligence. While operating a circular hand-saw, he severely injured a hand. Caulfield J. held that the defendants owed the plaintiff a duty of care as he fell within the "neighbour principle" enunciated in *Donoghue* v. *Stevenson*[38] and that this duty continued although the plaintiff was cutting a piece of wood for a fellow prisoner and was not using the machine in the interests of the prison service. The cause of the accident was that the plaintiff was wholly untrained in the use of the machine, and should not have been permitted to use it at all. In those circum-

[34] The above provisions are all contained in rule 28 Prison Rules 1964.
[35] *Ibid.*, rule 15.
[36] [1957] 1 W.L.R. 1186; [1957] 3 All E.R. 470.
[37] *The Times*, October 8, 1977.
[38] [1932] A.C. 562; [1932] All E.R. 1.

stances the plaintiff was entitled to succeed against the defendants and recovered £15,500 in damages.

**Statutory duties owed by the Prison Authorities**

In *Pullen* v. *Prison Commissioners*[39] Lord Goddard C.J. held that a prison workshop was not a "factory" within the meaning of section 151 of the Factories Act 1937, since re-enacted in section 175 of the Factories Act 1961. He observed that the Act was designed to apply to those working under a contract and not to prisoners employed on labour as a part of penal discipline. Thus no action can be brought, based upon any breach of the provisions of the Act. The Health and Safety at Work Act 1974 binds the Crown, but the Home Secretary may by order exempt the Crown from all or any of the provisions of Part I of the Act if it appears to him to be expedient to do so in the interests of persons lawfully detained. Moreover, few of the provisions of the Act apply to work carried out by prisoners since by section 52(1)(a) "work" means work as an employee under a contract of employment, and the observation of Lord Goddard summarised above suggests that prisoners would be excluded from the definition of "employee" in the Act. Finally, section 47(1) of the 1974 Act specifically provides that breaches of the duties contained in sections 2 to 8 will not confer any right of action in civil proceedings. So a prisoner wishing to claim damages for injuries sustained whilst working in the service of the prison authorities will probably be restricted to an action in negligence, and will be unable to add a claim for breach of statutory duty.

**Other compensation for injuries at work**

Prisoners are not able to take advantage of the industrial injuries scheme if injured at work. Any prisoner likely to be disabled after release as a result of his prison employment is examined by a Board set up by the Department of Health and Social Security, and he may be made payments at the statutory rates in lieu of disablement benefit if the Board so recommends.

## EDUCATION

The prison authorities are obliged by rule 29 of the Prison Rules 1964 to provide reasonable facilities for prisoners to improve their

[39] [1957] 1 W.L.R. 1186; [1957] 3 All E.R. 470.

education by correspondence courses or private study in their spare time. Programmes of evening educational classes must also be arranged at every prison. Despite these obligations the provision of educational classes and correspondence courses is in practice treated as a privilege, liable to forfeiture as a punishment. The rules also provide that special attention should be paid to the education of illiterate prisoners, and if necessary they may be taught during time when otherwise they would be working.[40]

Every prison must have a library, and subject to directions made by the Secretary of State, prisoners must be allowed to have and to exchange library books.[41] Again this has become a privilege rather than a right.

## EXERCISE

Subject to the views of the prison's medical officer, every prisoner held in a closed prison who is not engaged in outdoor work must be given a minimum of one hour's outdoor exercise every day, weather permitting. In special circumstances the Secretary of State may reduce that period to half an hour. Exercise consisting of physical training may be given indoors.[42] By implication, there is nothing to prevent a prisoner from being incarcerated in his cell for 23 out of every 24 hours. Indeed, that has proved to be the daily regime for many prisoners in recent years in local prisons and remand centres.

## RELIGION

By Section 7(1) of the Prison Act 1952 every prison must have a chaplain, and if the prison is large enough in the opinion of the Secretary of State to require it, an assistant chaplain may also be appointed.[43] Both must be clergymen of the Church of England, and are appointed by the Home Secretary. Notice of their nomination to a prison must be given within one month to the Bishop of the Diocese in which the prison is situated. They are only

[40] rule 29(3) Prison Rules 1964. See generally the Reports of the House of Commons Education Science and Arts Committee on Prison Education H.C. 45 and 453 H.M.S.O.

[41] *Ibid.*, rule 30.

[42] rule 27 Prison Rules 1964.

[43] s.7(3) of the Prison Act 1952.

permitted to officiate in the prison under the authority of a licence from the Bishop. A chaplain may serve as such in two prisons only if they are within convenient distance of each other, and are together designed to receive not more than 100 prisoners.[44] Substitute chaplains and prison ministers may be appointed.

The Act makes some provisions for prisoners who belong to other denominations; the Home Secretary may appoint a minister of another denomination to a prison if he considers that the number of prisoners of that denomination require it. Such a prison minister may be allowed to visit prisoners of his own denomination, though no prisoner may be so visited against his will.[45] Roman Catholic and Methodist ministers are appointed to every prison.

On reception to prison a prisoner's denomination must be recorded by the governor, although a prisoner may subsequently apply to have the record amended.[46] The special duties of chaplains and prison ministers are set out in rules 11 to 13 of the Prison Rules and may be summarised as follows:

(i) the interviewing of each prisoner of his denomination soon after his reception, and shortly before his release.
(ii) the reading of the burial service at the funeral of any prisoner of his denomination who dies in the prison unless other arrangements have been made.
(iii) daily visiting of all prisoners who are sick, under restraint, or undergoing cellular confinement.
(iv) regular visiting of prisoners.
(v) the chaplain must conduct services for Church of England prisoners at least once every Sunday, Christmas Day, and Good Friday. Other religious services may be arranged.

Arrangements must be made so as not to require prisoners of the Christian religion to do any unnecessary work on Sunday, Christmas Day, or Good Friday, or prisoners of other denominations on their recognised days of religious observance. Such religious books recognised by his denomination as are approved by the Home Secretary must be made available for the personal use of every prisoner so far as is reasonably practicable.

[44] *Ibid.*, s.9.
[45] *Ibid.*, s.10.
[46] s.10(5) of the Prison Act 1952, rule 10 Prison Rules 1964 as amended by (1974) S.I. No. 713.

By section 10(4) of the Prison Act 1952, prisoners not belonging to the Church of England must be allowed to attend chapel and to be visited by the prison chaplain in accordance with the arrangements made for the prison in which they are confined.

## PRISONERS' PROPERTY

Any cash which a prisoner has at a prison must be paid into an account under the governor's control, and the prisoner credited with the relevant amount in the books of the prison. Other property which the prisoner has but is not allowed to retain must be taken into the governor's custody. An inventory must be drawn up, and the prisoner required to sign it after having a proper opportunity to check it. Any article remaining unclaimed for more than three years after the prisoner leaves prison or dies may be sold or otherwise disposed of, and the proceeds paid to the National Association for the Care and Resettlement of Offenders ("NACRO").[47]

## MONEY AND ARTICLES RECEIVED BY POST

When cash, security for money, or other articles, are sent by post to a prisoner, the governor has a wide discretion as to how to deal with it. Cash itself may not be delivered to the prisoner but may be paid into an account under the governor's control, and the prisoner credited with the requisite amount in the books of the prison. Any other property or security for money may be delivered to the prisoner or placed with his property at the prison. Alternatively, anything sent to the prisoner may simply be returned to the sender, although where the sender's name and address are unknown the money may be paid to NACRO for its general purposes. A security may be cashed and dealt with in this way: likewise any other property may be sold and the net proceeds of sale so applied. The rules provide that the prisoner must be informed of the manner in which the money or property is dealt with, and if he has been committed to prison in default of payment of a sum of money, he must be informed of the receipt of any cash sent to him; unless he objects, the cash will be applied in total or partial satisfaction of the amount due.

[47] rule 41(1)–(3A), Prison Rules 1964.

It is clear from the above summary of rule 42 that the prisoner has no *right* to receive anything sent to him by post. In *Becker* v. *Home Office*[48] a cheque was sent to the plaintiff while she was in prison. The cheque was not dealt with in any of the ways prescribed by the rules. In fact it was held by the prison authorities and then eventually lost. The plaintiff claimed damages for the unlawful detention of the cheque. That part of her claim failed, and her appeal was dismissed by the Court of Appeal. Lord Denning M.R. stated:

> "A convicted prisoner, who is in custody, cannot claim to have delivered to him property which comes into the prison addressed to him. The prison authorities must be able to take possession of it whilst he is in custody, just as they can take possession of property found on him."

That passage alone would have been sufficient to dispose of Mrs. Becker's claim, but the Master of the Rolls went further in a passage much quoted in subsequent cases:

> "If the Courts were to entertain actions by disgruntled prisoners, the governor's life would be made intolerable. The discipline of the prison would be undermined. The Prison Rules are regulatory directions only. Even if they are not observed, they do not give rise to a cause of action."[49]

Edmund Davies L.J. concurred on the grounds, *inter alia*, that the disposal of the cheque was a matter for the governor's discretion, and that although the courses of action set out in rule 42 had not been followed, a breach of the rules did not *per se* create any civil liability.[50]

It is an offence against discipline for a prisoner to have in his cell or room or possession any unauthorised article.[51] Such an article, if found in his possession, may be confiscated by the governor.

## COMPLAINTS AND GRIEVANCES

If a prisoner wishes to make a formal complaint about any aspect of his imprisonment there are a number of avenues open to him.

[48] [1972] 2 Q.B. 407; [1972] 2 W.L.R. 1193; [1972] 2 All E.R. 676 C.A.
[49] [1972] 2 Q.B. 407 at p. 418.
[50] *Ibid.*, at p.420.
[51] rule 47(7) Prison Rules 1964.

It is a disciplinary offence repeatedly to make groundless complaints, and likewise to make a false and malicious allegation against a prison officer.[52] The following is a summary of the persons and bodies to whom complaints may be made.

(i) *The governor*

Every request by a prisoner to see the governor must be recorded by the officer to whom it is made and promptly passed on to the governor, who in turn must hear the applications of prisoners who have asked to see him on every day other than Sundays and public holidays.[53]

(ii) *A member of the Board of Visitors or a visiting officer of the Prison Department*

Requests by prisoners to see a Board member or Visiting Officer must be recorded in the same way as requests to see the governor. The governor must ensure that such persons are told of the request on their next visit to the prison.[54] One of the particular duties of members of the Board of Visitors under rule 95 of the Prison Rules is to hear any complaint which a prisoner wishes to make to them.

(iii) *The Home Secretary*

Although there is no statutory authority for the practice, prisoners may petition the Home Secretary. Indeed, this is the usual method of appeal against disciplinary adjudications by the governor or the Board of Visitors. Petition forms are provided by the prison authorities. Prior to December 1, 1981, administrative directives provided that, with certain exceptions, a prisoner could not petition if and so long as he was awaiting a reply to an earlier petition. This was relaxed from that date, and a prisoner may now submit a further petition if a month has elapsed from the date of the previous petition: on certain specified matters[55] he need not wait for this period to elapse but may petition forthwith. A reply to a petition is read out to the prisoner individually in the absence of other prisoners, and he is provided with a copy of such replies. Under the standing orders, governors are requested to

[52] Prison Rules 1964, r. 47(12).
[53] *Ibid.*, r. 8(1), (2).
[54] *Ibid.*, r. 8(3).
[55] These are matters concerning conviction and sentence, parole, deportation, interference with correspondence, and adjudications at which the prisoner was found guilty.

submit a reminder slip in respect of any petition which has remained unanswered for two months.

(iv) *Members of Parliament and the Ombudsman*

Although disenfranchised, a prisoner may write to a Member of Parliament complaining about his treatment. Moreover, the jurisdiction of the Parliamentary Commissioner for Administration (Ombudsman) extends to prisons,[56] so complaints by prisoners who claim to have suffered injustice as a result of maladministration may be referred to the Ombudsman by a Member of Parliament.

(v) *The European Commission of Human Rights*

Before any complaint can be made to the European Commission the prisoner must exhaust all domestic remedies, including a petition to the Home Secretary (*supra*). The complaint must be made within six months of the final domestic decision.[57]

An important aspect of the European Court's decision in *Silver* v. *United Kingdom*[58] was that none of the channels of complaint available to the prisoner, namely the Boards of Visitors, the Ombudsman, the Home Secretary, and applications for judicial review before the domestic courts, provided an effective remedy within the meaning of Article 13 of the European Convention. Article 13 provides:

> "Everyone whose rights and freedoms set forth in this Convention are violated shall have an effective remedy before a national authority, notwithstanding that the violation has been committed by persons acting in an official capacity."

The Court's reasoning was as follows:

(i) The *Boards of Visitors* could not enforce their conclusions in a particular case, being restricted to acting in an advisory capacity to the prison governor and the Home Secretary.
(ii) The *Ombudsman* had no power to render a binding decision granting redress: he was limited to reporting the results of his investigation.
(iii) The *Home Secretary* was insufficiently independent, being the effective author of the Prison Rules and standing orders.

[56] S.4(1) of and Sched. 2 to the Parliamentary Commissioner Act 1967.
[57] This is discussed in greater detail in Chapter 1, pp. 11–14, *ante*.
[58] (1980) 3 E.H.R.R. 475 (Euro. Comm.); (1983) 5 E.H.R.R. 347 (Euro. Court).

(iv) The *domestic courts* were endowed with limited jurisdiction to determine whether the prison authorities had exercised power arbitrarily, in bad faith, for an improper motive, or *ultra vires*. There was no suggestion that the English courts could have granted relief in respect of the various matters which the European Commission and Court had held to be violations of the Convention: the Convention itself was not incorporated into English domestic law.

Despite the Court's judgment, the English authorities have done nothing to introduce legislation to give effect to it.

## CUSTODY OUTSIDE PRISON

Most prisoners will have to be taken outside prison premises by the authorities at some stage. Apart from transfer between prisons, and the need on occasion for specialist medical treatment, many inmates will have to be taken to and from court for the purposes of their trial or appeal. By section 13 of the Prison Act 1952 a prisoner is deemed to be in the legal custody of the governor of the prison while he is being taken to or from prison, and while he is outside the prison in the custody or under the control of an officer of the prison.[59] This provision applies to prisoners who are kept in custody during their trial.

Rule 38(1) of the Prison Rules 1964 provides:

> "A person being taken to or from a prison in custody shall be exposed as little as possible to public observation and proper care shall be taken to protect him from curiosity and insult."

Such a prisoner must be kept in the custody of a prison officer or a police officer.[60] Where a prisoner is required to be taken in custody to court, he must be permitted to wear his own clothing, or, failing that, clothing different from usual prison attire.[61] The standing orders provide that a prisoner should be handcuffed in court only with the permission of the presiding judge, magistrate, etc.[62]

[59] See too section 6 of the Imprisonment (Temporary Provisions) Act 1980.
[60] Prison Rules 1964, r. 38(2).
[61] *Ibid.* r. 38(3).
[62] Standing Order 1G(6).

# Chapter 6

# CONTACT WITH THE OUTSIDE WORLD—CORRESPONDENCE, VISITS, AND ACCESS TO THE COURTS



It is difficult to separate the three strands represented by correspondence, visits, and access to the courts. Prisoners will often wish to correspond with, and receive visits from, their legal advisers, as well as wishing to see and communicate with their families and friends. As will be seen, the courts have come increasingly to regard unimpeded access to legal advice and assistance as an integral part of unimpeded access to the courts. It is intended in this chapter to trace the development of the law in all three areas over the past two decades, and to summarise the position as it now exists as a result of the body of case law which has emerged. The final part of the chapter deals with particular issues concerning the prisoner as litigant, and the various means of procuring or ensuring the attendance of a prisoner at court.

## Contact Generally

Rule 31 of the Prison Rules 1964 provides that special attention should be paid "to the maintenance of such relations between a prisoner and his family as are desirable in the best interests of both." It also requires that prisoners should be encouraged and assisted to establish and maintain such relations with persons outside prison as may, in the governor's opinion, best promote the interests of his family and his own rehabilitation. The specific issue of a prisoner marrying was considered in *Hamer* v. *United Kingdom*,[1] in which the European Commission found that to accord prisoners the right to marry, protected in general terms by Article 12 of the European Convention, involved no general threat to prison security, nor was it harmful to the public interest. If the English prison authorities were to prevent, or substantially to delay, the marriage of a prisoner eligible to marry, they would be in breach of Article 12 in the absence of any special circumstances justifying their action.

From the beginning of a prisoner's sentence, consideration must be given to his future and the assistance to be given to him on and after his release.[2] This must be done in consultation with the appropriate after-care authority. Towards this end, the prison department of the Home Office appoints voluntary prison visitors to meet and talk with the prisoner during the course of his sentence in some instances. These visitors are wholly separate from, and independent of, Boards of Visitors, and the two should not be confused.

If a prisoner has been detained in default of finding a surety or of payment of a sum of money, he may communicate with, and be visited at any reasonable time on a weekday by any friend or relative for the purpose of arranging payment of the sum owing, and the prisoner's release from prison.[3] Such communication or visit is not counted as part of the prisoner's entitlement under the rules outlined below.

## HISTORICAL DEVELOPMENT

### The position prior to Golder

In their unamended form, the Prison Rules 1964 made the following provisions in respect of letters, visits, and access to legal advice. Rules 33(1) and (2) together permitted the Home

[1] (1982) 4 E.H.R.R. 139.
[2] Prison Rules 1964, r. 32.
[3] *Ibid.*, r. 36.

Secretary "with a view to securing discipline or good order or the prevention of crime or in the interests of any persons" to impose restrictions upon communications between prisoners and other persons. Except as provided by the Rules, the prisoner was not permitted to communicate with any outside person, or that person with him, save with the leave of the Home Secretary. Rule 33(3) provided that every letter or communication to or from a prisoner "shall" be read and examined by a prison officer, although the mandatory reading of letters was relaxed in 1974 with the replacement of the word "shall" by "may."[4] In any event, the Standing Orders described below had provided prison governors with a discretion to subject specified domestic correspondence to a cursory examination only. The rules gave the governor power to stop any communication on the grounds that its contents were objectionable or that it was of inordinate length.[5]

As to the frequency of letters and visits, rule 34(2) entitled convicted prisoners to send and receive a letter on reception into prison and thereafter once a week, and to receive a visit once every four weeks. The governor had discretion to permit a prisoner additional letters or visits "where necessary for his welfare or that of his family," as did the Board of Visitors.[6] The governor could also permit a prisoner entitled to a visit to send and receive a letter instead.[7] These provisions were all subject to the important restriction in rule 34(8):

> "A prisoner shall not be entitled under this Rule to receive a visit from any person other than a relative or friend, except with the leave of the Secretary of State."

In relation to visits by legal advisers, rule 37 provided as follows:

> "(1) The legal adviser of a prisoner in any legal proceedings, civil or criminal, to which the prisoner is a party shall be afforded reasonable facilities for interviewing him in connection with those proceedings, and may do so out of hearing but in the sight of an officer.
> "(2) A prisoner's legal adviser may, with the leave of the Secretary of State, interview the prisoner in connection with

4 (1974) S.I. No. 713.
5 Prison Rules 1964. r. 33(3).
6 *Ibid.*, r. 34(3).
7 *Ibid*, r. 34(4).

any other legal business in the sight and hearing of an officer."

The Prison Rules were published and available to all, as is every statutory instrument. This availability was fortified by rule 7(1), which required that every prisoner should be provided in his cell or room with information in writing about those provisions of the rules which he needed to know. But the rules provided only the framework of control, and many aspects of prison life were in practice governed by standing orders and circular instructions issued by the Home Secretary to prison governors. These contained rules and guidance of a general and specific nature, concerning day-to-day administration of the prison. Although these documents were available to Members of Parliament, in that they were held in the libraries in the Houses of Parliament, neither the public nor individual prisoners had any form of direct access to them.

In so far as they concerned prisoners' correspondence, these directives were ostensibly aimed at securing uniformity of treatment throughout the prison system by governors. They did markedly restrict the exercise of the discretion apparently conferred upon governors by the rules, and introduced further fetters upon the ability of a prisoner to communicate with those outside. The most important provisions of the Orders and Instructions were as follows:

(i) The Standing Orders made with reference to rule 34(8) gave the governor discretion to forbid correspondence on the grounds of security and good order and discipline or in the interests of the prevention of crime. Generally, prisoners were only permitted to correspond with relatives and with friends known to them prior to their imprisonment, although the governor could permit communications with persons not known to the prisoner before he came into custody. There were certain categories of recipient with whom a prisoner was not permitted to correspond.

(ii) As to correspondence with legal advisers, this was subject to the necessity to petition the Home Secretary for permission to seek advice about or give instructions for the institution of civil proceedings (excluding certain divorce cases). For prisoners who had already commenced proceedings the position as regards visits was governed by rule 37(1), and as regards correspondence was relaxed in 1972 by the introduction of a new rule 37A, sub-rule (1) of which provided:

"A prisoner who is a party to any legal proceedings may correspond with his legal adviser in connection with the proceedings and unless the Governor has reason to suppose that any such correspondence contains matter not relating to the proceedings it shall not be read or stopped under rule 33."

By sub-rule (2), the prisoner was to be provided on request with writing materials necessary for this purpose, and provision was also made for a registered medical practitioner of the prisoner's choice to be afforded reasonable facilities for examining the prisoner in connection with the proceedings out of hearing but in the sight of a prisoner officer.[8]

The precise meaning of "legal proceedings" was considered by the Court of Appeal in *Guilfoyle* v. *Home Office*,[9] in which a prisoner had wished to correspond with his solicitor in order to lodge a petition with the European Commission of Human Rights. The solicitor wrote to the plaintiff enclosing a form for him to complete in order to apply for legal aid. This letter was stopped by the prison authorities. The solicitor then lodged a petition with the Commission. The plaintiff sought a declaration that he was a party to legal proceedings and thus entitled to the protection afforded by rule 37A(1). The Court of Appeal upheld the judge's dismissal of the plaintiff's claim. Lord Denning M.R. considered that proceedings in the European Commission (as opposed to the European Court) could not be described as legal proceedings as the Commission exercised no judicial function, being limited to reporting on the facts and stating an opinion. He also felt that an applicant would only become a "party" to proceedings in the Commission when the application was accepted as admissible.

(iii) Additional to the restrictions upon seeking legal advice and assistance described above, was the so-called "prior ventilation" rule. Rule 37A was restricted to prisoners who were already parties to legal proceedings. The prior ventilation rule provided that a complaint about prison treatment or an allegation against a prison officer could be contained or

8 rule 37A(1).
9 [1981] Q.B. 309; [1981] 2 W.L.R. 223; [1981] 1 All E.R. 943.

referred to only in correspondence with legal advisers or other specified individuals or bodies, and until the prisoner had ventilated his complaint through the proper internal channels and been given a definitive reply, such a letter would be stopped by the prison authorities. The internal channels consisted of petitioning the Home Secretary, or making application to the Board of Visitors, a visiting officer of the Home Secretary, or the prison governor. Therefore, before a prisoner could raise his complaint outside the prison walls, it had to have been raised and resolved internally.

(iv) Subject to the prior ventilation rule, prisoners could correspond with Members of Parliament and with certain specified organisations[10] without first requiring the leave of the Home Secretary or the prison governor. The only exception to the prior ventilation rule concerned correspondence with the European Commission.

(v) As to the quantity of correspondence, in addition to his entitlement under rule 34(2) to send and receive one letter per week (at public expense), the directives permitted the prisoner at his own expense to send at least one extra letter per week and to receive a reply.[11]

(vi) As to the content of correspondence there were many matters, which could not be mentioned in outgoing letters. Some of these (*e.g.* threats of or incitement to violence) were clearly aimed at the maintenance of order and discipline in prison, and/or the prevention of crime. The purpose of other categories of prohibited subjects was less easy to discern. For instance, letters containing objectionable references to people in public life, material intended for publication, begging requests, or attempts to stimulate public petition would be stopped.

(vii) There were also provisions in the directives relating to the business activities of prisoners. These are discussed elsewhere.

**Access to legal advice: The decision in and effect of Golder v. United Kingdom**[12]

Sydney Golder's case was the first occasion upon which the

[10] The National Council for Civil Liberties, "Justice," "Release" and the Howard League for Penal Reform.

[11] S.O. 5A3(8) Instr. 155/1968.

[12] (1975) 1 E.H.R.R. 524. Compare In re De Courcy (1968) 112 Sol. Jo. 329.

United Kingdom found itself to be a party in the European Court of Human Rights. The case was heard in October 1974, but arose out of a serious disturbance in Parkhurst prison on the evening of October 24, 1969. The following day a prison officer tentatively identified the applicant, a prisoner in the prison, as a participant. The applicant wrote to a Member of Parliament and a Chief Constable about the incident, but these letters were stopped by the prison governor. The prison officer concerned subsequently dropped the allegation he had made about the applicant's participation in the disturbance and supposed assault upon the officer. Disciplinary proceedings against the applicant were also dropped. The applicant wished to consult a solicitor about commencing libel proceedings against the officer. The authorities refused permission.

The applicant's complaint against the authorities in respect of stopping the two letters was ruled inadmissible by the Commission since the applicant had not exhausted the domestic remedies available to him. The Commission considered the applicant's complaints that the refusal to allow him access to a solicitor constituted violations of Articles 6 and 8 of the Convention. It upheld both complaints, and the matter was referred to the Court.

Article 6(1) of the Convention provides as follows:

> "In the determination of his civil rights and obligations or of any criminal charge against him, everyone is entitled to a fair and public hearing within a reasonable time by an independent and impartial tribunal established by law . . . "

The Court held by nine votes to three that there had been a breach of Article 6. By forbidding Golder contact with his solicitor, the Home Secretary had impeded the launching of the contemplated action. The right of access to the courts was an inherent element in the rights contained in Article 6. The right to have a claim relating to civil rights and obligations brought before a court or tribunal was not absolute, and admitted of implied limitations, although the Court declined to elaborate upon any general principle of admissible limitations. In the present case, Golder could justifiably wish to consult a solicitor with a view to commencing legal proceedings, and in refusing to grant permission, the Home Secretary had failed to respect the right conferred by the Article.

The Court was unanimous in upholding Golder's complaint under Article 8. That Article reads:

"1. Everyone has the right to respect for his private and family life, his home, and his correspondence.
2. There shall be no interference by a public authority with the exercise of this right except such as is in accordance with the law and is necessary in a democratic society in the interests of national security, public safety, or the economic well-being of the country, for the prevention of disorder or crime, for the protection of health or morals, or for the protection of the rights and freedoms of others."

The Court found that the refusal of Golder's petition had the direct and immediate effect of preventing Golder from contacting a solicitor. Impeding someone from initiating legal proceedings constituted the most far-reaching form of interference with the exercise of the right to respect for correspondence. As for any justification based upon paragraph 2, the Court accepted that it may be necessary to interfere with the exercise of the right of a convicted prisoner to respect for his correspondence having regard to the ordinary and reasonable requirements of imprisonment. Thus the "prevention of disorder or crime" might justify a wider interference with a prisoner's correspondence than in the case of someone at liberty. The Court was unable to see how the prevention of crime or disorder, the interests of public safety, or the protection of the rights and freedoms of others could have obliged the Home Secretary to prevent Golder from consulting a solicitor with a view to suing a prison officer for libel. Golder was seeking to exculpate himself from a charge made by that officer in the course of his duties and relating to an incident in prison. He could justifiably wish to write to a solicitor. It was not for the Home Secretary to appraise the prospects of the contemplated proceedings; it was for a solicitor to advise and a court to adjudicate upon. The Home Secretary's action was thus not "necessary in a democratic society," and the Government could not rely upon the provisions of paragraph 2 of Article 8.

As a direct result of the decision in *Golder*, the Government produced a new rule 37A(4) of the Prison Rules:

"Subject to any directions of the Secretary of State, a prisoner may correspond with a solicitor for the purpose of obtaining legal advice concerning any cause of action in relation to which the prisoner may become a party to civil proceedings

> or for the purpose of instructing the solicitor to issue such proceedings."

The retreat made by the Government was as limited as possible. Prisoners were not given an unimpeded right of access to solicitors, since they still had to apply in writing to the governor for the necessary facilities, still had to seek solicitor's advice before commencing legal proceedings, and, more significantly, the prior ventilation rule remained in place. Moreover correspondence with solicitors remained liable to be read by the prison authorities, a practice which would act as a powerful deterrent to prisoners wishing to complain about those authorities.

Although the immediate effect of the decision of the European Court in *Golder* was limited, the decision was a significant reverse for the Government, and for the policies of successive Governments, who had administered the prison system in an inaccessible manner. For the first time, internal decision-making became the subject of detailed scrutiny by a judicial body. Henceforth, the manner of administering the prison system was to alter radically and the decision in *Golder* made a wider impact than its immediate effects would suggest.

**Prisoners' correspondence: Decision in and effect of Silver v. United Kingdom**

In *Golder* the European Commission had ruled that complaints made by the applicant about the stopping of his letter to the Member of Parliament and the Chief Constable were inadmissible. The direct issue of the stopping and censorship of prisoners' correspondence was soon to be considered in detail both by the Commission and the European Court.

A concise summary of this decision, reported as *Silver* v. *United Kingdom*,[13] is impossible. For, in reality, it was not one case but seven, or viewed another way, 62. During the early 1970s, a large number of prisoners in British jails complained about the stopping and censorship of letters. The European Commission selected seven applications, covering a total of 62 letters, as a test case. These had all been written during the period between 1972 and 1976. The Commission's report was prepared in October 1980 and released for publication in May 1981.

[13] (1980) 3 E.H.R.R. 475. [Euro. Comm.); (1983) 5 E.H.R.R. 347 (Euro. Court).

Among the letters stopped by the authorities were ones written to legal advisers, Members of Parliament, fellow prisoners, journalists, and religious figures. The reasons for their being stopped were many and varied; a large number contained complaints about prison treatment without the prior ventilation rule having been complied with; some dealt with matters prohibited by the standing orders, such as the prisoner's trial, conviction or sentence, the offences of others, or the prisoner's business affairs; some contained improper or offensive language; some were intended for publication. In other cases, the identity of the recipient was unacceptable, as in the case of letters written to a fellow prisoner. In one instance a letter was stopped because the recipient, the Archbishop of Canterbury was not a relative or close friend of the applicant, until it was realised that the Archbishop was also a Member of Parliament. One letter was stopped as being an attempt to stimulate public petition, the prisoner concerned having been sentenced to life imprisonment for an offence of murder which he vigorously denied having committed. The above list is not exhaustive.

The Commission found the large majority of the prisoners' complaints to be justified. There was a clear prima facie breach of the terms of Article 8(1) of the Convention:

> " . . . a prisoner has the same right as a person at liberty to respect for his correspondence, the ordinary and reasonable requirements of imprisonment being of relevance in assessing the justification for any interference with that right under the exception permitted by Article 8(2)."[14]

In order to justify the interference with the prisoners' right to respect for their correspondence, the Government would have to show that such interference was "in accordance with the law," and was "necessary in a democratic society" for one of the stated purposes. In determining the meaning of the former phrase, the Commission adopted the European Court's explanation of it in *Sunday Times* v. *United Kingdom*,[15] that the relevant law must be adequately accessible to the ordinary citizen, and secondly that it must be formulated with sufficient precision to enable the citizen to regulate his conduct accordingly. The citizen must be able to foresee, to a reasonable degree, the consequences of a given action. To show that it had acted in accordance with the law, the

[14] (1980) 3 E.H.R.R. 475 at p. 496.
[15] *Sunday Times* v. *United Kingdom* (1979) 2 E.H.R.R. 245.

Government would have to satisfy these twin tests of foreseeability and accessibility, and then the third test of necessity. The Prison Rules satisfied the test of accessibility, whereas the unpublished standing orders and circular instructions did not. Unless the administrative restrictions could be reasonably deduced from the terms of the Prison Rules, they would also fail the test of foreseeability. As for the requirement of "necessity in a democratic society," this would be construed as requiring that the interference with the prisoners' right should be proportionate to the legitimate aim pursued by the interference, and involved striking a balance between the legitimate interests of the prison authorities of good order and security, and that of the rehabilitation of the prisoner.

The Commission found that the prior ventilation rule could not be reasonably foreseen, and was not in accordance with the law. Moreover, the need for a system of internal enquiry into prisoners' complaints did not justify the *priority* of such a system. The need to provide an immediate remedy for complaints about prison treatment would equally be satisfied by a simultaneous ventilation rule.

Dealing specifically with letters written by prisoners to their legal advisers, the Commission found that whilst the need for special leave under rule 34(8) for every letter to legal representatives was in accordance with the law, the sanction of stopping letters was disproportionate to the aim of the rule and so failed the test of necessity.

A number of the restrictions on correspondence were found not to be in accordance with the law in that they failed the foreseeability test described above. These included the prohibitions upon representations connected with a prisoner's trial conviction or sentence, complaints about prison treatment in general correspondence, grossly improper language, allegations against prison officers, and attempts to stimulate public petition. Likewise, a number of the restrictions could not be said to be necessary in a democratic society; these included the restrictions upon correspondence other than with relatives and friends, and upon communications in respect of legal and other business, and the prohibitions upon attempts to stimulate public petition, and upon complaints calculated to hold the prison authorities up to contempt.

*Changes introduced following the Commission's Report*

Following the Commission's Report, the British Government decided not to amend the Prison Rules themselves, but instead to revise the Standing Orders and Circular Instructions to take account of the Commission's findings. Revised Orders dealing with correspondence alone were drawn up, and the new regime based upon these came into force with effect from December 1, 1981. Matters of an administrative and management nature were removed from these Orders and were embodied in Instructions. The principal changes in practice were as follows:

(i) The Orders dealing with correspondence were published, thus removing the criticism of inaccessibility.

(ii) The restrictions upon the identity of those with whom a prisoner might correspond were largely abolished. Subject to certain exceptions, prisoners may now communicate with any person or organisation. These exceptions concern recipients who have requested that no further letters be sent to them, certain correspondence with other prisoners and ex-prisoners where security, discipline, or the sender's rehabilitation might be put in jeopardy, and other correspondence which might threaten the security or good order of a prison establishment.

(iii) Although the revised Orders do not provide for any increase in a prisoner's basic entitlement in respect of the number of letters he may send or receive, they do specify that additional extra letters should be allowed so far as is practicable.

(iv) Many of the prohibitions and restrictions upon the content of correspondence were swept away, and the revised list focuses more carefully upon matters concerned with security, good order and discipline, and the prevention of crime.

(v) The prior ventilation rule was replaced by the simultaneous ventilation rule; henceforth complaints about prison treatment could be included in letters as soon as such complaints had been raised internally through the prescribed procedure. The prisoner no longer had to wait until his complaint had been resolved internally before being able to raise it in correspondence.

*The reference to the European Court*

The Commission referred the case to the European Court. By

the time it was heard, the British Government had made the changes summarised above, and did not contest many of the Commission's findings, emphasising that the majority of the letters involved in the case would not have been stopped under the new regime. The compatibility of the new regime with the provisions of the Convention was not examined by the Court. The Court agreed with the reasoning of the Commission, and differed from its conclusions in respect of only a handful of letters. As for the administrative directives, the applicants contended that conditions and procedures governing interference with correspondence should be contained in the substantive law itself rather than in administrative guidelines. The Court rejected this contention.[16]

**Access to the courts: Raymond v. Honey**[17]

At the same time as the European Commission was preparing its Report in *Silver* v. *United Kingdom*,[18] the English Divisional Court was faced with an important application by a prisoner at Albany Prison to commit the prison governor for contempt of court. The matter arose as follows. A letter written by the applicant to a solicitor representing him in certain legal proceedings was stopped by the prison authorities because it contained an allegation of theft against the assistant governor. The applicant was told to rewrite it, omitting the offending allegation. Later the same month the applicant prepared a number of documents which together constituted an application to the High Court to commit the prison governor for contempt, for stopping the first letter. The governor stopped these documents too. The applicant then applied to the Divisional Court to commit the governor for contempt.

In March 1981 a two-judge Divisional Court found that the stopping of the first letter was not a contempt, but that the stopping of the committal documents did constitute contempt. The governor appealed, and the applicant cross-appealed. The matter went directly to the House of Lords, who dismissed both the appeal and cross-appeal, holding that the stopping of the committal documents was a contempt of court. Lord Wilberforce observed that a basic principle under English law was that a convicted prisoner, in spite of his imprisonment, retains all civil

[16] (1983) 5 E.H.R.R. 347 at p. 372–3.
[17] [1983] 1 A.C. 1; [1982] 2 W.L.R. 465; [1982] 1 All E.R. 756.
[18] (1980) 3 E.H.R.R. 475.

rights which are not taken away expressly or by necessary implication. Having reviewed the statutory provisions, and the relevant standing orders, he stated:

> " . . . there is nothing in the Prison Act 1952 that confers power to make regulations which would deny, or interfere with, the right of the respondent, as a prisoner, to have unimpeded access to a court. Section 47 . . . is a section concerned with the regulation and management of prisons and, in my opinion, is quite insufficient to authorise hindrance or interference with so basic a right. The rules themselves must be interpreted accordingly, otherwise they would be *ultra vires*. So interpreted, I am unable to conclude that either r. 34(8), which is expressed in very general terms, or r. 37A(4), whether taken by themselves or in conjunction with standing orders, is in any way sufficiently clear to justify the hindrance which took place. The standing orders, if they have any legislative force at all, cannot confer any greater powers than the regulations, which, as stated, must themselves be construed in accordance with the statutory power to make them."[19]

Lord Bridge, concurring, added that another basic principle was that a citizen's right to unimpeded access to the courts can only be taken away by express enactment. He continued:

> "Read in the context of rr. 34(8) and 37, as a matter of construction of the rules independently of the statutory power under which they were made, I find it impossible to exclude from the ambit of the prohibition (in rule 33(2)) communications between a prisoner and the courts. Indeed I think the rules, in their original form, which did not include r. 37A, were intended to give the Secretary of State an absolute discretion whether or not to allow a prisoner to institute legal proceedings. . . . "
>
> " . . . standing orders set out an elaborate procedure designed to discourage a prisoner from instituting proceedings in person, and impliedly assume that he requires the leave of the Secretary of State to do so, which the Secretary of State has an absolute discretion to give or withhold.
>
> "The only statutory provision relied on as empowering the Secretary of State to make rules imposing such fetters on a

[19] [1983] 1 A.C. 1 at p. 12.

prisoner's access to the courts as the rules, as I read them, purport to impose, is the power in section 47 of the Prison Act 1952 to make rules for the 'discipline and control' of prisoners. This rule-making power is manifestly insufficient for such a purpose and it follows that the rules, to the extent that they would fetter a prisoner's right of access to the courts, and in particular his right to institute proceedings in person, are *ultra vires*."[20]

**The short life of the simultaneous ventilation rule: R. v. Home Secretary ex p. Anderson**

Although the European Court had appeared to look with favour upon the concept of a simultaneous ventilation rule, at least in regard to letters to Members of Parliament, and although such a rule was introduced as part of the changes effected after the Report of the Commission in *Silver*, it was destined to have a short life by reason of the decision in *R.* v. *Home Secretary ex p. Anderson.*[20a] In June 1983 there was a disturbance in the prison in which the applicant was serving his sentence. The applicant was charged with a number of disciplinary offences, which were referred by the governor to the Board of Visitors. The applicant wished to receive a visit from his solicitor so that he could be advised about commencing civil proceedings against a prison officer in respect of an alleged assault by the officer upon him during the disturbance. Permission for this legal visit was refused because, in breach of the simultaneous ventilation rule, the applicant had made no written complaint to the prison governor about the alleged assault upon him. The Home Office confirmed this refusal. The applicant applied for judicial review of these decisions and for a declaration that the simultaneous ventilation rule was *ultra vires* and void.

A two-judge Divisional Court upheld his claim, reasoning as follows. From *Raymond* v. *Honey*[21] it was clear that a convicted prisoner retains all his civil rights not taken away expressly or by necessary implication, and there is nothing in the Prison Act 1952 which confers power to make regulations which would deny or interfere with the right of a prisoner to have unimpeded access to a court. If the regulations hindered or interfered with this right they were *ultra vires*. Although it was proper and inevitable that

[20] *Ibid.* at p. 15.
[20a] [1984] Q.B. 778; [1984] 2 W.L.R. 725; [1984] 1 All E.R. 920.
[21] [1983] 1 A.C. 1.

there would be some regulations over the circumstances in which prisoners would have access to solicitors, the simultaneous ventilation rule went beyond such regulation and constituted an impediment to the right of access to the courts. Unimpeded access to a solicitor for the purpose of receiving advice and assistance in connection with the possible institution of legal proceedings forms an inseparable part of the right of access to the courts themselves. The simultaneous ventilation rule was an impediment because it required the applicant to do something unnecessary for the purpose of seeing his solicitor. Indeed prisoners might be reluctant to make the necessary internal complaint for fear of bringing disciplinary proceedings upon their heads, since it was a disciplinary offence to make a false and malicious allegation against a prison officer. Further, it was inherent in the logic of *Raymond* v. *Honey* that an inmate's right of access to a solicitor for the purpose of obtaining advice and assistance with a view to instituting proceedings should be unimpeded in the same way as his right to initiate proceedings by sending the necessary documents for that purpose by post was unimpeded.[22]

## LETTERS AND VISITS: SUMMARY OF PRESENT POSITION

**Correspondence: frequency**

Rule 34(2)(a) remains unaltered in that a prisoner is entitled to send and to receive a letter on his reception to prison, and thereafter once a week. However, the standing orders specify that extra letters should be allowed where possible.

**Correspondence with solicitors**

In view of the decisions in *Raymond* v. *Honey* and *R.* v. *Home Secretary ex p. Anderson*,[23] it would seem that there can now be little or no restriction on the number of letters sent to or received from solicitors, certainly where such correspondence relates directly to actual or contemplated legal proceedings by or against the prisoner. Any attempt to prevent or delay such correspondence would expose the prison authorities to the risk of being found in contempt of court. It is unnecessary for the prisoner toraise any complaint about prison treatment internally before consulting his solicitor. Rule 37A(1) and (4) must be read subject to the above propositions.

[22] [1984] Q.B. 778 at p. 793–4.
[23] *Ibid.*

**Correspondence generally**

There are few restrictions upon the content of correspondence, or the identity of recipients. As to censorship of letters, although all letters may be read, outgoing domestic correspondence is not normally read or examined at open prisons. Elsewhere, while all correspondence is examined, it is not necessarily read.

**Visits: general**

The prisoner remains entitled to a minimum of one visit every four weeks by virtue of rule 34(2)(b). By rule 34(8), he is not entitled to receive a visit from any person other than a relative or friend without the leave of the Home Secretary.

The rules also provide for the conditions under which visits take place. They should be within the sight and hearing, of a prison officer unless the Home Secretary otherwise directs, although the strict observance of this rule is relaxed in all establishments. The Home Secretary may give directions, either generally or in relation to a particular visit or class of visits, concerning the days and times when a prisoner can be visited.

**Visits: legal**

Rule 37(1) entitles the prisoner's legal adviser to "reasonable facilities" for interviewing the prisoner where the latter is a party to such proceedings. This will be in the sight, but out of the hearing, of a prison officer. In connection with other business, rule 37(2) provides that such interview must be by the leave of the Home Secretary, and will be in the sight and hearing of a prison officer. By standing order 5A34 such visits are now allowed out of the hearing of the prison officer, provided that the subject-matter of the discussion is disclosed in advance to the governor: if it is not so disclosed, the prison officer will listen. In *Campbell and Fell* v. *United Kingdom*[24] the European Court countenanced the possibility that security considerations might justify restrictions upon the conditions of legal visits. In view of the decisions in *Raymond* v. *Honey* and *ex p. Anderson*,[25] the validity of rule 37(2) is open to doubt.

**Visits by police officers**

By rule 35 of the Prison Rules 1964 a police officer may interview any prisoner willing to see him, on production of an order issued by or on behalf of a chief officer of police.

[24] (1984) 7 E.H.R.R. 165.
[25] See *ante*, p. 85–88.

## The Prisoner as Litigant

### The writ of habeas corpus

A number of writs of habeas corpus are known to the common law, most of which are now obsolete. Their general object is to secure the production of an individual before a Court or judge for various purposes. The best known, and historically the most important, is the writ of habeas corpus ad subjiciendum, by which the Queen has the right to enquire into the causes for which any of her subjects are deprived of their liberty. By means of the writ the judges of the High Court command the production of the subject and enquire into the legal justification for his detention. If there is none, the prisoner must be released.

The usefulness of the writ of habeas corpus ad subjiciendum was increased by the Habeas Corpus Act 1679, which made the writ accessible during the vacation, and generally regulated the procedure surrounding the issue of the writ. This in turn was extended by the 1861 Act, and the modern procedure is governed by Order 54 of the Rules of the Supreme Court 1965. Application is made *ex parte* in the first instance; if leave is granted, the application is normally adjourned for notice to be served upon such persons as the Court directs. The application, since it is concerned with the liberty of the subject, is entitled to priority over all applications the same day.

### Applications for judicial review

Judicial review under Order 53 of the Rules of the Supreme Court provides the means whereby the High Court can exercise supervisory jurisdiction over the decisions and procedures of inferior courts and tribunals carrying out public duties. The High Court will intervene or quash or otherwise upset such decisions if they are reached in excess of jurisdiction (the doctrine of *ultra vires*), if there is an error of law upon the face of the record, if the inferior tribunal acted in breach of the principles of natural justice, or if the decision was one which no reasonable tribunal-,properly directing itself, could have reached.[26] Since the decision of the Court of Appeal in *ex p. St. Germain*,[27] the most common form of judicial review sought by prisoners has been the quashing of disciplinary awards made by Boards of Visitors. Prior to 1977 there were significant disadvantages in seeking the preroga-

[26] This is, of necessity, a simplified list. See generally de Smith's Judicial Review of Administrative Action (4th ed.) particularly pp. 26–28.

[27] [1979] Q.B. 425; [1979] 2 W.L.R. 42; [1979] 1 All E.R. 701.

tive orders of certiorari, mandamus and prohibition against Boards of Visitors or the other prison authorities. Whereas in an ordinary action a plaintiff could claim a declaration, damages and an injunction, these remedies were not available if the prerogative orders were sought. Nor were interrogatories, discovery, and the right of cross-examination available. In 1977 many of these anomalous disadvantages were swept away in radical changes to Order 53 of the Rules of the Supreme Court. Henceforth applicants for judicial review could combine claims for damages, injunctions, and declarations with a claim for one or more of the prerogative orders. Provision was also made for discovery, interrogatories, and cross-examination of the deponents of affidavits, although this was subject to the court's overriding discretion.

Even in its streamlined form the procedure for applying for judicial review still contained unattractive features for potential applicants. Leave was required to bring an application, so that wholly unmeritorious applications could be weeded out at an early stage, and before costs started to escalate. Secondly, there is now a time limit (in the absence of "good reason" for its extension) of three months within which to commence proceedings, whereas in the case of the old prerogative orders there had been a six-month time limit for certiorari only. Thirdly, the provisions as to discovery, interrogatories, and cross-examination of deponents of affidavits were subject to the court's discretion, rather than being automatic, as they would be in a private law action.

It was hardly surprising, therefore, that in a number of cases involving public law issues, applicants continued to try to seek declarations and damages rather than make their application under Order 53. In *Heywood* v. *Board of Visitors of Hull Prison and another*,[28] again a case arising out of the Hull prison riot and the subsequent disciplinary proceedings relating to it, the plaintiff sought a declaration in February 1980 that the adjudication of the Board of Visitors in October 1976 was void as being contrary to the principles of natural justice. Given the long delay before proceedings were commenced, the defendants would be in a stronger position if the plaintiff were to require leave to commence proceedings for judicial review. The defendants successfully sought an order that the action be stayed on the grounds that the plaintiff was indirectly seeking an order of judicial

[28] [1980] 1 W.L.R. 1386; [1980] 3 All E.R. 594.

review, and should not be able to obviate the need for obtaining leave by bringing a private law action in the Chancery Division.

*Heywood* was decided at a time when a division of judicial opinion was developing as to whether applicants in the public law arena were free to commence whatever type of proceedings they wished, or whether they were constrained to seek an order for judicial review.[29] This conflict ended with the House of Lords decision in *O'Reilly* v. *Mackman*,[30] yet another case brought by prisoners following an adjudication by the Board of Visitors arising out of the Hull prison riot. The judge at first instance refused to strike out the plaintiffs' claims for declaratory relief, but this decision was reversed by the Court of Appeal.[31] The House of Lords dismissed the prisoners' appeals. Lord Diplock, with whose speech the other law lords agreed, said:

> "Now that those disadvantages" (*i.e.* those of the pre-1977 provisions) "to applicants have been removed, and all remedies for infringement of rights protected by public law can be obtained on an application for judicial review, as can also remedies for infringements of rights under private law if such infringements should also be involved, it would in my view as a general rule be contrary to public policy, and as such an abuse of the process of the court, to permit a person seeking to establish that a decision of a public authority infringed rights to which he was entitled to protection under public law to proceed by way of an ordinary action and by this means to avoid the provisions of Ord. 53 for the protection of such authorities."[32]

He later described the actions as "blatant attempts to avoid the protections for respondents for which Ord. 53 provides."

As noted above, there is no *right* to cross-examine deponents of affidavits in judicial review hearings, notwithstanding the changes made in 1977. This is highlighted by the Divisional Court's decision in *R.* v. *Board of Visitors Nottingham Prison ex p. Moseley*,[33] in which a conflict between the affidavit of the prisoner

[29] See, *e.g. Thornton* v. *Kirklees Metropolitan B.C.* [1979] Q.B. 626, [1979] 3 W.L.R. 1; [1979] 2 All E.R. 349, *Uppal* v. *Home Office* (1978) *The Times*, October 21 and November 11, *de Falco* v. *Crawley B.C.* [1980] Q.B. 460, [1980] 2 W.L.R. 664; [1980] 1 All E.R. 913, and *Lambert* v. *Ealing London B.C.* [1982] 1 W.L.R. 550; [1982] 2 All E.R. 1038.

[30] [1983] 2 A.C. 237; [1982] 3 W.L.R. 1096; [1982] 3 All E.R. 1124.

[31] [1982] 3 W.L.R. 604; [1982] 3 All E.R. 680.

[32] [1983] 2 A.C. 237 at p. 285.

[33] *The Times*, January 23, 1981.

applicant and the chairman of the Board of Visitors was resolved without hearing oral evidence.

It is important that actions which properly belong in the province of private law should not be the subject of applications for judicial review. Thus in *R.* v. *Home Secretary ex p. Dew*[34] the applicant commenced proceedings for judicial review, seeking an order of mandamus requiring the Home Secretary and prison authorities to provide medical treatment to him. When the case came to be heard this treatment had been provided, and the applicant sought an order that the proceedings continue as if begun by writ. Instead the action was struck out by McNeill J. on the basis that it was essentially a claim for damages for negligence, and did not involve breach of any public law obligation.

**Service on prisoners**

If personal service is required, it is effected in the usual manner after application to the governor, who should provide facilities for such service. In *Danson* v. *Le Capelia and Steele*[35] the governor, in compliance with an order of the visiting justices, refused to permit service on a prisoner in his charge. The court granted a rule nisi for the attachment of the governor on condition that the rule was not to be served or acted upon unless he persisted in refusing to allow service. It would thus appear that governors refuse facilities to effect service at their peril. If personal service is not necessary, delivery to the prison authorities at the prison constitutes good service.

**Presence at court**

Several nineteenth-century authorities established that a prisoner who was a party to litigation was not entitled as of right to be present at court to argue his own case, certainly at the interlocutory stage. In *Benns* v. *Mosley*[36] the wife of the defendant moved for a writ of habeas corpus to bring her husband to court to move for a new trial. Cockburn C.J., having communicated with the other judges of Queen's Bench and Exchequer, held that the court had no power to do what was asked, and that any pre-existing practice to the contrary was erroneous.[37] Likewise in *Ford*

[34] [1987] 1 W.L.R. 881; [1987] 2 All E.R. 1049.
[35] (1852) 7 W. & H. Exch. 667.
[36] (1857) 2 C.B.N.S. 116.
[37] This decision was followed in *Weldon* v. *Neal* (1885) 15 Q.B.D. 471.

v. *Graham*,[38] the plaintiff prisoner commenced an action for trespass against the Home Secretary, who took out a summons for leave to plead certain matters. The plaintiff applied for habeas corpus to bring him up to oppose the summons. The judge refused and the plaintiff's appeal was dismissed, on the grounds that the matter was within the judge's discretion, and that unless the judge saw a very pressing reason for the plaintiff's attendance he was right to refuse the order sought.[39]

In view of the developments of recent years, and particularly the decision in *Raymond* v. *Honey*,[40] those decisions must now be looked at with some circumspection. The present position is governed by section 29(1) of the Criminal Justice Act 1961, which provides:

> "If the responsible Minister is satisfied, in the case of a person detained in any part of the United Kingdom in a prison . . . that the attendance of any person in any place in that or any other part of the United Kingdom is desirable in the interests of justice or for the purposes of any public enquiry the responsible minister may direct that person to be taken to that place."

Two modern cases have dealt with the issue of whether a prisoner is entitled to be brought to court free of charge. In *Becker* v. *Home Office*[41], the plaintiff applied to the Home Office for permission to leave prison in the custody of a warder to conduct an action which she had commenced whilst at liberty. She agreed in writing to pay the attendant costs of so doing. The Home Office granted permission under section 29(1). The plaintiff won the action, but on taxation she was not allowed the costs of the journeys to and from the court. The prison governor deducted the relevant sum from the moneys held by him on the plaintiff's

[38] (1850) 1 L.M. & P. 604.

[39] The following passage from the judgment of Maule J. is an illuminating example of how judicial attitudes can change over the years: "In contemplation of law a man in prison is put into a situation of considerable inconvenience; and if he was to be let out to conduct his business—whether the business happened to be an action at law or anything else—his creditor would have very little chance of getting his money . . . If we were to grant a habeas corpus in this case, we should next have applications for a habeas corpus to enable a prisoner to go to an election, or a race, or a regatta, or wheresoever else he might have business."

[40] [1983] 1 A.C. 1. [1983] A.C. 1; [1982] 2 W.L.R. 465; [1982] 1 All E.R. 756.

[41] [1972] 2 Q.B. 407; [1972] 2 W.L.R. 1193; [1972] 2 All E.R. 676.

behalf. She brought proceedings against the Home Office to recover this sum and succeeded before the County Court judge. The Home Office's appeal was allowed, the Court of Appeal holding unanimously that when exercising his discretion under section 29(1) of the 1961 Act, the Minister had power to impose conditions as to the payment of the expenses involved.

The problem arose in sharper focus in *R.* v. *Home Secretary ex p. Greenwood*,[42] in which the applicant prisoner had commenced a private prosecution against a police officer. He petitioned the Home Secretary for an order for his production, but was informed that he would have to bear his own costs. He was unable to do so, and his information was dismissed by the court in his absence. He sought judicial review of the decision to refuse to order his production. McPherson J. refused this application, holding that section 29 gave the Home Secretary an unfettered discretion, and that *Becker* v. *Home Office* established that the Minister could lawfully require payment of the transport expenses. There was no common law or statutory duty which compelled the Minister to assist, at no cost, in conveying a prisoner to court. The judge observed:

> "A prisoner contemplating non-legally aided litigation or prosecution must know, as Mr. Greenwood did expressly . . . what the score is and what are the conditions to which his decision to go to court would involve. No common law or statutory duty compels the Secretary of State in my judgment to assist at no cost a prisoner in custody in conveying his person to court. In this respect, apart from his inability to walk to court, Mr. Greenwood is no worse off than a person out of prison. And his inability to walk to court, because of his confinement, does not in my judgment mean that he must be taken there free. In fact of course, the journey would only be free to him. The taxpayer would be footing the bill for Mr. Greenwood and perhaps many others and I see no justice, in general terms, in that. I am bound to say, since I am asked to do so, that I see nothing unlawful or perverse or even unreasonable in the Secretary of State's general practice in demanding prepayment. Many would regard it as much more unreasonable in my judgment that impecunious prisoners should have the automatic right of free transport to court in any litigation which they choose to instigate."

[42] *The Times*, August 2, 1986.

## THE PRISONER AS WITNESS

If a party to litigation desires the attendance of a prisoner as a witness, there are three methods of securing this:

(i) *Writ of habeas corpus*

In order to compel a prisoner to attend to give evidence, the courts of common law developed the use of the writ of habeas corpus *ad testificandum*. This was directed to the gaoler or other person having custody of the prisoner to bring the prisoner before the court. The person seeking the writ was obliged to tender a reasonable sum to the gaoler to cover the expenses of such production.[43] The Habeas Corpus Acts of 1803 and 1804 gave statutory authority to this practice, the former making provision for awarding the writ to compel a prisoner's attendance at a court-martial, the latter dealing with ordinary courts. This has since been extended to proceedings before arbitrators and umpires. Applications for such writs are made on affidavit to a judge in chambers, and it matters not whether the prisoner is detained under civil or criminal process.

(ii) *Order of the judge*

Closely similar to the above procedure, is a simple application to a judge for a warrant or order. Section 9 of the Criminal Procedure Act 1853 provided that a judge of Queen's Bench or Common Pleas could issue a warrant or order in any case where he saw fit to do so "for bringing up any prisoner . . . before any court . . . to be examined in any cause or matter, civil or criminal . . . " The person so brought was to be dealt with in the same manner as a prisoner brought under a writ of habeas corpus. This was in time replaced by the Rules of the Supreme Court; the present Ord. 54 rule 9 provides that a judge of the High Court may by warrant or order compel the attendance of any prisoner (except a civil prisoner) before any court to be examined as a witness. Such an application is made on affidavit to a judge in chambers. Identical provision is made for the County Court by section 57(1) of the County Courts Act 1984.[44]

[43] *Anon.* (1663) 1 Keb. 566, *Dodd's case* (1858) 2 De G. & J. 510, at 532, 533.

[44] It would seem that a gaoler producing a prisoner without such an order or writ having been obtained may be liable for an action of false imprisonment: see *Bint* v. *Lavender* (1825) 1 C. & P. 659; 37 Digest (Repl.) 438.

(iii) *Order for production by Home Secretary*

The Home Secretary may make an order for production under section 29(1) of the Criminal Justice Act 1961, discussed above.

## THE PRISONER AS DEFENDANT

There are a number of ways by which a prisoner Defendant's attendance at his own trial may be secured.

(i) By section 10 of the Criminal Law (Amendment) Act 1867, where a person who has been granted bail in criminal proceedings is, while awaiting trial for the offence before a Crown Court, in prison on remand or under sentence for another offence, the court may, by written order, direct the governor to produce the prisoner for arraignment without a writ of habeas corpus, and the prison governor must obey such order.

(ii) By section 28 of the Criminal Justice Act 1961, a prisoner may be transferred from one part of the United Kingdom to another (including the Isle of Man and the Channel Islands), for the purpose of attending criminal proceedings against him. Likewise, if sentenced to imprisonment or detention in those proceedings, he may be transferred back to the original part of the United Kingdom (or island) to serve his sentence.

(iii) The prisoner himself, or those on his behalf, may apply for a writ of habeas corpus *ad respondendum*, which exists to bring up prisoners before magistrates or courts of record for trial or examination on any other charge. The procedure for obtaining this writ is identical to that for obtaining the writ of habeas corpus *ad testificandum*.

The problem of a prisoner Defendant who was not produced to answer to his bail confronted the House of Lords in *R.* v. *Governor of Brixton Prison ex p. Walsh*[45] in which the appellant had faced charges in two different magistrates' courts. He was remanded in custody by one court, and on bail by the other. He was not produced by the prison authorities to the latter court, because of staff shortages at the prison at which he was being held. He applied for a writ of habeas corpus *ad respondendum* and for judicial review for a declaration that the governor was bound to

[45] [1985] A.C. 154; [1984] 3 W.L.R. 205; [1984] 2 All E.R. 609.

produce him. The Divisional Court dismissed his application, and the House of Lords dismissed his appeal. The latter held that neither the Secretary of State nor the prison governor was under an unconditional duty to produce a prisoner in his custody who was on bail under the Magistrates' Courts Act 1980. The duty of both the Secretary of State and the governor was to consider whether they were satisfied that production was desirable under section 29(1) of the 1961 Act, and, if so, not unreasonably to refuse to produce the prisoner.[46]

## THE PRISONER AS APPELLANT

Appeal to the Court of Appeal (Criminal Division) is a two-tier process. A prisoner can appeal against his conviction and/or sentence only with the leave of the Court of Appeal or a certificate from the trial judge unless, in the case of an appeal against conviction, the appeal involves a question of law alone. Virtually all prospective appeals go through the screening process. A single judge of the High Court considers the relevant documents in the case, and grants or refuses leave, or alternatively refers the matter for consideration by the full court. If leave is refused by the single judge, the prisoner may renew his application before the full court, although at the risk of some or all of the time spent in prison pending the appeal being ordered to be "forfeit," *i.e.* not to count towards the sentence. The Court of Appeal makes such orders only rarely, where the appeal is considered frivolous, and they do not contravene the European Convention.[47]

If leave to appeal to the Court of Appeal is granted, the appellant becomes entitled to be present at the hearing, unless the appeal is purely on a question of law, or unless the prisoner is in custody by virtue of a verdict of not guilty by reason of insanity, or of a finding of disability. In these cases the leave of the Court of Appeal is required for the prisoner to attend. Nor can the prisoner attend at an application for leave to appeal, or proceedings preliminary or incidental to the appeal, without such leave.[48]

[46] *Ibid.* at p. 165.
[47] *Monnell and Morris* v. *United Kingdom*, (1988) 10 E.H.R.R. 205 (Euro. Court).
[48] s.22 Criminal Appeal Act 1968.

A prisoner who is appealing to the House of Lords is not entitled to be present at the hearing of the appeal, or any preliminary or incidental hearings, without the leave of that Court or of the Court of Appeal.[49]

[49] *Ibid*. s.38.

*Chapter 7*

# DISCIPLINE IN PRISON



The importance and difficulties of maintaining discipline in a penal establishment are obvious. Many people are held against their will in an institution in which their freedom is greatly curtailed. They are people who have already shown their disrespect for the rules of society as a whole. Some are dishonest, some violent, and some mentally unstable. Some see little or no prospect of release, while others, by the nature of the offences of which they were convicted, are liable to attack by fellow prisoners. The prison system must contain these and many more.

The methods by which good order and discipline are designed to be achieved are various. Parole and remission hold out the prospect of early release based upon good behaviour. The system of privileges and job distribution is at least partially operated so as to secure tranquillity of prison life. Privileges may be withheld without any need for a formal disciplinary hearing. Troublemakers may be transferred to other establishments, and security classifications altered. Finally, for those prisoners whose behaviour remains unaffected by the methods set out above, there is a broad range of disciplinary measures available to the prison authorities. It is with these measures that this chapter is concerned.

As for general provisions, rule 2 of the Prison Rules 1964 states that "order and discipline shall be maintained with firmness, but with no more restriction than is required for safe custody and a well ordered community life," and expresses the hope that prison officers should seek to influence prisoners by example and leadership, and enlist their willing co-operation.

## The tools of discipline

(i) *Search and confiscation*

As noted elsewhere, prisoners must be searched on reception into prison, and the governor can order further searches, either of the prisoner himself or of his cell, whenever it is considered necessary. One of the complaints made by the plaintiff in *Williams* v. *Home Office (No. 2)* was that he and his cell were too frequently searched.[1] Tudor Evans J. stressed the necessity for carrying out searches for security reasons and to ensure compliance with the rules, holding that the frequency of searches depended on the governor and that he (the judge) was not satisfied that the frequency of searching in the control unit was different from the remainder of the prison system.[2]

By rule 41(4) of the Prison Rules 1964, a governor may confiscate any unauthorised article found in a prisoner's possession, or concealed or deposited anywhere in a prison.

(ii) *The use of force*

Prison officers have the same right as ordinary citizens to use reasonable force in self-defence if they are attacked or in immediate danger of attack. In addition, by section 3(1) of the Criminal Law Act 1967, a person may use reasonable force in the prevention of crime, or in effecting a lawful arrest. By section 8 of the Prison Act 1952, prison officers whilst acting as such have the

[1] [1981] 1 All E.R. 1211 at p. 1222.
[2] *Ibid.* at p. 1237.

powers of constables, and so have the same rights of arrest as constables.[3]

The extent to which force may be used to ensure the execution of a lawful order by a prison officer, as opposed to its use in self-defence, the prevention of crime, or the effecting of a lawful arrest, is uncertain. Rule 44(1) of the Prison Rules 1964 provides:

> "An officer in dealing with a prisoner shall not use force unnecessarily and, when the application of force to a prisoner is necessary, no more force than is necessary shall be used."

It would seem obvious that there must be circumstances in which prison officers are entitled to use force to secure compliance with a lawful order, for instance, when an unwilling inmate has to be moved from one part of the prison to another. What is less clear is whether a subjective or objective test should he applied in determining the necessity of using force. Some guidance is to be found in the Canadian case of *R.* v. *Berrie and others*,[4] in which a prisoner had disobeyed an order by the Director of the Penitentiary to shave off his beard. A number of prison officers tried to shave the prisoner forcibly. The latter resisted, and sustained some injury. The officers were charged with assault, and Govan Prov.C.J. held that there was no authority, either under statute or at common law, to justify this trespass to the person. He observed that

> "the use of brute force would not be reasonable to accomplish the enforcement of a mere regulation of this sort."[5]

In effect therefore, the use of force was considered unnecessary, and the degree of force unreasonable bearing in mind the regulation which was being enforced and the formal disciplinary measures available. It is to be hoped that the English Courts, if called upon to adjudicate, would adopt a similar objective approach to the question of whether the use of force was necessary.

(iii) *Removal from association : rule 43*

Rule 43(1) of the Prison Rules 1964 provides as follows:

> "Where it appears desirable, for the maintenance of good

[3] As to which, see Police and Criminal Evidence Act 1984, sections 24–33

[4] (1975) 24 C.C.C. 66 (B.C.)

[5] *Ibid.* at p. 72.

order or discipline or in his own interests, that a prisoner should not associate with other prisoners, either generally or for particular purposes, the governor may arrange for the prisoner's removal from association accordingly."

Safeguards upon the use of this power to remove prisoners from association with other prisoners are contained in rule 43(2). This provides that prisoners shall not be so removed for more than 24 hours without the authority of a member of the Board of Visitors, or of the Home Secretary. Such authority remains in force for one month, but may be renewed from month to month. The governor may arrange for a prisoner removed under the rule to resume association, and must do so if the medical officer so advises on medical grounds.

In practice, the rule is used for two entirely different categories of prisoner. First there are many prisoners who would be in danger if they were to associate freely with their fellow inmates. Examples of this category are police informers and so-called "supergrasses," ex-policemen who have fallen foul of the criminal law, some sexual offenders, and those who have been convicted of offences involving children.[6] The second category consists of those prisoners who pose an immediate threat to good order and discipline, and whose removal is deemed to be necessary in the interest of the stability of the prison as a whole. It was with such a prisoner that the Control Unit case was concerned.

**The Control Unit case**

The plaintiff in *Williams* v. *Home Office (No. 2)*[7] was serving a sentence of 14 years' imprisonment imposed in February 1981. He was a Category "A" prisoner, and by the summer of 1974 he was considered by the prison authorities to be a "subversive and dedicated troublemaker." In 1974 a control unit was established at Wakefield Prison, designed to contain and control prisoners who were considered to be troublemakers. The regime of the unit was divided into two stages, each of 90 days. During stage one the prisoner was confined mainly to his cell, and associated with other prisoners only during his one hour's exercise per day. He was not obliged to work, but he could only proceed to stage two if he did so. At stage two he was allowed a greater degree of

[6] Such prisoners often request to be "put on" rule 43 for their own protection.
[7] [1981] 1 All E.R. 1211.

association, but if he failed to work or caused trouble he reverted to the first stage. Having completed the two stages he qualified for return to normal prison life.

The plaintiff was transferred to the control unit on August 23 1974, under the provisions of rule 43. This transfer was ordered by the control unit committee acting on behalf of the Home Secretary, following a request by the prison governor. The committee did not meet to review the case until early February 1975, and then authorised the plaintiff's return to normal prison life as from February 18, *i.e.* 180 days after his transfer to the unit. The plaintiff claimed damages for false imprisonment and a declaration that the Home Office had acted *ultra vires* and unlawfully in setting up and controlling the unit.

The following were the main contentions advanced on the plaintiff's behalf:

(i) Detention in the control unit was unlawful because the nature and quality of that detention was different from and worse than that practised in the rest of the prison system, and constituted a breach of the Prison Rules.
(ii) The Secretary of State had no power to act under rule 43; the only person who had such power was the governor.
(iii) The detention after the first month was unlawful, since there was no review of his case under rule 43(2).
(iv) The detention constituted a "cruel and unusual" punishment prohibited by the Bill of Rights 1688.

The plaintiff's claim failed. Tudor Evans J. held that the sentence of the court and the provisions of section 12(1) of the Prison Act 1952 always afforded a defence to an action for false imprisonment. The lawfulness of the plaintiff's detention could not be affected by the conditions of that detention, which were essentially a matter for the Home Secretary. Having reviewed the authorities, the judge held that there was no authority in modern law to support the proposition that although a detention was lawful it could become unlawful if the nature (*i.e.* the conditions) of the imprisonment changed. Any breach of the Prison Rules could not be relevant to the question whether the defendants could justify in law the detention of the plaintiff.

Having dealt with the principle of transferring the plaintiff into the control unit, the judge examined the operation in practice. He held that the Secretary of State, as well as the governor, had the power to act under rule 43, and that power was validly exercised for one month by the control unit committee, acting as his duly authorised agents. The regime of the unit was held not to be devised to punish, it was not punitive in character, nor was the plaintiff being punished when sent there. The judge observed that punishment was not within the ambit of rule 43, and that if the rule were used merely as a device to punish a prisoner it would be highly improper and there would be a breach of the rule.

There was, therefore, no breach of the rules in transferring the plaintiff to the unit in the first place. There remained to consider however, the process of renewal in view of the provisions of rule 43(2). The judge found as a fact that there was a predetermined policy to detain the plaintiff for the period of each stage of the regime, but that this policy did not preclude the plaintiff's release should circumstances require it. The renewal, however, from month to month was effected automatically. This was a breach of rule 43(2), as the renewal provisions required consideration of the facts, and the renewing authority should at least look at what had happened in the preceding month and ask themselves whether anything had changed. This breach did not affect the lawfulness of the plaintiff's detention, nor, following *Arbon* v. *Anderson*,[8] did it give rise to an action.

As for the argument based upon contravention of the Bill of Rights, the judge, having taken into account the provisions of the European Convention, the United Nations Declaration of Human Rights, and the United Nations Standard Minimum Rules, held that the control unit regime was neither cruel nor unusual, and did not fall below the irreducible minimum standard of public morality.

It is somewhat difficult to reconcile the judge's finding that an alteration in the conditions of imprisonment could not render the imprisonment itself unlawful with his clear acceptance that there exists an irreducible minimum standard below which imprisonment would amount to a cruel and unusual punishment, and thus presumably be unlawful as contravening the provisions of the Bill of Rights. Later cases have suggested that imprisonment can be unlawful if the conditions in which the prisoner is held are such as to fall below this undefined minimum standard.

The judge also considered the extent to which the rules of natural justice applied:

[8] [1943] K.B. 252; [1943] 1 All E.R. 154.

> "It seems to me that Parliament, as reflected in the Prison Act and the Prison Rules drew a clear distinction between r. 43 cases and cases of offences against discipline. In the former case the prisoner has no voice in the decision which is to be taken. When a man is transferred to a segregation unit he is not able to make any representation. . . .
>
> " . . . I do not think that the fact that the control unit committee failed to follow the procedural steps shows that they acted unfairly or that they should have given the plaintiff the right to make representations . . .
>
> " . . . I do not consider that the principles of natural justice required that the plaintiff should have given notice of what was intended and the opportunity to make representations that he should not be transferred to the unit. Such a step is not within the contemplation of the Prison Act or the Prison Rules and would be damaging to the exercise of the administrative power under r. 43. Nor do I think that the principles of natural justice required that he should have had the opportunity to make representations when his detention was renewed month by month.
>
> " . . . I hold that the principles of natural justice required the control unit committee to consider the request to transfer the plaintiff fairly and in accordance with the prescribed criteria. It is not suggested that they failed . . . "[9]

The Court of Appeal dismissed the plaintiff's appeal (as it was invited to by the plaintiff's legal representatives) on technical grounds. Leave to appeal to the House of Lords was refused, but both Cumming-Bruce and Brightman L.JJ. accepted that the question whether breach of the provisions of rule 43 gives a right of action would be an arguable point in the House of Lords.

(iv) *Temporary confinement*

Rule 45 of the Prison Rules 1964 gives the governor power to order a refractory or violent prisoner to be confined temporarily in a special cell. The prisoner must not be so confined as a punishment, nor after he has ceased to be violent or refractory.

[9] [1981] 1 All E.R. 1211 at pp. 1247–8. See also *App. No. 9907/82* v. *U.K.* (1984) 6 E.H.R.R. 576.

The Prison Act 1952 requires every prison to have special cells for the confinement of such prisoners.[10]

(v) *Restraint*

The use of restraints constitutes a serious interference with a prisoner's person, and rule 46 of the Prison Rules, which permits their use, is formulated in detailed terms. The two most common forms of restraining devices are the loose canvas jacket, which may be used only upon the written authority of the prison's medical officer, and the body belt, a leather belt with handcuffs. Standing Orders require that the person issuing the restraint order must see the inmate personally before authorising the action. Both the governor and the medical officer must visit the inmate at least twice a day and the inmate must be observed by a prison officer at least every 15 minutes.

A prisoner may be put under restraint in the following circumstances:

(a) By order of the governor, where it is necessary to prevent the prisoner from injuring himself or others, damaging property or creating a disturbance.
(b) For safe custody during removal.
(c) On medical grounds by direction of the medical officer. The rule expressly forbids the use of restraints as a punishment.

Where a prisoner is put under restraint by order of the governor in the circumstances outlined at (a) above, this must be recorded forthwith, and notice of it must be given without delay to a member of the Board of Visitors and the medical officer : the latter must inform the governor whether he concurs in the order, and the governor is bound to give effect to any recommendation made by the medical officer. The prisoner must be kept under restraint for no longer than necessary, and cannot be so kept for longer than 24 hours without the written direction of a member of the Board of Visitors or an officer of the Secretary of State. This direction must state the grounds for the restraint, and the duration of its continuance.

10 "Three separately designated kinds of cell are used to confine prisoners deemed to be in need of physical restraint and isolation: the stripped cell (usually an ordinary cell equipped only with a mattress): the special cell (usually equipped with a double door, soundproofing and furniture which cannot cause injury); and the protected room (with a double door, soundproofing, padded walls and no furniture)" : Plotnikoff—*Prison Rules, a Working Guide*, p. 79.

(vi) *Invoking the criminal law*

If a prisoner is suspected of having committed a criminal offence (which will inevitably also be an offence against discipline), the prison authorities may call in the police to conduct an investigation.[11] Where the criminal offence is also an offence against discipline, the prisoner may in theory be dealt with both internally and in the criminal courts. This is the effect of *R.* v. *Hogan*,[12] in which two prisoners who had escaped were recaptured and dealt with by the authorities (in fact, by the now defunct visiting committee) for the disciplinary offence of escape. They were later tried for and convicted of prison breach, and argued on appeal that the internal disciplinary measures taken against them precluded the later criminal prosecution. This argument failed, but Lord Parker C.J. did observe that the fact of an internal punishment was a matter for the trial judge to take into account in passing sentence. In practice, if the prisoner is dealt with under the criminal law the disciplinary charge is not proceeded with.

## OFFENCES AGAINST DISCIPLINE AND AWARDS AVAILABLE

There are three categories of offences against discipline contained in the Prison Rules 1964.[13] The significance of the distinctions between them lies in the seriousness of the offences, the methods of dealing with each category, and the awards available if the charge is proved. Every charge, however serious, must be enquired into in the first instance by the governor. The three categories, in descending order of gravity, are as follows.

(i) *Exceptionally grave offences*

Only three offences fall into this category:

(a) mutiny and incitement to mutiny. In *R.* v. *Home Secretary ex p. Tarrant*,[14] Webster J., with the agreement of counsel for both parties, quoted Lord Goddard C.J.'s

[11] The Prison Department's policy is set out in a memorandum entitled "Notes for guidance on the handling of certain offences under the Prison Rules." Although the seriousness of the alleged offence is the most important single consideration, issues are often far from straightforward. For instance, a life sentence prisoner may have more to fear by way of prison disciplinary sanctions than by way of a meaningless additional prison sentence from a court.

[12] [1960] 2 Q.B. 513; [1960] 3 W.L.R. 426; [1960] 3 All E.R. 149

[13] Prison Rules 1964 r. 52.

[14] [1985] Q.B. 251; [1984] 2 W.L.R. 613; [1984] 1 All E.R. 799.

definition of mutiny as "an offence which deals with collective insubordination, collective defiance or disregard of authority or refusal to obey authority."

(b) doing gross personal violence to a prison officer.

Where a prisoner is charged with an offence in this category, the governor must inform the Home Secretary forthwith, and refer the charge to the Board of Visitors unless otherwise directed. The chairman of the Board must then summon a special meeting at which three, four or five members may be present, including at least two Justices of the Peace. The Board thus constituted must then enquire into the charge.

*Awards.* If the charge is proved, all awards available in the case of graver offences (see below) are available to the Board of Visitors, save that in the case of exceptionally grave offences, there is no limit to the amount of remission which the Board may order to be forfeited. The only other difference is that where an exceptionally grave offence is proved, the Board must impose one of the penalties available to it, whereas in the case of graver offences the imposition of a penalty is discretionary.

*Legal representation.* As will be seen below,[15] a prisoner should invariably be granted the right to legal representation when charged with an exceptionally grave offence.

(ii) *Graver offences*[16]

The following offences fall into this category:

(a) escaping or attempting to escape from prison or lawful custody.
(b) assaulting a prison officer.
(c) doing gross personal violence to any person not being an officer.
(d) where the prisoner is charged with a serious or repeated offence against discipline for which the awards available to the governor appear to be insufficient, the latter may, after investigation, refer the charge to the Board of Visitors.

The meaning of "serious or repeated offence against discipline" was considered in *R.* v. *Board of Visitors Dartmoor Prison ex p. Seray-Wurie.*[17] The applicant was serving a sentence of four years'

[15] *Infra* pp 121–126.
[16] Prison Rules 1964 r. 51.
[17] *The Times*, February 5, 1982.

imprisonment and had already forfeited 249 days of remission for a variety of offences. In August 1981 he was charged with assaulting a fellow prisoner, neither a grave nor an exceptionally grave offence under the Rules. The governor referred the matter to the Board of Visitors on the basis that the applicant had been charged with repeated offences and his (the governor's) powers of punishment seemed insufficient. The Board duly adjudicated on the matter, and the applicant sought judicial review of its decision, claiming that the offence was neither serious nor repeated in that he had never previously been convicted of an offence of assault. In dismissing the application Forbes J. held that the purpose of the Rule was that there might come a time when the governor regarded his powers of punishment as inadequate. That could be either because the offence was serious, or because the prisoner's prison record showed that he had committed repeated offences against prison discipline and the time had come for a sharper punishment.

In the case of these offences, the governor must, unless he dismisses the charge, inform the Home Secretary and refer the charge to the Board of Visitors unless directed otherwise. The Chairman of the Board must then summon a meeting at which two, three, four or five members may be present.

*Awards.* If after enquiries the charge is proved, one or more of the following awards are available to the Board[18]:

(i) caution.
(ii) forfeiture or postponement of any privileges for any period.
(iii) exclusion from associated work, and/or stoppage of all or a stated proportion of earnings for a maximum period of 56 days.
(iv) cellular confinement for a maximum period of 56 days, provided that the prison medical officer has certified that the prisoner is in a fit state of health to be so punished.
(v) forfeiture of remission for a maximum period of 180 days. Such an award would remain valid even though the prisoner's sentence was subsequently reduced on appeal.[19]

[18] Prison Rules 1964 r. 51(4).
[19] *Hancock* v. *Prison Commissioners* [1960] 1 Q.B. 117; [1959] 3 W.L.R. 583; [1959] 3 All E.R. 513.

(vi) in the case of an unconvicted prisoner forfeiture of the right to have the articles referred to in rule 41(1) of the Prison Rules 1964.

(vii) in the case of an unconvicted prisoner guilty of escaping or of attempting to escape, forfeiture for any period of the right to wear his own clothing.

The Home Secretary may require any charge in this category to be referred to him rather than to the Board of Visitors. If so, it will be investigated by an officer of the Home Secretary (who may not be a prison officer). If the charge is found proved, the officer may make any of the above awards.[20]

(iii) *Other offences*[21]

The vast majority of disciplinary offences fall into this category, and are dealt with by the governor rather than the Board of Visitors. Rule 47 of the Prison Rules 1964 provides that a prisoner shall be guilty of an offence against discipline if he:

(a) commits any assault.

(b) absents himself without permission from any place where he is required to be, whether within or outside prison.

(c) has in his cell or room or in his possession any unauthorised article, or attempts to obtain such an article. The meaning of this offence was considered by the Court of Appeal in *R.* v. *Deputy Governor Camp Hill Prison ex p. King*,[22] in which the deputy governor found the charge against the applicant proved on the basis that the applicant had been in his cell knowing that there was a hypodermic syringe in there. The Court of Appeal held that this was a misconstruction of the meaning of the offence. Mere knowledge of the presence of the forbidden article was insufficient: the offence envisaged a degree of control over the needle.

(d) delivers to, or receives from, any person any unauthorised article.

(e) sells or delivers to any person without permission, anything which he is allowed to have only for his own use.

[20] Prison Rules 1964 r. 51(5).
[21] *Ibid*. r. 47.
[22] [1985] Q.B. 735; [1985] 2 W.L.R. 36; [1984] 3 All E.R. 897.

(f) takes improperly or is in authorised possession of any article belonging to another person or to a prison.
(g) wilfully damages or disfigures any part of the prison or any property not his own.
(h) makes any false or malicious allegation against an officer. This offence is directed towards allegations of fact, rather than statements of opinion, the use of insulting language, or comment : it related to accusations which within the laws of libel would need to be defended as true.[23]
(i) treats with disrespect any officer or any person visiting a prison.
(j) uses any abusive, insolent, threatening or other improper language.
(k) is indecent in language, act or gesture.
(l) repeatedly makes groundless complaints.
(m) is idle careless or negligent at work, or being required to work, refuses to do so.
(n) disobeys any lawful order or refuses or neglects to conform to any rule or regulation of the prison.
(o) attempts to do any of the foregoing things.
(p) in any way offends against good order and discipline. This offence has the unfortunate appearance of a "sweep up" provision, and has received criticism. It was charged and found proved against the applicant in *R.* v. *Board of Visitors High Point Prison ex p. McConkey*.[24] He had remained in the same room as other prisoners while they were smoking cannabis. McCullough J. observed that since strong similarities existed between the disciplinary provisions of the Prison Rules and the criminal law, the rules should not be construed so harshly that they were brought into conflict with accepted ideas about criminal responsibility. The decision was quashed because the applicant had not been informed fully of the allegation against him, which was, in effect, that he had actively encouraged the prisoners to smoke the controlled drug.
(q) does not return to prison when he should have returned after being temporarily released from prison

[23] *R.* v. *Board of Visitors of Thorpe Arch Prison ex p. De Houghton, The Times,* October 22, 1987, D.C.
[24] *The Times,* September 23, 1982.

under rule 6 of the rules, or does not comply with any condition upon which he was so released.

*Awards.* All of the above offences, unless referred by the governor to the Board of Visitors (see (ii)(d) above), are dealt with by the governor. If he finds the charge proved, the range of awards available to him is similar to, but milder than, those available to the Board. They are as follows:

(i) caution.
(ii) forfeiture or postponement of any privileges for a maximum period of 28 days.
(iii) exclusion from associated work for a maximum period of 14 days and/or stoppage of all or a stated proportion of earnings for a maximum period of 28 days.
(iv) cellular confinement for a maximum period of three days subject to the medical officer's certificate under rule 53(2). Since the governor can order loss of privileges, including exercise, and can order exclusion from associated work for up to 14 days, he has in reality power to impose cellular confinement for 14 rather than three days.
(v) forfeiture of remission for a maximum period of 28 days.
(vi) and (vii) identical awards in respect of unconvicted prisoners are available to the governor as to the Board of Visitors.

*Consecutive awards.* Both the governor and the Board of Visitors have power to impose consecutive awards when more than one offence has been proved. They can also combine two or more awards in respect of one offence. Awards of forfeiture of remission are treated as cumulative, although the governor or Board may order that they be treated as concurrent. Standing orders provide that punishment should take effect at once, unless an inmate already undergoing one punishment receives another, or two punishments of the same kind are awarded at the same time.

*"Suspended sentences."*[25] Since 1974 the governor or Board of Visitors have had power to suspend any award (except a caution) for a maximum of six months. This is done by directing that the award shall not take effect unless within a specified period of six months the prisoner commits another offence. If the prisoner

[25] Prison Rules 1964 r. 55, introduced by (1974) S.I. No. 713.

does commit another offence during the period of suspension, the governor or Board may make one of the following directions:

(a) activation of the suspended award.
(b) activation of the suspended award reduced as deemed appropriate.
(c) re-suspending the award for a further period of up to six months.
(d) making no direction as to the suspended award. In this case the award simply remains in being if the period of suspension has not elapsed.

*Remission and mitigation of awards.*[26] The Home Secretary may remit or reduce any disciplinary award and/or may substitute for it another award which is, in his opinion, less severe. A Board of Visitors may remit or mitigate any award; so too can a governor in respect of awards which are made by him or another governor.

*Prospective forfeiture of remission.* Rule 54 of the Prison Rules 1964 permits awards of forfeiture of remission to be made in respect of prisoners detained on remand or awaiting sentence. Such an award takes effect only where a sentence of imprisonment or youth custody is subsequently imposed which is reduced by Section 67 of the Criminal Justice Act 1967 by a period which includes the time when the offence against discipline was committed.

## STATUTORY PROVISIONS GOVERNING DISCIPLINARY HEARINGS[27]

Section 47(2) of the Prison Act 1952 provides that rules made thereunder must make provision for ensuring that a prisoner charged with a disciplinary offence shall be given a proper opportunity of presenting his case. Rule 49(2) of the Prison Rules 1964 accordingly states as follows:

> "At any enquiry into a charge against a prisoner he shall be given a full opportunity of hearing what is alleged against him and of presenting his own case."

In *R.* v. *Board of Visitors of Swansea Prison ex p. Scales,*[28] Hodgson

[26] *Ibid.* r. 56, also introduced in 1974.
[27] A detailed summary of the practice adopted under the standing orders and circular instructions is to be found at Appendix 4 of the Prior Report on the Prison Disciplinary System (1985) Cmnd. 9641, and in particular paragraphs 47–78.
[28] *The Times,* February 21, 1985.

J. recommended that the form charging a prisoner with the breach of one of the Prison Rules should set out brief particulars of the offence in addition to the words of the relevant rule.

Rules 48 and 49 of the Prison Rules 1964 provide that where a person is to be charged with a disciplinary offence the charge shall be laid as soon as possible. This requirement is mandatory rather than directory, and failure to comply with it will invalidate subsequent disciplinary proceedings.[29] The charge must first be enquired into by the governor not later than the day after it is laid, excluding Sundays and Bank Holidays. The prisoner must be informed of the charge as soon as possible, and in any event before the enquiry made by the governor. The prisoner may be kept apart from other prisoners pending adjudication. In addition, where the prisoner is charged with a grave or exceptionally grave offence the governor must inform the Home Secretary, and the procedure outlined above must be followed.

## JUDICIAL REVIEW OF DISCIPLINARY HEARINGS

Until 1978 no judicial control existed over the conduct of disciplinary proceedings by governors or Boards of Visitors. They were free to make their own rules of procedure, and to conduct the hearings much as they wished. In the late summer of 1976 a serious riot occurred in Hull Prison, a riot which caused enormous damage to the fabric of the prison and to relationships between staff and inmates. It was also responsible for a historic judicial decision which opened up prison life to judicial scrutiny.

### Hearings by Boards of Visitors: the Hull Prison case

Arising out of the Hull Prison riot, a number of prisoners were charged with serious disciplinary offences, most of which were found proved by the Board of Visitors in due course. Severe awards were made, including in some cases forfeiture of long periods of remission. Seven prisoners applied to the Divisional Court for orders of certiorari to quash the Board's decisions on the ground of failure to comply with the rules of natural justice. At the start of the hearing, counsel for the Board raised the preliminary point of law that the remedy of certiorari was not available to quash adjudications of Boards of Visitors.

[29] *R.* v. *Board of Visitors Dartmoor Prison ex p. Smith* [1987] Q.B. 106; [1986] 3 W.L.R. 61; [1986] 2 All E.R. 651.

The three-judge Divisional Court agreed, holding that the Board of Visitors was not subject to the control of the High Court.[30] Although the court considered that in performing its disciplinary functions the Board was acting as a judicial body and was under a duty to act judicially, Lord Widgery C.J. considered that the jurisdiction of the court did not extend to private disciplinary proceedings of a closed body, which enjoyed its own form of discipline and its own rules. Both he and Cumming Bruce L.J. emphasised the considerations of public policy which drove them to their conclusions.

The Court of Appeal unanimously allowed the applicants' appeal[31] and held that the courts had jurisdiction to review decisions of Boards of Visitors and to grant the remedy of certiorari in appropriate cases. Megaw L.J., with whom Waller L.J. agreed, emphasised that the Board was carrying out a judicial function which was separate and distinct from its other functions. As such, the Board's decisions were subject to judicial control in certain circumstances. However, the interference of the courts would be justified only where there was a failure to act fairly, and where such unfairness could reasonably be regarded as having caused a substantial, as distinct from a trivial or merely technical, injustice which was capable of remedy. In a judgment, echoes of which could clearly be heard in the later House of Lords' decision in *Raymond* v. *Honey*,[32] and which ultimately received fulsome tributes from the House of Lords in *Leech* v. *Deputy Governor of Parkhurst Prison*,[33] Shaw L.J. set out the role of the courts as he saw it:

> "Now the rights of a citizen, however circumscribed by a penal sentence or otherwise, must always be the concern of the Courts unless their jurisdiction is clearly excluded by some statutory provision. The Courts are in general the ultimate custodians of the rights and liberties of the subject whatever his status and however attenuated those rights and liberties may be as the result of some punitive or other process. . . . Once it is acknowledged that such rights exist the Courts have function and jurisdiction. It is irrelevant that the Secretary of State may afford redress where the rules

30 [1978] Q.B. 678; [1978] 2 W.L.R. 598; [1978] 2 All E.R. 198 D.C.
31 [1979] Q.B. 425; [1979] 2 W.L.R. 42; [1979] 1 All E.R. 701.
32 [1983] 1 A.C. 1; [1982] 2 W.L.R. 465; [1982] 1 All E.R. 756.
33 [1988] 2 W.L.R. 290; [1988] 1 All E.R. 405.

have been infringed or their application has been irregular or unduly harsh. An essential characteristic of the right of a subject is that it carries with it a right of recourse to the Courts unless some statute decrees otherwise. What should be the nature and measure of the relief accorded must be a matter for the Courts. Public policy or expediency as well as merit may be factors to consider and they may influence the answer to any application for relief; but to deny jurisdiction on the ground of expediency seems to me, with all respect to the views expressed in the judgment of Lord Widgery C.J. in the Divisional Court, to be tantamount to abdicating a primary function of the judiciary."

Shaw L.J. recognised the dangers of capricious complaints by prisoners, and the stultifying effect upon prison discipline which recourse to the courts might create. However, the courts possessed discretion in the exercise of their powers, and " . . . all the arguments advanced in opposing these appeals appeared to me to go to discretion and not to jurisdiction." As for Lord Denning M.R.'s observation in *Becker* v. *Home Office* that if the courts were to entertain actions by disgruntled prisoners, the governor's life would be made intolerable, Shaw L.J. observed "However, disgruntled prisoners may have serious grounds for complaint of some award which is not only peremptory but also arbitrary."

A stamp of approval upon the Court of Appeal's decision in the *Hull Prison* case was provided by Lord Diplock in the House of Lords' in *O'Reilly* v. *Mackman*.[34] Lord Diplock, in a speech with which all the other members of the court agreed, considered that the decision was "clearly right." This observation was *obiter* however, and the Home Office could have sought to have the *Hull Prison* decision reversed by the House of Lords in *Leech* v. *Deputy Governor of Parkhurst Prison*. By then, however, the Home Office accepted that supervision by the courts of awards of Boards of Visitors was right and desirable.[35]

After the preliminary point of law in the *Hull Prison* case was decided favourably to the applicants, the applications were referred to the Divisional Court for hearing and determination. The judgment of the court, *R.* v. *Hull Prison Board of Visitors ex p. St. Germain (Number 2)*[36] contained observations about the extent

[34] [1983] 2 A.C. 237; [1982] 3 W.L.R. 1096; [1982] 3 All E.R. 1124.
[35] [1988] 2 W.L.R. 290 at 301.
[36] [1979] 1 W.L.R. 1401; [1979] 3 All E.R. 545.

of the rules of natural justice in proceedings before Boards of Visitors. These will be discussed below.

**Hearings by the governor**

While the courts were first considering in the *Hull Prison* case whether decisions of the Boards of Visitors should be subject to judicial review, it was inevitable that arguments would be advanced and judicial views expressed upon the issue of whether governors' adjudications would likewise be subject to review. In the Divisional Court, both Lord Widgery C.J. and Cumming Bruce L.J. rejected any suggestion that a governor's decision should be subject to certiorari. In the Court of Appeal there was disagreement. Megaw L.J. clearly supported the views of the Divisional Court judges, equating the position of the prison governor with that of a military commander or schoolmaster enforcing internal discipline, whilst Waller L.J., although officially reserving his decision, found it "difficult to visualise any circumstances in which certiorari would lie against the governor." Shaw L.J. on the other hand, could see no real distinction between disciplinary proceedings conducted by the Board of Visitors and those conducted by the governor. By implication he would have held that governors' adjudications should be subject to judicial review.

The issue of judicial review of governors' adjudications arose directly in *R.* v. *Deputy Governor of Camp Hill Prison ex p. King*.[37] The applicant was charged under rule 47(7) of the Prison Rules 1964 with having in his cell or room or in his possession a prohibited article, namely a hypodermic needle found hidden in his cell. He denied knowledge of this, but the deputy governor found the charge proved. The Court of Appeal ultimately held that the deputy governor had misconstrued the relevant rule, but that the decision made by him could not be the subject of judicial review. At first instance, the two-judge Divisional Court was equally divided, and its decision is unreported. The Court of Appeal was unanimous in its view that judicial review was not available, even though two of the judges (Griffiths and Browne-Wilkinson L.JJ.) recognised the difficulty of drawing a logical distinction between hearings before the Boards of Visitors on the one hand and those before prison governors on the other, and all of the judges emphasised policy considerations.

[37] [1985] Q.B. 735; [1985] 2 W.L.R. 36; [1984] 3 All E.R. 897.

These were essentially two-fold. Firstly, both the internal system of prison discipline and the authority of the governor would be undermined if the governor's decisions could be challenged in the courts as suggested. Secondly, to permit the principle of judicial review would open the way to a large number of unmeritorious applications, and further damage morale and discipline in prisons. The court found a solution to its logical difficulty in the provisions of Section 4 of the Prison Act, concluding that the governor was accountable to the Home Secretary rather than to the courts, and observing that the prisoner's remedy lay by way of petition to the Home Secretary. If upon such a petition, the Secretary of State misconstrued the correct meaning of the relevant rule, the prisoner would then be in a position to apply for judicial review of that decision. This elevation of Section 4 of the Act to oust the court's jurisdiction emerged during the hearing of the appeal, and had not been argued in the Divisional Court.

After the Court of Appeal decision in *ex p. King*, the Court of Appeal in Northern Ireland reached a contrary conclusion in *R.* v. *Governor of the Maze Prison ex p. McKiernan*[37a]. Leave to appeal to the House of Lords in *ex p. King* had been refused by the English Court of Appeal, and it was thus important that the conflict between the two Courts of Appeal be resolved. This was eventually effected by the House of Lords in *Leech* v. *Deputy Governor of Parkhurst Prison*,[38] in which their Lordships overruled *ex p. King*, vigorously affirming that governors' adjudications could be the subject of judicial review.

The prison authorities had again sought to rely upon the argument that Section 4 of the 1952 Act had imposed upon the Home Secretary the duty to ensure compliance with the Act, and that intervention by the courts prior to failure by the Home Secretary to perform his statutory duty was unnecessary. Both Lord Bridge and Lord Oliver, who gave the only reasoned speeches, described this argument as fallacious. Lord Bridge said:

> "The Governor's duty to act in accordance with the rules of natural justice is clearly spelt out in the Rules and has never been in question. Thus a Governor adjudicating on a charge of an offence against prison discipline bears on his face all the classic hallmarks of an authority subject to judicial review. To invoke the Secretary of State's general statutory duty to

[37a] (1985) 6 N.I.J.B. 6.
[38] [1988] 2 W.L.R. 290; [1988] 1 All E.R. 405.

ensure compliance with prison legislation to oust the jurisdiction of the Court on the ground that the Secretary of State's duty obviates the need for any such jurisdiction in relation to the Governor's awards is to stand the doctrine by which the limits of jurisdiction in this field are determined on its head. When the Court comes to the question of how to exercise its discretion, it may well be proper to ask whether in the particular case, the Court's intervention is needed but neither principle nor authority lend any support to the view that the Court must identify some element of necessity on the basis of its jurisdiction."

Likewise, Lord Oliver recalled the words of Lord Bridge in *Raymond* v. *Honey* that a citizen's rights to unimpeded access to the courts can only be taken away by express enactment. Whatever else Section 4 (2) of the 1952 Act did, it did not constitute a clear and unambiguous expression of the will of Parliament that the prima facie right to apply for judicial review should be removed.

"It has never previously, so far as I am aware, been suggested that the mere existence of an alternative remedy, of itself and by itself, ousts the jurisdiction of the Court, though it may be a powerful factor when it comes to the question of whether the discretion to review should be exercised."

Their Lordships were not in any event impressed by the adequacy of the alternative remedy provided by petition to the Home Secretary. In the words of Lord Oliver:

"A review of a Governor's decision by, effectively, a civil servant with access only to the paper record, even assuming that the Secretary of State has the power, which he has previously disclaimed, not only to remit an award but to expunge a conviction, must in its very nature be less than satisfactory in many cases. One has to postulate, for the question to be a live one at all, that there has been an error of law or an abuse or excess of power—one hopes an unlikely occurrence, but that is the postulate. That may and almost certainly will in some cases involve questions of fact which are inevitably more appropriately dealt with by the Court."

Lord Bridge was unimpressed with an argument which had

found favour with Lawton L.J. in the Court of Appeal *ex p. King*, namely that the governor's adjudicatory functions were somehow indivisible from his ordinary managerial functions:

> "The day to day management of the prison is one thing, the adjudication of charges against prisoners of specific offences and the award of punishments for those offences is another. Of course the two functions are related, but insofar as it is relevant to do so, I see no greater difficulty in drawing a distinction between them than in the parallel case of Boards of Visitors whose disciplinary functions are distinct from other functions they perform under the Act of 1952 and the Rules of 1964."

Essentially therefore "the decision of a governor of a disciplinary charge against a prisoner is one which has all the attributes of the kind of decision which is amenable to the Courts' jurisdiction to review." Their Lordships dealt with arguments that governors' authority would be undermined, and problems of maintenance of discipline would be aggravated if governors' adjudications were to be the subject of judicial review. These consequences were speculative, and on the other side unfair treatment of prisoners by the prison authorities could itself generate unrest and undermine discipline. Moreover, the experience of the courts since judicial review of decisions of Boards of Visitors in England and those of governors in Northern Ireland since *McKiernan* did not bear out these fears:

> "For my part, therefore, I think that the spectre of the Courts being flooded with frivolous applications for leave to apply for judicial review is likely to be more illusory than real."[38a]

## LEGAL REPRESENTATION AT DISCIPLINARY HEARINGS

The opening shots in the battle to secure legal representation for prisoners facing disciplinary charges before Boards of Visitors were fired in *Fraser* v. *Mudge*.[39] The plaintiff had been charged with assaulting a prison officer, but before the Board of Visitors met to hear the charge, he applied *ex parte* for a declaration that he was entitled to legal representation and an injunction preventing the Board from enquiring into the charge until he could appear

[38a] *Ibid* per Lord Oliver at 325.
[39] [1975] 1 W.L.R. 1132; [1975] 3 All E.R. 78 C.A.

before it by lawyers. Both Chapman J. and the Court of Appeal refused to grant the relief sought. In a short unreserved judgment Lord Denning M.R. held that there was no right of legal representation in such circumstances. The other Court of Appeal judges agreed. The court did not consider whether the Board had any discretion to permit legal representation.

There, in the English courts at least, the matter rested for almost a decade. Boards of Visitors conducted their affairs in the belief that prisoners had no right to legal representation, and that they, the Boards, had no power to grant it. The picture altered dramatically in October 1983 when five prisoners sought to challenge this belief. The cases are reported under the umbrella of *R.* v. *Home Secretary ex p. Tarrant.*[40] Two of the applicants had been charged with mutiny (an "exceptionally grave offence" under the rules), and the others with various "grave" offences, including assaults on prison officers. At their respective hearings before the Boards, each applicant requested legal representation, while two had also sought the assistance of a friend or adviser. All of these requests had been refused.

By the time the case came before the court, the European Commission in *Campbell and Fell* v. *United Kingdom*[41] had reported that two "exceptionally grave" offences constituted "criminal charges" within the meaning of the European Convention, entitling the prisoner to legal representation under Article 6 of the Convention. Judgment from the European Court was pending, and the English court in *ex p. Tarrant* was therefore faced on the one hand by binding Court of Appeal authority, in the shape of *Fraser* v. *Mudge*, that there was no right to legal representation, and on the other by persuasive reasoning from the European Commission to exactly the opposite effect.

The English court succeeded in treading a delicate path between the two decisions. It held that it was bound by *Fraser* v. *Mudge* to decide that the applicants had no right to legal representation. Unlike the Court of Appeal in that case, it went on to consider whether the Boards had any discretion to permit such representation. It answered that question in the affirmative, citing two principal reasons. Webster J. having considered the authorities in detail, observed that there was no rule or decision of common law which limited the power of the Board of Visitors to be the master of its own proceedings so as to deprive it of its

[40] [1985] Q.B. 251; [1984] 2 W.L.R. 613; [1984] 1 All E.R. 799.
[41] [1982] 5 E.H.R.R. 207.

necessary inherent jurisdiction to permit legal representation. Likewise, Kerr L.J. pointed out that there was no statutory authority which fettered the Boards. Secondly, the grant of legal representation must in some cases follow from the statutory requirements that prisoners charged with disciplinary offences must be given a proper and full opportunity to present their cases.[42] There might well be circumstances in which a Board of Visitors felt that this statutory requirement could only be complied with if the prisoner was legally represented. The court also held that this discretion was not confined to any particular category of offence (such as those described in the Rules as "exceptionally grave"), but existed in respect of any hearing before the Boards. Finally, the same reasoning as that set out above led the court to conclude that the Boards had an identical discretion to permit representation or assistance by lay advisers.[43]

Once the court had determined that the discretion to permit legal representation existed, it was common ground between the parties that in the case of each applicant the Board concerned had failed to exercise the discretion, believing that it had no power to permit representation. Webster J. enumerated a number of matters which Boards should take into account in deciding whether to exercise their discretion in the prisoner's favour:

(i) the seriousness of the charge and the potential penalty.
(ii) whether any points of law are likely to arise. The judge singled out the offence of mutiny as being particularly likely to fall into this category.
(iii) the capacity of a particular prisoner to present his own case.
(iv) procedural difficulties. These include the fact that pending adjudication the prisoner may have been segregated from other prisoners under rule 48(2), thus inhibiting the preparation of his defence. Likewise, some prisoners will have difficulty in cross-examining a witness at short notice, particularly if the evidence is of an expert nature.
(v) the need for reasonable speed in making the adjudication.

[42] Section 47 Prison Act 1952, and rule 49(2) Prison Rules 1964.
[43] Often referred to as "McKenzie men" after the decision in *McKenzie* v. *McKenzie* [1971] P. 33. Kerr L.J. said: "for myself I would not exclude this in cases where (i) the prisoner asks for this form of assistance, (ii) it appears to the Board appropriate to grant it and (iii) the request relates to a suitable person who is readily available and willing to assist, namely, not a fellow prisoner, but, for instance, a probation officer, social worker, or clergyman acquainted with the prisoner."

(vi) the need for fairness as between prisoners and as between prisoners and prison officers.[44]

Webster J. went on to consider the definition of mutiny, and the questions which might arise out of it. Having done so he concluded that no Board of Visitors properly directing itself could reasonably have decided not to grant legal representation to the two applicants charged with that offence. As for the other applicants, the judge concluded that it could not be said that any Board properly directing itself would be bound to grant legal representation or assistance by a lay adviser. Other specific criticisms made by the applicants about the detail of the conduct of the proceedings before the Boards have been noted elsewhere.

**Exceptionally grave offences: impact of Campbell and Fell** v. **United Kingdom**

During September 1976 both applicants made a sit-down protest during an incident in Albany Prison. They were removed by prison officers after a struggle, and the applicant Campbell was charged with the disciplinary offences of mutiny and causing gross personal violence to a prison officer. He requested, but was denied, legal representation. Thereafter, he refused to attend the hearing before the Board of Visitors, was convicted in his absence by the Board, and was ordered to forfeit a total of 570 days of remission. He alleged that there had been various breaches of the European Convention, the most significant being the refusal by the Board to grant his request for legal representation, and an attack upon the role and impartiality of the Board itself.

By Article 6 (1) of the Convention "in the determination of . . . any criminal charge against him everyone is entitled to a fair and public hearing within a reasonable time by an independent and impartial tribunal established by law."

By Article 6 (3) of the Convention:

> "Everyone charged with a criminal offence has the following minimum rights:
>
> (b) . . . to have adequate time and facilities for the preparation of his defence;
>
> (c) . . . to defend himself in person or through legal assistance of his own choosing, or if he has not sufficient

[44] R. v. *Secretary of State for the Home Department, ex p. Tarrant* [1985] Q.B. 251 at 284.

> means to pay for legal assistance, to be given it free when the interests of justice so require."

In order to succeed in his contention that he was entitled to legal representation, the applicant had to establish that the disciplinary charges against him also constituted criminal charges. Both the Commission and the Court found that the disciplinary charges were indeed criminal in nature. In determining the question, the Commission relied upon the criteria set out in *Engel* v. *Netherlands*,[45] namely whether the proceedings defining the offence belonged to the criminal law or disciplinary law of the state concerned, or both; the "very nature" of the offence; and the severity of the penalty risked by the citizen. As to the first criterion, it was clear that the offences of mutiny and causing gross personal violence to an officer were either themselves criminal offences (assault occasioning actual bodily harm) or alleged facts upon which criminal charges could be founded (in the case of mutiny, a criminal conspiracy). As for the penalty risked by the citizen, the Commission rejected any suggestion that prisoners had a right to remission, or that forfeiture of remission involved the imposition of a new sentence:

> "The Commission for its part does not consider that an award of loss of remission can be regarded as equivalent to a further sentence of imprisonment . . .
> "However, the present case differs from those which the Commission has previously had to consider in that the penalties which could be awarded . . . were very much more severe . . . the loss of remission which the Board of Visitors could award was not subject to any limit under the rules."[46]

The European Court, when it came to consider the case, did not specifically comment upon the Commission's approach, but noted the Court of Appeal's approach to remission in the *Hull Prison* case. It concluded:

> "The Court is of the opinion that the forfeiture of remission which Mr. Campbell risked incurring and the forfeiture actually awarded involved such serious consequences as regards the length of his detention that these penalties have to be regarded, for Convention purposes, as 'criminal.'

45 [1976] 1 E.H.R.R. 647.
46 [1982] 5 E.H.R.R. 207 at p. 213.

> "The sanction came close to, even if it did not actually represent, deprivation of liberty, and the object and purpose of the Convention require that the imposition of a measure of such gravity should be accompanied by the guarantee of Article 6."[47]

There was thus a general right to legal representation for prisoners charged with the two offences considered by the court. The logical conclusion is that for each of the exceptionally grave offences listed in the Prison Rules, European judicial authorities would conclude that Article 6 applies. However, in view of Webster J.'s observations about the offence of mutiny in *ex p. Tarrant* the difference of approach between the English and European courts may prove not to be of any lasting significance in respect of exceptionally grave offences. There may still be a significant divergence of views as regards the remainder, in the light of the House of Lords decision in the case discussed in the next paragraph.

**R. v. Board of Visitors Maze Prison ex. p. Hone**

The correctness of *Fraser* v. *Mudge* (at least in so far as it relates to all disciplinary offences other than those in the "exceptionally grave" category) was affirmed by the House of Lords in two conjoined appeals from the Northern Ireland Court of Appeal in *R.* v. *Maze Prison Board of Visitors ex p. Hone.*[48] The prisoners had been charged with assaults upon prison officers. Each contended that he was entitled as of right to legal representation at his hearing before the Board of Visitors, and each failed at every stage of the judicial process. Under r. 30(2) of the Prison Rules (Northern Ireland) 1982, a prisoner must be given a "full opportunity . . . of presenting his own case." The appellants' assertions that this must include the right to legal representation and that *Fraser* v. *Mudge* was wrongly decided, found no favour with the House of Lords:

> "No doubt it is also correct that a board of visitors is bound to give effect to the rules of natural justice. But it does not follow that, simply because a charge before a disciplinary tribunal such as a board of visitors relates to facts which in law constitute a crime, the rules of natural justice require the tribunal to grant legal representation. Indeed if this were the

[47] [1984] 7 E.H.R.R. 165 at p. 197.
[48] [1988] 2 W.L.R. 177; [1988] 1 All E.R. 321.

case then as Roskill L.J. pointed out in *Fraser* v. *Mudge* exactly the same submission could be made in respect of disciplinary proceedings before the governor of a prison. . . . In the nature of things, it is difficult to imagine that the rules of natural justice would ever require legal representation before the governor. But though the rules of natural justice may require legal representation before a board of visitors, I can see no basis for the submission of counsel for the appellants that they should do so in every case as of right. Everything must depend on the circumstances of the particular case, as is amply demonstrated by the circumstances so carefully listed by Webster J. in (*ex p. Tarrant*) as matters which boards of visitors should take into account. But it is easy to envisage circumstances in which the rules of natural justice do not call for representation, even though the disciplinary charge relates to a matter which constitutes in law a crime, as may well happen in the case of a simple assault where no question of law arises, and where the prisoner charged is capable of presenting his own case. To hold otherwise would result in wholly unnecessary delays in many cases, to the detriment of all concerned including the prisoner charged, and a wholly unnecessary waste of time and money, contrary to the public interest."[48a]

Nor was Lord Goff impressed by any argument based upon Article 6(3) of the European Convention:

"It is not surprising therefore to discover that the provision has been the subject of interpretation by the European Court of Human Rights to ensure that its application does not exceed the bounds of common sense. This the Court has achieved by imposing a restrictive meaning on the expression 'criminal offence' in Art. 6."

Having analysed *Engel* v. *Netherlands* and *Campbell and Fell* v. *United Kingdom*,[49] he concluded:

"Now in English law, the objective which is sought to be achieved is, in my opinion, indeed harmonious with Art. 6 of the Convention as interpreted by the court. It is only the technique which is different. In English law we are fortunate in having available to us a discretionary power, so often

[48a] *Ibid* per Lord Goff at p. 185–186.
[49] [1976] 1 E.H.R.R. 647, and (1984) 7 E.H.R.R. 165.

employed when it is necessary to weigh the effect of different factors; and it is established that disciplinary tribunals have, in the exercise of their discretion, and having regard to a broad range of factors including those mentioned by the European Court, to decide whether natural justice requires that a person appearing before the tribunal should be legally represented. The European Court . . . is striving, as I see it, to achieve the same flexibility . . . It follows that I cannot, for my part, see that recourse to the convention can assist the appellants in the present case."

Once the discretion of Boards of Visitors to allow legal representation was recognised, two practical problems immediately appeared. If one side was to be permitted legal representation, what of the other? Soon after the decision in *ex p. Tarrant* the Home Office announced that in all cases where the prisoner was to be legally represented before the Board, the governor would be similarly represented. Secondly, since the vast majority of prisoners would be unable to afford the cost of legal representation, what provision was to be made for this? Under an extension of the green form scheme, prisoners are now eligible for Legal Aid, under arrangements called "Assistance by way of legal representation," which are swifter in operation than conventional Legal Aid.

Apart from exceptional or unusual cases, it would seem that a Board of Visitors is under no duty to consider exercising its discretion to grant legal representation unless the prisoner specifically requests such representation. The Board itself is under no duty to enquire of the prisoner whether he wishes to be represented.[50]

## PRISON DISCIPLINARY HEARINGS: ASPECTS OF THE REQUIREMENTS OF NATURAL JUSTICE

The principles of natural justice, enshrined in the statutory provisions noted above, entitle a prisoner to a fair hearing before a Board of Visitors or a prison governor. Since decisions of the Boards have been subject to a judicial control only since 1978, and those of the governor since shortly before publication of this book, it is as yet impossible to formulate any sort of comprehen-

[50] See *R.* v. *Board of Visitors Swansea Prison ex. p. McGrath. The Times,* November 21, 1984.

sive code dealing with the rights of prisoners at such hearings. Summarised below are some specific issues which have been raised in the various cases which have come before the High Court in judicial review proceedings. Useful general guidance was provided by Hodgson J. in *R. v. Board of Visitors Gartree Prison, ex p. Mealy.*[51] He stressed that a prisoner was likely to be at a substantial disadvantage compared with somebody facing an ordinary criminal charge: the prisoner was likely to be unrepresented, to be segregated pending the hearing, and to feel that he was appearing in a hostile environment. It was thus important that chairmen of Boards of Visitors should follow the provisions of the explanatory card[52] issued to prisoners as strictly as possible, and to explain any departures from it. Allowance should also be made for the fact that a prisoner may not distinguish clearly between matters of substantive defence and matters of mitigation.

**The rule against bias**

It is one of the most important principles of natural justice that a judge is disqualified from determining any case in which he may be, or may fairly suspected (by the ubiquitous reasonable man) to be, biased.[53] In *R. v. Board of Visitors Frankland Prison, ex p. Lewis,*[54] the applicant had been found guilty by a Board of Visitors of having a controlled drug in his cell. He was legally represented at the hearing before the Board, and made no objection to the constitution of the adjudicating tribunal. Some time later he realised that the chairman of the Board had been a member of the local review committee which had considered his application for parole some three weeks before the Board of Visitors hearing. Of particular significance was the fact that the applicant was serving a sentence for a drugs offence, and his defence to the disciplinary charge was that he was unaware of the presence of the drugs in his cell. Although the chairman had recognised the applicant at the disciplinary tribunal hearing, he had forgotten the details about the applicant which he had learned as a member of the local review committee.

The applicant sought an order of certiorari to quash the finding against him made by the Board of Visitors. He argued that justice

[51] *The Times*, November 14, 1981.
[52] Entitled "Explanation of Procedure."
[53] See generally de Smith's Judicial Review of Administrative Action 4th ed. pp. 248–276.
[54] [1986] 1 W.L.R. 130; [1986] 1 All E.R. 272.

had not been seen to have been done, and that the hearing had offended the rule against bias. Woolf J. rejected this contention. He found guidance in the position of a magistrate sitting hearing charges against a defendant who had previously appeared before him:

> "The very functions which (the boards of visitors) are required to perform under the Prison Rules 1964 means that they must inevitably and frequently have a considerable knowledge of the background of a particular prisoner."

In a later passage, he set out the relevant criteria:

> " . . . it is important, in considering whether or not there has been a departure from the rules of natural justice that two principles be borne in mind. First of all, a board of visitors, like justices, undoubtedly has a discretion not to proceed . . . if it considers that it is not possible to proceed fairly and justly having regard to its background knowledge. Secondly, when exercising that discretion, it should take into account the functions that it has to perform, which I have described as being of an administrative nature and bear in mind that these offences are ones that it is required to adjudicate upon because Parliament through the Prison Act 1952 and the Secretary of State through the Prison Rules 1964 have concluded that is the most appropriate body to deal with offences of that sort . . . With regard to the second principle as I have described it, the board of visitors should not be too ready to regard a general background knowledge of a particular prisoner as being something which makes it desirable for it not to continue with the adjudication on a particular charge. In deciding whether or not it is possible for a particular member of a board to adjudicate fairly . . . the reasonable and fair-minded bystander would have to take into account the nature of the proceedings and the nature of the duties which the board has to perform."[55]

**The right of the prisoner to know the extent of the case against him and to have a fair opportunity to contradict or correct it**

This is a fundamental principle of natural justice, and, as noted above, rule 49(2) of the Prison Rules 1964 provides that a prisoner must have a full opportunity of hearing what is alleged against

[55] *Ibid.* at p. 135. See too *R.* v. *Board of Visitors Walton Prison exp. Weldon* (1985) Crim. L.R. 514.

him. Hodgson J. suggested in R. v. *Board of Visitors Swansea Prison ex p. Scales,*[56] that the form giving notice to the prisoner that he was being charged with a breach of the rules should set out brief particulars of the offence charged. The importance of the general principle was underlined by Geoffrey Lane L.J., who gave the judgment of the Divisional Court in R. v. *Hull Prison Board of Visitors ex p. St. Germain (No. 2),*[57] and who observed:

> "In our judgment the statutory obligation to make the rules, and rule 49(2) in particular, are merely declaratory of one of the basic rules of natural justice, namely that every party to the controversy has a right to a fair hearing. He must know what evidence has been given and what statements have been made affecting him; and he must then be given a fair opportunity to correct or contradict them"

Basic to the right to "correct or contradict" is the right to cross-examine witnesses. Indeed in R. v. *Home Secretary ex p. Tarrant*[57a] the Divisional Court was critical of the refusal by a Board of Visitors to permit one of the applicants to cross-examine a witness. Although it was proper for the Board's chairman to insist that questions should be put through him,

> " . . . if a prisoner is to receive a full opportunity of hearing what is alleged against him and of presenting his case, he must be allowed to ask his own questions unless he abuses that right, which in my view (the prisoner) was not doing on this occasion."[58]

A proper opportunity to contradict the evidence of a witness may require the production of a record of the evidence given by that witness on an earlier occasion. In R. v. *Gartree Prison Board of Visitors ex p. Mealy,*[59] the prisoner alleged that a witness who gave evidence before the Board had made a different statement at a hearing before the deputy governor of the prison. He asked that the record of the earlier hearing be made available. This request was refused by the Board's chairman. In quashing the Board's decision Hodgson J. held that it was not unfair that the record of the earlier hearing was not made available as a matter of routine practice. However, when an issue of inconsistency arose, the

[56] *The Times,* February 21, 1985.
[57] [1979] 1 W.L.R. 1401; [1979] 3 All E.R. 545.
[57a] [1985] Q.B. 251; [1984] 2 W.L.R. 613; [1984] 1 All E.R. 799.
[58] *Ibid.* at p. 289.
[59] *The Times,* November 14, 1981.

prisoner was entitled to call for production of the record, and unless the application was frivolous, the chairman would be expected to make it available.

In *R.* v. *Board of Visitors Wandsworth Prison ex p. Raymond,*[60] Webster J. appeared to go further. A Welfare Report upon the applicant was before the Board; the judge found that the applicant had not asked to see it, but that it was desirable in the interests of justice being seen to be done for the applicant to be shown a copy. The judge felt it inappropriate to lay down hard and fast rules, as there may be circumstances in which withholding such a report would be justified, but if it were to be withheld, the Board would be obliged to take it into account to the maximum possible extent in the prisoner's favour.

**The Admissibility and Treatment of Hearsay Evidence**

In the *Hull Prison (Number 2)* case Geoffrey Lane L.J. dealt with the correct approach to be adopted towards hearsay evidence by a Board of Visitors. It was entitled to admit such evidence, subject to its overriding obligation to provide the prisoner with a fair hearing. This obligation might oblige the Board not only to inform the prisoner of the nature of the evidence, but also to afford him an opportunity to deal with it. This in turn might involve the cross-examination of the witness whose evidence was initially before the Board in the form of hearsay. There might, however, be insuperable difficulties in arranging for such cross-examination. If so, the Board should refuse to admit the hearsay evidence, or, if already admitted, should disregard it.[60a]

**The right of the prisoner to call witnesses**

In the *Hull Prison (No. 2)* case, the Divisional Court also had to consider the extent to which a prisoner should be entitled to call witnesses on his own behalf. Geoffrey Lane L.J. sounded a note of caution;

> "Those who appear before the board of visitors on charges are, ex hypothesi, those who are serving sentences in prison. Many of such offenders might well seek to render the adjudications by the board of visitors quite impossible if they had the same liberty to conduct their own defences as they would have in an ordinary criminal trial. In our judgment the chairman's discretion is necessary as part of a proper procedure

[60] *The Times*, June 17, 1985.
[60a] [1979] 1 W.L.R. 1401 at p. 1409–10.

> for dealing with alleged offences against discipline by prisoners.
>
> "However that discretion has to be exercised reasonably, in good faith and on proper grounds. It would clearly be wrong if, as has been alleged in one instance before us, the basis for a refusal to allow a prisoner to call witnesses was that the chairman considered that there was ample evidence against the accused. It would equally be an improper exercise of the discretion if the refusal was based on an erroneous understanding of the prisoner's defence . . . "[61]

The judge also felt that mere administrative difficulties in obtaining the attendance of witnesses, or in arranging the attendance of large numbers of witnesses, would not justify the refusal to permit a witness to be called. Later in his judgment he underlined the cardinal importance of permitting prisoners to call all relevant evidence:

> "In the instant cases what was being considered was alleged serious disciplinary offences, which,if established, could and did result in a very substantial loss of liberty. In such a situation it would be a mockery to say that an accused had been 'given a proper opportunity of presenting his case' . . . if he had been denied the opportunity of calling evidence which was likely to assist in establishing the vital facts at issue."[62]

Further specific guidance upon the issue of whether and to what extent Boards of Visitors should permit the calling of witnesses by accused prisoners is to be obtained from *R.* v. *Home Secretary ex p. Tarrant.*[63] Three of the applicants complained of breaches of natural justice in the refusal of the Boards to permit them to call hopefully relevant evidence. In each case the court found the complaint justified.

(i) The applicant Leyland wished to call eight witnesses. During discussions the chairwoman of the Board said that the Board might feel that he did not need all of these to support his defence. The hearing was adjourned. At the resumed hearing the applicant asked to be allowed to call three witnesses. He was permitted to call only one of these. The

[61] [1979] 1 W.L.R. 1401 at 1406.
[62] *Ibid.* at p. 1408.
[63] [1985] Q.B. 251; [1984] 2 W.L.R. 613; [1984] 1 All E.R. 799.

court held the Board to be in breach of its duty to give the applicant a full opportunity to present his own case. At least one of the witnesses whom the applicant wished to call might have been able to give evidence upon a matter in respect of which the applicant had been wrongly prevented from cross-examining another witness.

(ii) The applicant Tangney wished to call six witnesses. The Board allowed him to call three of these, of whom two could not assist with relevant evidence. The applicant asked if he could have "replacement" witnesses. He was permitted one, who failed to give relevant evidence. He then sought to call two or three more prisoners and a prison officer to give evidence. He was allowed to call only the latter. Webster J. observed:

"... it should have been apparent to the board that Tangney had been kept apart from other prisoners under r. 48(2) of the 1964 rules, that he might, as he said was the case, not have had any contact with any of them and that it might therefore be necessary for him to call a number of witnesses before finding more than one who would have witnessed the scene. In these circumstances I do not see how the board could have been satisfied that none of the other witnesses whom Tangney wished to call would be able to give useful evidence should they be called; nor, applying Geoffrey Lane L.J.'s test in *Ex p. St. Germain (No. 2)*, do I see how they could have concluded that Tangney's wish to call more evidence was an attempt to render the hearing impracticable or that it was unnecessary to call so many witnesses to establish the point at issue."

(iii) The applicant Clark wished to call nine witnesses in support of his alibi defence. By the time of the hearing four of these had been transferred to other penal establishments. Because the Board felt that these four men could not add to the evidence of the five available, the applicant's application to adjourn was refused. Once again the court held that this was an improper exercise of the Board's discretion:

"... whether or not the board would have been entitled, having heard the first five witnesses, to refuse to allow the other four (a matter about which I have some doubt), they were not entitled to take that view at least until they had heard those five. Having heard those five, if they accepted their evidence they could, quite properly, be satisfied that the further four would not be able to give useful evidence. If, however, having heard those five, they did not believe them, or they were left in some doubt about whether or not to accept their evidence then, as it seems to me, they could not, without more, have been satisfied that the other four would not be able to give useful evidence unless they made some assumptions such that either the case charged was made out (which would have been a premature decision) or that those other witnesses would be unreliable (an assumption which they would not be entitled to make)."[64]

It would seem to be self-evident that a right to call a witness presupposed a right to question that witness. However, in the-*Gartree Prison* case (*supra*) the applicant called the prison's medical officer to give evidence on his behalf. The chairman of the Board put questions to the medical officer, but refused to permit the applicant to do so. Hodgson J. held that it was impossible to contend that the chairman had been acting fairly in acting in this way: he should at least have discovered what evidence the applicant wished to adduce from the medical officer.

**Duty of the prison authorities to inform the prisoner of the existence and identity of potential witnesses**

This duty was effectively laid down by Phillips J. in *R.* v. *Board of Visitors of Blundeston Prison ex p. Fox-Taylor*.[65] The applicant, who was charged with assaulting a fellow prisoner, gave evidence before the Board of Visitors, but called no witnesses on his behalf, believing there were none. In fact, a witness had seen the incident out of which the charge arose, and had reported what he had seen to the prison officer in charge of the case, who had told him to see a senior officer. The prison authorities had not brought the existence of the potential witness to the notice of the applicant or the Board of Visitors. Phillips J. quashed the decision of the Board, observing:

"Where there is an inquiry on foot it seems to me that there must be some (it is very difficult to say what the extent of it is) obligation on (the prison authorities) to take reasonable steps to see that the existence of potential witnesses comes to the notice of the board of visitors. I, for my part, cannot see

64 [1985] Q.B. 251 at p. 293.
65 [1982] 1 All E.R. 646.

> otherwise how the board of visitors are ever going to be able to make effective enquiries or conduct an effective enquiry if they are limited to those witnesses who, as it were, the officer in charge of the case chooses to put before them."
> " . . . It is not only a question of whether the witness wishes to give evidence, it is a matter of some and perhaps greater importance whether the board of visitors or the person charged wishes to call the witness."[66]

Hearings before a Board of Visitors are essentially inquisitorial in nature, and it is of crucial importance that the Board should know the identity of all potential witnesses. Moreover, the prisoner is usually in no position to make the relevant enquiries himself. Not only will he be denied access to legal advice in the vast majority of cases, but he will often have been segregated from other prisoners between the occurrence of the incident and the hearing of the charge.

**The standard of proof**

Curiously, in none of the Home Office regulations or guides to Boards of Visitors was there originally any reference to a question of crucial importance; whether in hearing disciplinary allegations against prisoners, the Boards and governors should adopt the civil (balance of probabilities) or criminal (beyond reasonable doubt) standard of proof. The omission ended in the Divisional Court in *ex p. Tarrant*[67] in which Webster J. said:

> "Before us however Counsel for the Boards conceded, rightly in my view, that the standard of proof to be applied is a criminal one, and although he does not appear on behalf of the Secretary of State for Home Affairs, I have no doubt that he would not have made that concession without the Home Office's approval. It seems reasonable to infer therefore, that for the future, either by an amendment to the guide or in some other way, Boards will be advised to apply the criminal standard of proof."

As a result of this judgment, the matter was rectified in revised manuals for Boards of Visitors and governors issued during 1985.

**There is no jurisdiction to convict a prisoner of a different offence to that, or those, charged**

This principle emerges from the Court of Appeal decision in *R.*

[66] *Ibid.* at p. 649.
[67] [1985] Q.B. 251 at p. 285; [1984] 2 W.L.R. 613; [1984] 1 All E.R. 799.

v. *Board of Visitors of Dartmoor Prison ex p. Smith*,[68] which arose out of an incident in Dartmoor Prison in February 1984. The applicant was charged with doing gross personal violence to a prison officer, an "exceptionally grave offence" under rule 52(1)(b) of the Prison Rules. The Board of Visitors enquired into the charge on May 2, dismissed it following a submission of no case to answer by the applicant's counsel, but then directed that the lesser charge of assault be laid instead. The applicant challenged this procedure in judicial review proceedings. McCullough J. held[69] that in view of the division of disciplinary offences into three categories, the varying powers of punishment for each category, and the fact that there was no express provision in the Rules for convicting of a lesser disciplinary offence than that charged, it would not have been open to the Board to convict of assault while enquiring into an allegation of doing gross personal violence to a prison officer. As for the laying of the less serious charge of assault, this offended the requirement of rule 48(1) that disciplinary charges should be laid "as soon as possible."

The Court of Appeal upheld the judge's decision on both bases, using similar reasoning. Ralph Gibson L.J., after noting that there was nothing in the Prison Rules to prohibit the laying of alternative charges, stated[70]:

> "No power to convict of a lesser included offence is conferred on the board of visitors by the rules. If it had been intended to confer that power there would have been express reference to it, and, no doubt, provision would have been made for dealing with the situations discussed above, where, on reference to a 'graver' offence under r. 52, the panel proceeded to convict of a lesser included offence, so that the limits of its powers of punishment would have been made clear beyond doubt . . . It seems to me that, where powers to try charges of disciplinary offences, and to impose penalties on proof of the charge, are conferred on a board by legislation, the powers of the board are limited to those expressly provided by the legislation unless the intention to confer some further or additional power can be shown as necessary to give effect to

[68] [1987] Q.B. 106; [1986] 3 W.L.R. 61; [1986] 2 All E.R. 651.
[69] *The Times*, July 12, 1984.
[70] [1987] Q.B. 106 at 121–2.

the rules as enacted. I see no necessity to imply the additional power contended for, and much to indicate that it was not intended to be given."

The court also agreed with McCullough J. that the provision of rule 48(1) for a disciplinary charge to be laid "as soon as possible" was mandatory rather than merely directory, and that, on the facts of the case, the new charge of assault had not been laid as soon as possible.

## Appeals against disciplinary awards

(i) *Against "conviction"*

The Prison Rules 1964 make no provision for an appeal against a finding of guilt by either the governor or the Board of Visitors. Although the Home Secretary may remit an award, he has no power under the Rules as presently formulated to quash the finding of guilt. In *Leech* v. *Deputy Governor Parkhurst Prison*,[71] Lord Bridge stated:

> "One manifest inadequacy of the remedy by petition is the absence of any power in the Secretary of State to quash the adjudication. This may seem of minor significance. If the award has been remitted, it may perhaps be of little consequence that the adjudication of guilt has not been set aside. But when the prisoner's record shows merely that the punishment awarded for an offence has been remitted by the Secretary of State, those who have to take account of the record, as for example when the prisoner's eligibility for parole is under consideration, will not know, in a case such as that of Leech, that the proceedings leading to the award were wholly invalid and it is at least possible that the record may operate to his prejudice. This is a lacuna in the rules which can readily be cured by amendment and it is very desirable that it should be."

(ii) *Against the severity of the award*

(a) *The Home Secretary*: by rule 56(1) of the Prison Rules 1964 " the Secretary of State may remit a disciplinary award, or may mitigate it either by reducing it or by substituting another award which is, in his opinion,

[71] [1988] 2 W.L.R. 290; [1988] 1 All E.R. 405.

less severe." The standard method of appealing against the severity of an award is by petition to the Home Secretary. In its evidence to the Prior Committee the Home Office told the Committee that in the event of a petition, the Prison Department of the Home Office investigated whether any procedural errors prejudicial to the prisoner's defence had been made, whether any new matters created a reasonable doubt as to guilt, and whether the finding was indefensible in that no reasonable person could have reached it on the evidence.

(b) *The Governor and Board of Visitors*: since 1974, and subject to any direction of the Home Secretary, the Board of Visitors may remit or mitigate any award, and the governor may do so in respect of awards made by him or another governor.[72] Written directions made by the Home Secretary make it clear that the Board or governor are not acting in an appellate capacity when exercising their discretion under the provision. The appellate function is carried out by the Home Secretary as described above. The directions provide that at least nine months should normally elapse before an application for the restoration of forfeited remission is considered. It would not normally be sufficient that the prisoner had not reoffended in the meantime: some evidence of a genuine change of heart would be required. Moreover, only in exceptional circumstances will the whole amount of a substantial forfeiture of remission be restored.

[72] Rule 56(2) Prison Rules 1964.

*Chapter 8*

# TRANSFER AND RELEASE



## Transfer between Prisons

The Home Secretary is given power by section 12(2) of the Prison Act 1952 to determine the prison to which a prisoner is committed, and to direct the removal of a prisoner from the prison in which he is held to any other prison. The preceding subsection provides that a prisoner, whether serving a sentence or on remand, may be lawfully confined in any prison.

Section 12 therefore presents the Secretary of State with an apparently wide discretion. In the *Hull Prison case*, Waller L.J. suggested that a decision to transfer a prisoner to another prison would not be subject to judicial review.[1] However, the Divisional Court had to consider the matter directly in *R.* v. *Home Secretary, ex p. McAvoy*.[2] The applicant had been arrested and held on remand at Brixton prison, charged with very serious offences. Six

[1] *R.* v. *Board of Visitors of Hull Prison, ex p. St. Germain* [1979] Q.B. 425 at 465.
[2] [1984] 1 W.L.R. 1408; [1984] 3 All E.R. 417.

months later (approximately one month after his committal for trial to the Central Criminal Court), the Home Secretary ordered his removal to Winchester prison, some 60 miles away. He sought judicial review of this decision on the grounds that his right to a fair trial would be prejudiced as his lawyers (particularly leading counsel already instructed) would find it much more difficult to arrange suitable visits, that the prison had inadequate facilities for legal consultations, and that due to ill health his parents would be unable to visit him. A principal in the Prison Department of the Home Office swore an affidavit stating that it was considered essential to move the applicant from Brixton for operational and security reasons, and that the only potentially suitable alternative in London (the applicant being a category 'A' prisoner), Wormwood Scrubs, was not considered appropriate.

Whilst accepting that the Secretary of State's powers under section 12 of the 1952 Act were very wide, Webster J. held that a decision made under the section would be reviewable if it could be shown that the Secretary of State had misdirected himself in law. He regarded the reasons given for the transfer as being good and sufficient, save that the reason given for rejecting Wormwood Scrubs was not sufficient for the purposes of an application for judicial review. This defect was cured during the course of the hearing by the submission of a second affidavit from the Home Office employee, who deposed that the "inappropriateness" of Wormwood Scrubs referred to the operational and security reasons which had governed the original decision to transfer.

As for the detail of the reasons given by the authorities for the decision to transfer, Webster J. considered it to be "undesirable if not impossible" for the Court to examine operational reasons for decisions made under section 12, and to examine security reasons would be "dangerous and contrary to the policy of that particular statutory provision". However:

> "... the power is none the less reviewable in principle and one that can be reviewed if it can be shown that the Secretary of State has misdirected himself in law. It would be a misdirection if the Secretary of State took the view that he was entitled to exercise his powers under that section without regard to such rights as a prisoner has in relation to visits by his family, friends, and lawyers."[3]

[3] *Ibid.* at p. 423.

It is submitted that the Courts will rarely if ever wish to examine the reasons behind a decision to move a prisoner out of a particular penal establishment. Such reasons will almost inevitably fall within the "operational and security" blanket, under which the Courts will not be prepared to peep. *McAvoy* does indicate that the Courts may be prepared to intervene to force the authorities to justify, and perhaps reconsider, the choice of prison *to* which a prisoner is transferred. To that limited extent, decisions made under section 12 may, in practice, be reviewable. There would seem to be no likelihood of successful challenge to a decision to transfer based upon the grounds that a prisoner should be entitled to some sort of hearing prior to the decision being made.[4]

## TRANSFER BETWEEN JURISDICTIONS WITHIN THE UNITED KINGDOM

Part III of the Criminal Justice Act 1961 was enacted to facilitate the movement of prisoners across existing jurisdictional limits within the British Isles. (*i.e.* the United Kingdom, Channel Islands and the Isle of Man). By section 26 of the Act,[5] the Secretary of State may order the prisoner's transfer from one part of the British Isles to another. Having been so transferred to serve the remainder of his sentence, the prisoner must be treated for the purposes of his detention, recall, release or otherwise as if he had been sentenced in that part of the United Kingdom to which he has been transferred. In general (save where the prisoner has been sentenced in the Channel Islands or the Isle of Man), these powers of transfer may be exercised only upon the application of the prisoner. Section 27 of the Act gives the Secretary of State power to order the temporary transfer of a prisoner upon the latter's application.

## TRANSFER BETWEEN JURISDICTIONS: THE REPATRIATION OF PRISONERS ACT 1984

This Act, which came into force on April 15, 1985, permitted for

[4] There is no direct English authority on the point, but both the American and Canadian Courts have concluded that there is no such duty of prior consultation: see Additional references for *Re Anaskan and R* (1977) 34 C.C.C. (2d) 361; 76 D.L.R. (3d) 350; 15 O.R. (2d) 515, *Canadian Penitentiary Service* v. *Marcotte* (1977) 1 F.C. 297, *Meachum* v. *Fano* 427 U.S. 215 (1976) and *Montayne* v. *Haynes* 427 U.S. 236 (1976).

[5] As amended by the Criminal Law Act 1977, s.65(4) Sched. 12.

the first time widescale movements of prisoners between jurisdictions. Thus, though sentenced abroad, offenders may serve their sentences in their own countries. The Act provides for transfers both into and out of the United Kingdom, and applies to persons detained in prisons, hospitals, or other institutions, either by virtue of the exercise by a court or tribunal of its criminal jurisdiction or under the provisions of the Act itself or equivalent provisions abroad.

**Prerequisites of transfer**

Under section 1(1) of the Act there are three preconditions which must be satisfied before the Home Secretary can issue a warrant providing for the transfer into or out of the United Kingdom:

(i) The United Kingdom must be a party to relevant international arrangements. By this in practice is meant the International Convention on the Transfer of Sentenced Persons 1983.

(ii) The Home Secretary and the appropriate authority of the other party to the transfer ("the other transferring country") must each have agreed to the transfer of the prisoner concerned. By section 1(2) the Home Secretary need not issue a warrant, and may revoke any warrant already issued, if circumstances arise or are brought to his attention, making it inappropriate for the transfer to take place.

(iii) The prisoner must consent to the transfer. The Act contains detailed provisions as to this. The Home Secretary must be satisfied that such consent is given in a manner authorised by the international arrangements, either by the prisoner himself, or by an appropriate person on his behalf. Moreover, the Home Secretary must also be satisfied that all reasonable steps have been taken to inform the prisoner of certain specified and relevant matters in writing in his own language. However, if given, the consent cannot be withdrawn once the warrant has been issued.[6]

**Transfer out of the United Kingdom: section 2**

Once issued, the warrant authorises the taking of the prisoner to any place in any part of the United Kingdom, his delivery at the

[6] Repatriation of Prisoners Act 1984, s.1(6).

point of departure from the United Kingdom into the custody of the representative of the other transferring country, and the removal of the prisoner outside the United Kingdom. The Act provides that the order which justified detention in the United Kingdom at the time the warrant was issued ("the original detention order") continues in force after the transfer, so as to apply again if the prisoner returns to the United Kingdom at any time when under the order he could be detained. The Home Secretary has power in order to give effect to the international arrangements under which the prisoner is transferred, to direct that the original detention order be varied or quashed. This enables him, *inter alia*, to provide for release on licence. Different provision is made for hospital orders.

**Transfer into the United Kingdom: sections 1(3) and 3**

The Home Secretary may not issue a warrant for transfer into the United Kingdom unless either the prisoner is a British citizen, or the transfer appears appropriate to the Home Secretary having regard to any close ties which the prisoner has with the United Kingdom. The warrant, once issued, authorises the bringing of the prisoner into the United Kingdom, taking him to the place of detention, and his subsequent detention in any part of the United Kingdom in accordance with the provisions of the warrant. Such provisions will usually relate to the length of the sentence to be served here.

**Miscellaneous**

Whilst being transferred to or from any place under the warrant the prisoner is deemed to be in the lawful custody of the Home Secretary, who may designate any person as authorised to take the prisoner under the warrant. If the latter escapes or is unlawfully at large, he can be arrested without warrant by a constable.

The Act also contains provisions for the temporary return of prisoners to or from the United Kingdom, for the revocation of warrants, and for the payment of the expenses incurred in effecting the transfer of prisoners.[7]

**R. v. Home Secretary ex p. Read**

The first, and so far only, case dealing with the meaning of the 1984 Act and the Convention arose out of a transfer from Spain to

[7] *Ibid.* ss.4, 6 and 7.

the United Kingdom. In *R.* v. *Home Secretary ex p. Read,*[8] the applicant was convicted of introducing counterfeit currency into Spain. He was sentenced to imprisonment for 12 years and one day. This was the *minimum* sentence for the offence. The Spanish sentencing court announced that it would request its government to halve the sentence, because the amount of currency involved was not large. However, no decision was ever made by the government. In January 1986, the applicant applied for transfer to the United Kingdom under the provisions of the 1984 Act. In February 1987 he was duly transferred to Wandsworth prison, under a warrant which specified that the time to be served in the United Kingdom was 2,847 days.

This calculation was made by the Home Secretary on the following basis: the United Kingdom had determined to apply Article 10 of the Convention, by which it continued to enforce the original sentence, and had excluded the operation of Article 11 which would have permitted the conversion of the Spanish sentence into an English sentence. Article 10 of the Convention reads as follows:

> "(1) In the case of continuing enforcement the administering state shall be bound by the legal nature and duration of the sentence as determined by the sentencing state.
>
> (2) If however this sentence is by its nature or duration incompatible with the law of the administering state, or its law so requires, that state may, by a court or administrative order, adapt the sanction to the punishment or measure prescribed by its own law for a similar offence. As to its nature, the punishment or measure shall, as far as possible, correspond with that imposed by the sentence to be enforced. It shall not aggravate, by its nature or duration, the sanction imposed by the sentencing state, nor exceed the maximum prescribed by the law of the administering state."

The appropriate "similar offence" within the meaning of Article 10(2) was one under section 15(1) of the Forgery and Counterfeiting Act 1981. For this offence the maximum sentence was 10 years' imprisonment. The Home Secretary thus reduced the sentence of 12 years and a day to one of 10 years imprisonment, and deducted from that the period spent in custody in Spain by the applicant.

[8] [1988] 2 W.L.R. 236; [1988] 1 All E.R. 759.

The two-judge Divisional Court found that the Home Secretary had erred. Parker L.J. dealt with the matter as follows:

> "Since the 10 year sentence under section 15 is to be reserved for the gravest offence and the Spanish offence was far from the gravest, it must in my view follow that in fixing the term to be served on the basis of a 10 year sentence, the Secretary of State has infringed the final prohibition" (*i.e.* that contained in the final sentence of Article 10(2))
>
> "In the instant case the punishment prescribed by law for an offence under section 15 is imprisonment not exceeding 10 years. It is not 10 years. To find the term prescribed by law in this country one has in my view to resort to the decisions of the courts. No other course is possible. The term so prescribed for the offence is certainly not 10 years, for that term is only to be imposed for the gravest cases. It therefore appears to me that adaptation can involve reduction below the maximum permitted by statute."

And later:

> " . . . I have no hesitation in saying that in my judgment it cannot have been the intention of Parliament to have required the Secretary of State to enforce a sentence considered by the sentencing court to be manifestly excessive and which in my judgment would also be held to be manifestly excessive by the courts of this country."[8a]

The Court also dealt with the question of remission. In Spain, remission must be the subject of an approved grant, in contrast to the English practice that remission is seen as a right unless forfeited. Article 2(b) of the Convention requires the sentencing state to inform the administering state of any remission earned by the prisoner. Although sought, no such information had been forthcoming from the Spanish government. The Home Secretary had based the applicant's earliest release date upon remission only in respect of the period served in England. Parker L.J. held that although the Home Secretary could not be said to have erred: "In the light of Article 12 of the Convention however I see no reason why, if he chooses to do so, the Secretary of State should not base earliest release date on a third of the whole period."

There are acute difficulties with the Divisional Court's decision, which, although designed to meet the justice of the partic-

8a *Ibid* at p. 243.

ular case, may have a dampening effect upon the desire of foreign states to consent to the transfer of prisoners into the United Kingdom. The case is to be considered by the House of Lords.

## RELEASE: REMISSION

By section 25(1) of the Prison Act 1952, Rules may be made allowing for the grant of remission of part of a sentence on the grounds of a prisoner's industry or good conduct. As originally framed, the Prison Rules 1964 provided for remission for prisoners serving terms of more than one month's imprisonment, but this was reduced in 1981 to five days.[9] Rule 5 of the Prison Rules, as amended in 1968 and 1981, provides that a prisoner serving a sentence of more than five days may be granted remission on account of his industry and good conduct, although such remission cannot permit the reduction of the actual term served below five days. A prisoner who has been released on licence and recalled to prison cannot be released before the thirtieth day following his return to prison. The maximum amount of remission available to a prisoner serving a sentence of more than 12 months imprisonment is one third of his total term[10] and any period taken into account under section 67 of the Criminal Justice Act 1967. Pressure of overcrowding in prisons led to a relaxation of the remission provisions for short sentence prisoners in 1987. By the Prison (Amendment) Rules 1987,[10a] the maximum amount of remission available for sentences of 12 months or less was increased to one half of the length of the sentence. Similar provision was made for those serving sentences of youth custody.[10b] For prisoners who were under 21 when their sentence was passed or subject to extended sentence certificates, and who have been released on licence and then recalled to prison, the amount of remission available cannot exceed one third of the unexpired period of the sentence calculated as at the date of recall. Where a prisoner is serving a partially suspended sentence, the part served in prison will be subject to remission in the usual way: likewise if such a prisoner is released, but part of the sentence is subsequently restored, the restored part will be subject to remission.[11]

[9] 1981 S.I. No. 70.
[10] Prison Rules 1964 r. 5(2), as amended by 1968 S.I. No. 440.
[10a] 1987 S.I. No. 1256.
[10b] 1987 S.I. No. 1257.
[11] Prison Rules 1964 r. 5(2)(A), introduced by 1982 S.I. No. 260.

Apart from the above, when a prisoner is released from prison in pursuance of the grant of remission, the sentence automatically expires.[12]

On the face of the Rules, the grant of refusal of remission is entirely within the discretion of the Home Secretary, and there can be no enforceable right to remission. This was certainly the view of the courts in *Morris* v. *Winter*[13] and *Hancock* v. *Prison Commissioners*.[14] In the former case, Horridge J. found the question a difficult one, but concluded that if it had been intended to confer a legal right on prisoners, clear words would have been used. The statute itself only provided that Rules might be made, and the Rules themselves did not say that prisoners were entitled to remission. In *Hancock*, Winn J. perceived no such difficulty in analysing the legal basis of remission. He described as "wholly fallacious" the view that a sentence was to last for only two thirds of its stated period: it was only by virtue and indulgence of the Prison Rules, an administrative provision, that in practice well-behaved prisoners usually found themselves serving only two thirds of the stated sentence. That being so, it was "within the administrative and uncontrolled discretion" of the prison authorities as to whether or not a prisoner would be considered for remission. In a later passage Winn J. said:

> "I would not think of interfering in any way whatsoever with the entirely unfettered power and discretion of the prison commissioners in this matter."[15]

It is, to say the least, doubtful whether Winn J.'s views represent the modern law. At the outset of his sentence every prisoner is given his estimated date of release, calculated by reference to the maximum possible remission, and he will be released upon that date unless remission is forfeited in disciplinary proceedings. This contrasts with an earlier system (under which *Morris* v. *Winter* was decided) by which remission was earned on a daily basis by good conduct and diligence at work. The modern system bears a close similarity to a scheme of entitlement rather than discretion, and has provoked comment in the courts. In the *Hull Prison* case Waller L.J. stated:

[12] Prison Act 1952, s.25(1).
[13] [1930] 1 K.B. 243.
[14] [1960] 1 Q.B. 117; [1959] 3 W.L.R. 583; [1959] 3 All E.R. 513.
[15] *Ibid*. at p. 128.

"... it was common ground between the parties that a prisoner is credited with his full remission when he arrives in prison after sentence and he is told then his earliest date of release. Whether it is a right or a privilege a prisoner can expect to be released on that date unless he is ordered to forfeit some remission. Lord Reid quoted deprivation 'of rights or privileges' as of equal importance, and I respectfully agree with him. Whether remission is a right or a privilege is in my opinion immaterial."[16]

This statement was noted by the European Court in *Campbell and Fell* v. *United Kingdom*,[17] which also observed:

"The Court, for its part, does not find that the distinction between privilege and right is of great assistance. What is more important is that the practice of granting remission—whereby a prisoner will be set free on the estimated date of release given to him at the outset of his sentence—creates in him a legitimate expectation that he will recover his liberty before the end of the term of his imprisonment. Forfeiture of remission thus has the effect of causing the detention to continue beyond the period corresponding to that expectation."

The development of the doctrine of legitimate expectation in recent years has drawn much of the sting from the issue of whether remission can truly be seen as a right or a privilege. As Lord Scarman observed in *Findlay* v. *Home Secretary*[18]:

"... the doctrine of legitimate expectation has an important place in the developing law of judicial review ... a legitimate expectation can provide a sufficient interest to enable one who cannot point to the existence of a substantive right to obtain the leave of the court to apply for judicial review."

In *Leech* v. *Deputy Governor Parkhurst Prison*,[19-21] Lord Bridge echoed those words:

"Although remission of sentence is not a right but, in theory, a reward for 'industry and good conduct' under rule 5 of the Rules of 1964, long standing practice gives prisoners

[16] [1979] Q.B. 425 at 464. See too *Re Savundra* [1973] 1 W.L.R. 1147.
[17] [1984] 7 E.H.R.R. 165.
[18] [1985] A.C. 318; [1984] 3 W.L.R. 1159; [1984] 3 All E.R. 801.
[19-21] [1988] 2 W.L.R. 290; [1988] 1 All E.R. 405.

a legitimate expectation that they will granted maximum remission under the disciplinary code."

## TEMPORARY RELEASE

Wide powers are given to the prison authorities by rule 6 of the Prison Rules 1964 to permit the temporary release of prisoners serving sentences. Such prisoners may be released at any time during their sentence for any period, and subject to any conditions. The reasons for permitting temporary release are many, though the most important are probably the following:

(i) To enable the prisoner to engage in employment, or receive instruction or training. Many prisoners serving long sentences are considered for the pre-release employment scheme during the last few months of their sentences, which enables them to work outside for a private employer.

(ii) To assist the prisoner in the transition from prison life to freedom. Many prisoners are thus permitted one or two short periods of home leave towards the end of their sentence.

(iii) Compassionate considerations may persuade the prison authorities to permit the temporary release of a prisoner to visit sick relatives, or to attend funerals or weddings of close relatives.

A prisoner who has been temporarily released in accordance with the rule may be recalled at any time, irrespective of whether or not he has broken any of the conditions of the release.

**Temporary release for ill-health**

Section 28 of the Prison Act empowers the Home Secretary to order a prisoner's temporary release from prison, where,

> "by reason of a prisoner's health it is undesirable to detain him in prison, but that, such condition of health being due in whole or in part to the prisoner's own conduct in prison, it is desirable that the release should be temporary and conditional only . . . "

Under such discharge, the order may contain conditions, with which the prisoner must comply, and he must return to prison at the expiration of the period stated in the order, or at the end of any extended period fixed by subsequent order. If he fails to do so he may be arrested without warrant. While he is out of prison, the sentence is suspended.

## PAROLE AND EARLY RELEASE

**Prisoners serving determinate sentences**

Prior to 1967, there was no system whereby prisoners serving determinate sentences could be released on licence, or "parole" as it has become known. Provisions for such release were introduced in the Criminal Justice Act 1967. Section 60(1) of that Act provided that the Secretary of State could, if recommended to do so by the Parole Board, release on licence a person serving a determinate sentence of imprisonment after he had served not less than one third of the sentence, or 12 months from the date of sentence, whichever was the longer. In effect, therefore, sentences of 18 months or less were excluded from the system, for an 18 month sentence would normally entail release with full remission after 12 months, whereas those prisoners who had forfeited remission would normally be unlikely candidates for parole.

The pressure of overcrowding in prisons throughout the 1970s and early 1980s led to a significant alteration to the position by the Criminal Justice Act 1982. Section 33 of the Act conferred power on the Home Secretary to reduce the minimum period for eligibility below 12 months. This power was to be exercisable only by order laid before Parliament and approved by a resolution of both Houses. By the Eligibility for Release on Licence Order, which came into force on July 1, 1984, the minimum period was reduced to six months from the date of sentence. The parole system now extends in practice to all sentences of more than nine months.

The "parolee" may be released subject to conditions specified in the licence, and by section 60(4) of the 1967 Act, he must comply with such conditions. The licence terminates when the prisoner would otherwise have been entitled to release, and this date must be specified in the licence.

**Prisoners serving life sentences**

In contrast to those serving determinate sentences, life sentence prisoners were eligible for release on licence by reason of the Prison Act 1952. Section 27(1) granted a discretion to the Secretary of State to release such prisoners at any time if he thought fit, subject to compliance with such conditions (if any) as he determined. By section 27(2) of the Act the Secretary of State was permitted to recall to prison any person so released without prejudice to the power to release on licence again at a later stage.

This position was modified and somewhat restricted by section 61 of the Criminal Justice Act 1967, which made the Secretary of State's power to release subject to a positive recommendation to that effect by the Parole Board. Moreover, the Secretary of State was now obliged to consult with the Lord Chief Justice and, if available, the trial judge, before ordering the release on licence of life sentence prisoners. Subject to his duty to act fairly, the Secretary of State has a complete discretion as to whether to release a prisoner following a positive recommendation by the Parole Board, but cannot order release if the Board has recommended otherwise. Although the trial judge has power under the Murder (Abolition of the Death Penalty) Act 1965 to recommend the minimum period that should be served in custody by a life sentence prisoner, that recommendation does not form part of the sentence, and both the Parole Board and the Secretary of State are free to disregard it in making their own assessments of the case.

In 1973 the Secretary of State appointed a joint committee of the Home Office and the Parole Board to consider at what stage the case of a life sentence prisoner should first be sent to the relevant Local Review Committee for a first review. The joint committee was disbanded following the change of parole policy announced by the Secretary of State in October 1983 discussed below. As a result, he now decides the date of the first reference of a case to the local review committee following initial consultation with the judiciary. The practice after the 1983 policy statement (see p. 157) was for the Home Secretary to wait three to four years from the date of the sentence before consulting with the judiciary upon the time ("the tariff period") which should be served by the prisoner to satisfy the requirements of retribution and deterrence. The prisoner's case would then be referred to the local review committee for the first time three years before the end of the tariff period. In *R.* v. *Home Secretary ex p. Handscomb and others*,[22] the Divisional court could find no logic in the three to four year delay before asking the trial judge for his view of the tariff period. It created a danger that the prisoner would serve longer than he

[22] *The Times*, March 4, 1987, D.C.

should, and was unlawful. Moreover, the Home Secretary was obliged to accept the judicial view of the tariff period.

Life sentence prisoners released as set out above, remain on licence for the rest of their natural lives. Revocation of such licences is governed by section 62 of the 1967 Act, discussed below.

**The mechanism for release on licence**

The structure invented by the Criminal Justice Act 1967 to deal with the selection of prisoners to be released on licence involves three separate stages.

(i) *The first stage: consideration by a local review committee*

Local review committees exist to review and report upon a prisoner's suitability for release on licence. Their composition and procedures are principally governed by the Local Review Committee Rules 1967 made under section 59(6) of the Criminal Justice Act 1967.[22a] Every prison must have such a committee, consisting of the prison governor and not less than four other members appointed by the Secretary of State. The governor is the only prison officer on the committee. The committee must review the case of every prisoner serving a determinate sentence of two years or more at some time before he becomes eligible for parole, and thereafter at intervals of between 10 and 14 months from the previous review. Where a person eligible for parole is received into prison, and his case has not been reviewed, the committee must review it as soon as possible after reception and thereafter at the same intervals as set out above. The committee is *not* however obliged to consider a prisoner's case:

(a) while criminal or disciplinary proceedings are outstanding against him.
(b) while he is serving a period of cellular confinement as a punishment.
(c) if it appears that he will be released within 16 months of the previous review.
(d) if it appears that he will be released within 13 months of the date of the imposition of his sentence.
(e) if he wishes his case not to be reviewed.

[22a] 1967 S.I. No 1462 as amended by 1973 S.I. No 4 and 1983 S.I. No 622. The same provisions apply to youth custody centres.

In these circumstances the Secretary of State must be notified. Subsequent reviews of the case remain unaffected.

*The rights of the prisoner.* The Local Committee Rules specifically confer the following rights upon the prisoner who wishes his case to be reviewed in accordance with the procedure described above:

1. Before the review a member of the committee (other than the prison governor) must interview the prisoner if he is willing.
2. At such an interview the prisoner must be given a reasonable opportunity to make any representations which he wishes to have considered by the committee.
3. The prisoner has the right to make written representations to the committee, which in turn must consider such representations upon reviewing the case. The prisoner must be informed of the existence of this right.
4. The interviewing member of the committee must make a written report of the interview which must be considered by the committee when it reviews the case, and which must be sent to the Secretary of State with the committee's report upon the prisoner's suitability for release on licence.

*Release upon recommendation by the committee: the leapfrog procedure.* Under the original procedures set up by the 1967 Act, it was necessary for every case to be considered by the Parole Board after the review by the local review committee, before in turn the case was considered by the Secretary of State. This proved to be unnecessarily cumbersome and time-consuming in the more straightforward cases. Thus by section 35 of the Criminal Justice Act 1972, the Secretary of State became empowered, after consultation with the Parole Board, to determine classes of case in which he could act directly upon the recommendations of the local review committee, without the necessity of involving the Board in the process. Since January 1976 those classes of case have been:

(i) Where the sentence is of four years or less in the case of offences other than those involving violence, sex, arson or drug trafficking, or two years or less in such cases; and
(ii) Where the local review committee is unanimous.

Thus for all sentences of four years or more, and for sentences of two years or more where the offences concerned involved violence, sex, arson or drug trafficking, the matter must still be referred to the Board irrespective of whether the local review committee has reached a unanimous recommendation.

(ii) *The second stage: consideration by the Parole Board*

Having been reviewed by the Local Review Committee, the prisoner's case is then referred by the Secretary of State to the Parole Board, whose constitution, membership and functions are governed by section 59 of and Schedule 2 to the Criminal Justice Act 1967. By section 59(3) it is the Board's duty to advise the Secretary of State with respect to:

(a) The release on licence, and subsequent recall, of prisoners whose cases have been referred to it.
(b) The imposition, variation and cancellation of conditions of the licence.
(c) Any other matters referred to it which are connected with the release on licence or recall of such prisoners.

*The rights of the prisoner.* Unlike the Local Review Committee, consideration of a prisoner's case by the Parole Board is not governed by Rules designed to maximise his opportunity to make representations in support of his application for release on licence. Indeed, subject to its duty to act fairly, the Board has an almost complete discretion in arriving at its recommendation to the Secretary of State. The only obligations cast upon the Board by the 1967 Act are:

(a) To deal with the case on consideration of any documents given to it by the Secretary of State, and of any oral or written information which it has obtained.
(b) To consider any written representations made by the prisoner in connection with or since his last interview with a member of the Local Review Committee acting in that capacity.
(c) The Board may also request one of its members to interview the prisoner if it considers it necessary; if this is done, the Board must take account of that member's report of the interview. The interviewing of the prisoner is wholly within the discretion of the Board.

In *Payne* v. *Lord Harris of Greenwich*,[23] the Plaintiff, who had

[23] [1981] 2 All E.R. 842; [1981] 1 W.L.R. 754.

been sentenced to life imprisonment for murder in 1968, unsuccessfully applied for release on licence several times from the mid-1970s onward. While in prison he had behaved impeccably, and had been placed in security category "D". He commenced proceedings against the chairman of the Parole Board, the chairman of the relevant Local Review Committee, and the Secretary of State, seeking various declarations, including one that he should be acquainted with the reasons for the Board's decision not to recommend him for release on licence. The Court of Appeal unanimously dismissed his appeal against McNeill J.'s refusal to grant him the declarations sought. The Court held that the relevant provisions of the Criminal Justice Act, together with the Rules made thereunder, formed a comprehensive code in respect of release on licence. No "right to know" was conferred on the prisoner by that code, and none could be properly implied. The Court went on to consider whether the duty to act fairly and in accordance with the principles of natural justice, which, it was accepted, lay upon the Board, required the Board to furnish reasons for its decisions. Each of the judges set out considerations of policy which rendered the disclosure of reasons unnecessary, unhelpful to the prisoner, or impracticable. Lord Denning M.R. concluded:

> "In the end I think the problem comes down to this: what does public policy demand as best be done? . . . I think that in the interests of the man himself, as a human being facing indefinite detention, it would be better for him to be told the reasons. But, in the interests of society at large, including the administration of the parole system, it would be best not to give them."[24]

The decision in *Payne* is clearly supported by the way in which the legislation is framed, in particular the *express* duty to give reasons for a recall to prison under section 62(3) of the 1967 Act. It is also justifiable on grounds of policy and practicality, but nevertheless raises difficult questions. Although the Parole Board is under a duty to act fairly, it is hard to see how this duty can possibly be enforced. If a prisoner is not to be entitled to know the reasons which impel the Board to decline to recommend release on licence, that prisoner will in practice find it almost impossible to establish that the Board has acted unfairly. The practical consequence of the decision in *Payne* is, it is submitted, effectively to

[24] *Ibid.* at p. 846.

remove the deliberations of the Parole Board from the public domain, and to ensure that those deliberations, and the decisions arising out of them, cannot be investigated or challenged.[24a]

(iii) *The third stage: consideration by the Secretary of State*

It has already been noted that, save in the "leapfrog" cases, the Secretary of State can order the release of prisoners on licence only following a positive recommendation to that effect from the Parole Board. In the case of life sentence prisoners an additional safeguard is afforded by the necessity for the Secretary of State to consult with the Lord Chief Justice and trial judge before ordering release. Successive Home Secretaries almost invariably acted upon the recommendations of the Parole Board, save presumably in those cases where the release of a prisoner might have proved politically sensitive to the Government of the day.

As can be seen from the summary of the history of the parole provisions set out above, the caution enshrined in the original legislation slowly gave way to legislative provisions which permitted swifter release for larger numbers of prisoners. This proved to be the policy of successive Home Secretaries, and in 1975 the then Home Secretary announced new guidelines discussed with the Parole Board designed to increase the number of prisoners released on licence and the amount of time for which they were to be so released.

This steady trend came to an end in October 1983 with the announcement by the Secretary of State[25-26] of a major change in parole policy:

(i) As regards life sentence prisoners, the existing Home Office/Parole Board joint committee was to be disbanded, and the Secretary of State was henceforth to discuss with the judiciary when such a prisoner's case should first be reviewed by a local review committee. Certain categories of life sentence prisoner would normally spend at least 20 years in prison.

(ii) Prisoners serving determinate sentences of more than five years imprisonment for offences of violence or drug trafficking would, save in exceptional circumstances, be granted parole only when release under supervision for a

[24a] See though *Weeks* v. *United Kingdom, The Times* March 5, 1987 (Euro. Court).

[25-26] This announcement was first made to the Conservative Party conference, and then on November 30, to Parliament: 49 H.C. Official Report (6th series) Written Answers col. 513.

few months at the end of the sentence would be likely to reduce the long-term risk to the public.

Prior to making this announcement, the Secretary of State did not consult the Parole Board, although in subsequent discussions it was agreed that he would continue to refer the same number of cases to the Board as previously, but that the Board would make its recommendations in accordance with the new policy.

The effect of these changes was that for certain categories of prisoner the likelihood of being released on licence was very much more remote than it had been hitherto, and that those prisoners were likely to remain in prison for a longer period than would formerly have been anticipated. As a result, four prisoners applied to the Courts for judicial review of the Home Secretary's policy statement, claiming that it constituted an abuse or excess of the discretion afforded to him by the statutory provisions.[26a] Two of the applicants were serving life sentences, and had been transferred from open to closed prisons as a result of the change of policy. Of the remaining two applicants, each was serving a determinate sentence of more than five years' imprisonment, one for an offence of violence, the other for an offence involving drug trafficking.

The matter first came before a two-judge Divisional Court. The judges disagreed about the lawfulness of the policy statement, and the applicants treated this as a dismissal of their claim rather than insisting upon a new trial before a three-judge court. The Court of Appeal, by a majority, dismissed the appeal.

The reasoning of Browne-Wilkinson L.J., in his dissenting judgment, is worthy of note. He regarded the new policy as unlawful on two counts. First, individual consideration of each case was an essential feature of any system of parole. Unless regard was had to the conduct and circumstances of each prisoner since conviction, the system was not one of parole, but of remission. All relevant circumstances had to be weighed: however, the Home Secretary's statement involved disregarding all relevant circumstances except the nature of the original offence, and he was not entitled to negate the weighing process. Although the judge accepted that as a matter of policy the Home Secretary could decide to attach more importance to one relevant factor (*e.g.* the nature of the original offence and the deterrent

[26a] *Findlay* v. *Home Secretary* [1985] A.C. 318; [1984] 3 W.L.R. 1159; [1984] 3 All E.R. 801.

effect of the sentence) than to others, the policy statement had gone further than this, and was not saved by the proviso "save in genuinely exceptional circumstances." The policy had created a presumption against parole, and had deprived the prisoner of his right to individual consideration of his case.

The second objection to the policy as it was to be excuted, was that the Board's practice in making its recommendations in accordance with the new policy caused its own advice and recommendations to be unlawful:

> "It appears that the Home Secretary was making it a condition of the exercise of his discretion to refer to the Board cases falling within the new policy statement that it would in giving *its* advice and recommendation give effect to *his* policy . . .
>
> " . . . It is in my judgment of the essence of the system established by the 1967 agreement that, if a case is referred to the Board, the Board reaches its own conclusion on its own criteria according to its own judgment."

In essence therefore, the judge found that the implementation of the policy undermined the independence of the Board.

The House of Lords unanimously dismissed the appeal and affirmed the legality of the new policy, without hearing argument from the Home Secretary's legal representatives. The leading speech was that of Lord Scarman, in which the rest of the House concurred. The applicants' first, but subsidiary, contention was that the failure to consult the Parole Board before formulating the policy was unlawful. This contention found favour with Forbes J. in the Divisional Court, but had been rejected by all of the judges in the Court of Appeal. Lord Scarman observed that there was no express statutory requirement for such consultation, and that it was impossible to imply such a requirement. Nor was the Home Secretary unreasonable in his failure to consult:

> "in deciding to adopt the new policy without consulting the board the Secretary of State took into account the factors of deterrence retribution and public confidence in the administration of criminal justice. These were plainly material matters for his consideration in the exercise of his discretion."

The applicants' main contentions were that the formulation of the policy was unlawful in that it offended against the purpose of the legislation that every prisoner should have his case individually considered; that the classification of prisoners according to offence and length of sentence created a presumption against parole, which denied the prisoner his legitimate expectation of individual consideration, and which effectively operated as a punishment not authorised by law; and that the policy compromised the independence of the Board. These were largely the propositions which had found favour with Browne-Wilkinson L.J. in the Court of Appeal. Lord Scarman commenced by seeking out the legislative purpose in the statutory provisions:

> "The statute gives little, and at best only indirect, guidance as to the factors which the Secretary of State has to consider in the exercise of his power to grant parole or as to the weight to be given them. But they are many, and they are by no means confined to the particular circumstances or record of the prisoner. If the public interest is to be served, they must include some matters of policy, *e.g.* the weight to be given to the factors of deterrence, retribution and public confidence in the system and to consistency of treatment as between one prisoner and another.
>
> "For myself, I have difficulty in understanding how a Secretary of State could properly manage the complexities of his statutory duty without a policy."

The legitimacy of adopting a policy in the exercise of an administrative discretion had been recognised by the courts, and the policy adopted by the Home Secretary did not constitute a refusal to consider individual cases:

> "Consideration of a case is not excluded by a policy which provides that exceptional circumstances or compelling reasons must be shown because of the weight to be attached to the nature of the offence, the length of the sentence, and the factors of deterrence, retribution and public confidence, all of which it was the duty of the Secretary of State to consider."[26b]

Lord Scarman thus differed fundamentally from Browne-Wilkinson L.J. in his view of the "exceptional circumstances" proviso.[27] He saw no objection in the classification of offenders according to the character and gravity of their offences provided

[26b] [1985] A.C. 318 at p. 336.
[27] See now *R.* v. *Home Secretary ex p., Handscomb, The Times*, March 4, 1987.

that this did not preclude consideration of other relevant factors. The presumption against parole was inevitable and presumably intended, but did not preclude consideration of other factors. The disappointment of the expectation that prisoners would not have to serve the whole of their sentences in prison was not a punishment which went beyond the sentence of the court.

Finally, dealing with the argument that the policy undermined the independence of the Parole Board, Lord Scarman said:

> "Granted the separate responsibilities of minister and board which . . . the statute plainly envisages, I think it good sense and in the public interest that the board should know the release policy of the minister when conducting its own review of individual cases . . . . Since the Secretary of State has the final responsibility for release, the board needs to know his policy if its advice is to be relevant and of value."[27a]

**Revocation of licences**

There are two basic methods by which a prisoner's licence may be revoked:

(a) *By the Secretary of State:* if he considers it expedient and in the public interest to do so without consulting the Parole Board, the Home Secretary may do so. In other cases he may revoke the licence and order the prisoner's recall to prison upon the recommendation of the Board. In either event the prisoner is specifically granted the right to make written representations with regard to his recall, and must be informed of the reasons for it.[28] The extent of this latter duty was considered in *R.* v. *Home Secretary ex p. Gunnell.*[29] The applicant, a life sentence prisoner, had been released on licence in March 1981. He was recalled to prison in early 1983, after his behaviour had given cause for concern. The reasons for his recall were explained orally to him by the assistant governor, and later by a member of the Local Review Committee. The Parole Board recommended that he be released at the end of April 1983, subject to acceptable release plans, which were to include residence and supervision at a hostel. He was not released, and sought judicial review of this decision. It was contended on his behalf that he should have been supplied with written reasons for his recall, and should have

27a [1985] A.C. 318 at p. 337–8.
28 See generally Criminal Justice Act 1967, s.62.
29 (1985) Crim.L.R. 105.

been granted a full hearing before the Parole Board, including an opportunity for legal representation and cross examination, together with access to the reports and documents before the Board. The Court of Appeal, upholding the dismissal of the application by the Divisional Court, held that in respect of informing a prisoner of the reasons for his recall, there was no obligation to do more than to see whether the prisoner understood why he had been recalled. There was no requirement to furnish him with written reasons for the recall.[30]

Where the prisoner is recalled to prison without prior consultation between the Secretary of State and the Parole Board, or where the prisoner has exercised his right to make representations with regard to his recall, the Secretary of State must refer the case to the Board. If the Board then recommends immediate release, the Secretary of State must give effect to that recommendation. In *ex p. Gunnell* it was contended that the Board's recommendation was for immediate release. This was rejected by the Court of Appeal, which held that the recommendation was for conditional release on a medical plan being drawn up.

(b) *By the Courts:* if a prisoner on licence is convicted by a Magistrates' Court of an offence punishable on indictment by imprisonment, the Court may commit him on bail or in custody to the Crown Court for sentence but cannot itself revoke the licence. On the other hand the Magistrates may make no order, in which case the licence continues as before, subject to the Secretary of State's power to order recall. If a prisoner on licence is convicted on indictment of an imprisonable offence, or is committed for sentence as aforesaid, the Court concerned (usually the Crown Court), may revoke the licence irrespective of any other sentence which it imposes. The revocation of a licence by the Crown Court in these circumstances constitutes a sentence within the meaning of section 9 of the Criminal Appeal Act 1968, and can properly be the subject of an appeal to the Court of Appeal.[31] By section 62(10) of the 1967 Act, if the Crown Court revokes the licence of a prisoner serving a determinate sentence, he must not again be released on licence until one year, or one-third of the remaining licence period (whichever is the longer) has elapsed from the date of revocation. The meaning of this provision was considered by the Court of Appeal in *R.* v. *McKinnon*[32] in which the appellant

[30] See now *Weeks* v. *United Kingdom, The Times* March 5, 1987 (Euro. Court).
[31] *R.* v. *Welch* [1982] 1 W.L.R. 976; [1982] 2 All E.R. 824; 75 Crim. App. Rep. 207.
[32] [1987] 1 W.L.R. 234, C.A.; [1987] 2 All E.R. 21.

had been released on licence in March 1986. He had abided by the terms of the licence, but in April he was imprisoned for other offences, committed prior to the offences for which the earlier term of imprisonment had been imposed. The Court of Appeal held that section 62(10) should be interpreted as meaning that.

> "the embargo on any further parole during the one year period is not confined to the sentence in respect of which the revoked parole licence was imposed. If that is likely to result in injustice, the answer is for the court not to exercise the optional power of revocation when an offender is convicted and sentenced to a second term of imprisonment, despite the apparent illogicality."

There was therefore an absolute embargo on parole for one year after the revocation, and the appellant could not have been paroled in respect of the second sentence for one year. Faced with this illogicality, the Court quashed the revocation order.

### EARLY RELEASE

Acute overcrowding in Britain's prisons led not only to the extension of the parole scheme noted above, but also to the introduction of the system of early release. Section 32 of the Criminal Justice Act 1982 confers power upon the Home Secretary to order the early release of prisoners serving sentences for certain categories of offence. Most serious offences are excluded from the provisions by Schedule 1 to the Act, and if a prisoner is serving more than one sentence of imprisonment, including such a sentence for an excluded offence, he will not be eligible for early release.

Provided that the prisoner is eligible for early release, the Secretary of State may order his release not more than six months earlier than he would otherwise have been released. The Secretary of State may not do so however, "unless he is satisfied that it is necessary to do so in order to make the best use of the places available for detention." The effect of an order for early release is that, save in the cases of prisoners serving extended sentences, the sentence expires upon release.

The mechanism by which the Home Secretary is empowered to exercise this power is by order laid before Parliament, approved by resolution of each House. In urgent cases the Secretary of State can release prisoners in the last month of their sentence without such order.

## FORMALITIES OF RELEASE

By section 30 of the Prison Act 1952 as replaced by section 66(3) of the Criminal Justice Act 1967, the Home Secretary may make such payments to or in respect of persons released or about to be released from prison as he may, with Treasury consent, determine. Upon release, the prisoner may be provided where necessary with suitable and adequate clothing.[33]

## SUPERVISION AND AFTER-CARE

Save as regards prisoners released on licence, there is no specific statutory provision for any sort of after-care by the authorities for those prisoners who were 21 or over when sentenced. Rule 32 of the Prison Rules 1964 provides that from the beginning of the sentence consideration must be given to the prisoner's future and the assistance to be given to him on and after release. Such a provision is by its nature unenforceable, and is expressed perhaps more in hope than expectation. As for prisoners released on licence, provision will be made in the licence for contact to be maintained between the prisoner and a probation officer. By section 60(4) of the Criminal Justice Act 1967 the parolee must comply with any conditions specified in his licence.

## THE ROYAL PREROGATIVE

A prisoner may be released by exercise of the royal prerogative of mercy. This is exercised either by the grant of a free pardon, or, more typically, by a reduction of all or part of the outstanding sentence. The prerogative is invoked in only a tiny proportion of cases. The independence of the legal system from executive intereference in part dictates this. There are a number of circumstances in which the prerogative is exercised. Perhaps the most typical examples are the medical condition of the prisoner or a close relative, the emergence of fresh evidence throwing doubt upon the correctness of the prisoner's conviction, and as a form of reward to the prisoner for the provision of valuable assistance to the authorities.

The meaning and effect of a free pardon was considered by the Court of Appeal in *R.* v. *Foster*.[34] The Court's conclusion was that constitutionally the Crown did not have a prerogative of justice,

[33] Rule 20(5) of the Prison Rules 1964.
[34] [1985] Q.B. 115; [1984] 3 W.L.R. 401; [1984] 2 All E.R. 679.

only a prerogative of mercy. It could not therefore remove a conviction, but only its effects. Even after a free pardon, the conviction remained until quashed by the Court of Appeal.

*Ex gratia payments by the Home Office*

Although there is no statutory basis for the practice, *ex gratia* payments are usually made by the Home Office in those cases where prisoners have been granted a free pardon in respect of the crimes for which they were convicted, or where the Court of Appeal has quashed a conviction following a reference by the Home Secretary. The decision as to whether such a payment is to be made is not subject to any sort of review, nor are the reasons upon which the decision is based either published or discussed. The assessment of quantum is usually made by the chairman of the Criminal Injuries Compensation Board, upon principles analagous to those governing the assessment of damages for civil wrongs. Thus pecuniary (*e.g.* losses of earnings, and earning capacity, legal expenses etc.) and non-pecuniary (damage to reputation, mental anguish etc.) losses are taken into account. Likewise, any contributory conduct of the prisoner may reduce the award. The award, if made, is not subject to any appeal or judicial scrutiny, and in accepting it, the recipient will sign a form undertaking not to make any other claim whatsoever arising out of the circumstances of his prosecution or conviction, or his detention in either or both of these connections.

## ESCAPE AND PERSONS UNLAWFULLY AT LARGE

*Escape*

It is hardly surprising to find that to escape from prison or lawful custody, or to attempt to do so, is a disciplinary offence under the Prison Rules 1964. These fall within the category of "grave" offences, with which the Board of Visitors would usually deal.[35] There are also a number of criminal offences connected with escape from prison:

(i) Escape from prison is a common law offence, irrespective of whether it is effected forcibly. Those who assist such escape may be convicted as principals of this offence.
(ii) Prison breach is another common law offence, and is committed by somebody who, while in lawful custody, escapes

[35] Rules 47(5)(19) and 51(1)(a) Prison Rules 1964.

by force from the prison or other place in which he is confined. There must be an actual breaking, although this need not be intentional.[36] Otherwise the offence would be one of escape.

(iii) By section 39 of the Prison Act 1952, it is an offence to aid a prisoner to escape or attempt to escape from a prison[37] or, with intent to facilitate such escape, to convey any thing into a prison or to a prisoner, or to place any thing outside a prison with a view to its coming into the possession of a prisoner.

(iv) By section 22 of the Criminal Justice Act 1961, it is an offence knowingly to harbour an escaped prisoner.

*Persons unlawfully at large*

Section 49(1) of the Prison Act 1952 empowers a constable to arrest without warrant a prisoner unlawfully at large, and to return him to the place at which he is liable to be detained.[38] A magistrate may issue a warrant, on sworn information, to arrest and bring before the court an escaped prisoner, and must, if satisfied as to the facts, order him to be returned to the institution where he is liable, or required, to be detained.[39]

While a prisoner is unlawfully at large, whether by escape, failure to return after temporary release, or after a recall order, time metaphorically stands still. Section 49(2) of the Prison Act 1952 provides that where a prisoner is unlawfully at large, no account shall be taken of any period during which he is absent from prison in calculating the period for which he is liable to be detained, unless the Home Secretary otherwise directs. In *R.* v. *Governor of Leeds Prison ex p. Stafford*,[40] the applicant escaped from prison in November 1956. He was arrested in Trinidad in April 1957, and was held in custody until June, when he was returned to the United Kingdom. On an application for habeas corpus, the court held that the whole period of absence from prison, rather than just the period between November 1956 and April 1957,

[36] *R.* v. *Burridge* (1735) 3 P.Wms. 439, *R.* v. *Haswell* (1821) R. & R. 458.

[37] "Prison" being strictly construed: *R.* v. *Holden* (1965) 115 L.J. 450, and *R.* v. *Harte and Moss* (1985) 82 Cr.App.R. 116 C.A.

[38] See too the provisions of Criminal Justice Act 1961, s.30 which extends the operation of Prison Act 1952, s.49 throughout the United Kingdom, Isle of Man and Channel Islands, and makes reciprocal arrangements.

[39] Criminal Justice Act 1967, s.72.

[40] [1964] 2 Q.B. 625; [1964] 2 W.L.R. 731; [1964] 1 All E.R. 610.

should be disregarded in calculating the period during which the applicant could be detained pursuant to the original sentence of the English court. The day of escape and the day of recapture both constitute days of imprisonment and count towards the sentence.

### DEATH OF A PRISONER

Upon the death of a prisoner, the prison governor is obliged by rule 19(1) of the Prison Rules immediately to inform the deceased's spouse or next of kin where he knows that person's address, "and also any person who the prisoner may reasonably have asked should be informed." The governor must also give immediate notice to the coroner having jurisdiction, who would then be under a duty to hold an inquest, to the Board of Visitors, and to the Secretary of State. The chaplain or prison minister will conduct the burial service of any prisoner of the appropriate denomination if no other arrangements have been made.

*Chapter 9*

# THE EFFECT OF A SENTENCE OF IMPRISONMENT UPON LIFE OUTSIDE



## Imprisonment and the Prisoner's Job

A sentence of imprisonment will inevitably affect the contract of employment under which the prisoner was working prior to his arrest or sentence. Usually that contract will be brought to an end, although the courts have not been consistent in their analysis of precisely how this occurs. There are essentially four ways in which a contract of employment can be brought to an end; namely by agreement, by frustration, or by termination either on the part of the employer or of the employee. In theory there is nothing to prevent the parties to a contract of employment from agreeing that if the employee is convicted of a criminal offence or sentenced to an immediate term of imprisonment, the contract shall forthwith determine. In practice this is rarely done: at the outset of such a contract, neither party wishes to envisage such circumstances.

In the absence of such express agreement, there are two possible legal interpretations of the legal effect of a sentence of imprisonment upon a contract of employment. The first is that further performance of the contract is rendered impossible and the contract is frustrated. The second is that by committing the relevant offence, or by being sentenced, the employee repudiates the contract: the employer then has the option of accepting the repudiation and dismissing the employee, or of refusing to accept it, and treating the contract as still in existence. The distinction between frustration and repudiation is of crucial practical significance. For if the contract is frustrated, there is in law no dismissal by the employer, and the employee will be unable to claim either that he has been wrongfully dismissed (within the general principles of the common law) or unfairly dismissed (under the relevant statutory provisions).

A detailed discussion of the distinction between wrongful and unfair dismissal falls outside the scope of this book. In essence wrongful dismissal is a dismissal which constitutes a breach of contract by the employer, for which the employee is entitled to be compensated in damages. The usual measure of damages is the amount that the employee would have earned during the period until the employer could lawfully have dismissed him, *i.e.* the notice period agreed between the parties or imposed by statute. Such entitlement to damages is subject to the employee's duty to mitigate his loss by, if appropriate, accepting alternative employment within the relevant period. The concept of unfair dismissal was first introduced by the Industrial Relations Act 1971 and is entirely a creature of statute. Under the Employment Consolidation (Protection) Act 1978 as amended, the employer has to show firstly what was the reason for the dismissal and secondly that it was a reason falling within a statutory list of reasons justifying dismissal. The Industrial Tribunal must then determine whether he acted reasonably in relying upon that as a sufficient reason to dismiss the employee. If the dismissal is held to be unfair, the employee will generally (though by no means invariably) be awarded a higher level of compensation by an Industrial Tribunal than would be the case in a wrongful dismissal claim.

Where an employee is sentenced to a long prison term and does not appeal, no real problem can arise: common sense dictates that the contract must come to an end as the employee will be prevented from working for a considerable period. Difficulties do arise where the sentence is a short one. In such cases the employee is likely to be away for only a few months, equivalent to a moderately long sickness absence. Indeed, in the case of very short sentences, the employee may be absent for a period equivalent to or less than his annual holiday entitlement. Further difficulties are presented by the appeal process. If a conviction is quashed on appeal, the appellant is treated as never having been convicted of the offence, even if the appeal succeeds only for technical legal reasons. In the meantime the employee may well have been dismissed, or the contract deemed to be frustrated by the employer. It is not easy to fit all such problems into a legal straitjacket. In their attempts to do so, the courts have not been successful.

**Imprisonment and the doctrine of frustration**

The first occasion upon which the Court of Appeal had to consider the correct approach towards an employee who had lost his job due to being sentenced to a term of imprisonment was in *Hare* v. *Murphy Bros.*[1] The applicant, who had worked for the respondents for 25 years, was involved in a brawl away from work. He was sentenced to 12 months' imprisonment. Before his trial his employers told him that if he did not receive a custodial sentence his job would remain open for him, but if he was sent to prison, the position would be reconsidered upon his release. After his release he asked his employers when they would like him to return, but was told that his old job had been filled and that there were no alternatives.

In the Court of Appeal, Lord Denning M.R. held that there had been no breach of contract by the applicant. The brawl had taken place away from work and had no connection with it. The sentence of imprisonment was not a breach of contract by the applicant but was an act of the court. Lord Denning, however, considered the sentence of imprisonment to be a frustrating event. Although brought about by the applicant's own act, "the event was so unforeseen and the delay so long that the contract of employment was brought automatically to an end when the sentence was imposed." He gave some guidance as to how the problem should be approached:

> "In the case of a contract of employment you must look at the length of time he has been employed, the position which he held, and, of course, most important of all, the length of time which he is likely to be away from his work and unable to perform it and the importance of getting someone else to do his job meanwhile ... If it then appears that his job has effectively been brought to an end, the contract is frustrated."

It would appear that the judge was not suggesting that all sentences of imprisonment had the effect of frustrating the contract, but that each case must be viewed in the light of its own particular facts. The other judges of the court made no finding as to whether the sentence frustrated the contract, simply holding that the contract was terminated by the sentence, and that no claim for unfair dismissal could lie, since at that date the Industrial Relations Act 1971 was not in force.

[1] [1974] 3 All E.R. 940; [1974] I.C.R. 603; [1974] I.R.L.R. 342.

Although upon a close reading of the judgments of the Court of Appeal in *Hare* v. *Murphy Bros.*, Lord Denning M.R. was the only judge to hold that the sentence of imprisonment operated to frustrate the contract of employment, his reasoning was followed by the Employment Appeal Tribunal in two later cases. Both raised the difficult question of the relevance of the criminal appeal process in such circumstances. In *Harrington* v. *Kent County Council*,[2] the applicant was a teacher employed by the respondents. He was charged with and convicted of offences of indecency involving young female pupils of the school at which he was teaching. Soon after his conviction, the respondents wrote informing him that his employment was regarded as automatically terminated by the sentence. Two months later his appeal against conviction was successful, and his conviction quashed. The Employment Appeal Tribunal, following *Hare* v. *Murphy Bros.*, held that the fact of the sentence frustrated the contract, and that knowledge on the respondents' part that an appeal had been launched could not affect this.

A slightly different result was reached in *Chakki* v. *United Yeast Co. Ltd.*,[3] in which the applicant had been sentenced to a total of 11 months' imprisonment. The following day he was released on bail pending an appeal against sentence, but the employers had by then already terminated his contract. The Industrial Tribunal held that the contract had been frustrated by the sentence, even though in the event the appeal had been successful, and the applicant placed on probation. The Employment Appeal Tribunal allowed the applicant's appeal and remitted the case to an Industrial Tribunal for further consideration. Neill J. considered that the sentence of imprisonment was a *potentially* frustrating event rather than a cause of *immediate* frustration, for, as matters had turned out, the applicant need never have informed his employers of the passing of the sentence upon him. He formulated three questions to resolve the issue of whether the contract had in fact been frustrated:

> "(1) Looking at the matter from a practical commercial point of view, when was it necessary for the employers to decide as to the employee's future and as to whether a replacement driver would have to be engaged? (2) At the time when the decision had to be taken, what would a reasonable employer

[2] [1980] I.R.L.R. 353, E.A.T.
[3] [1982] 2 All E.R. 446; [1982] I.C.R. 141.

> have considered to be the likely length of the employee's absence over the next few months? (3) If in the light of his likely absence it appeared necessary to engage a replacement, was it reasonable to engage a permanent replacement rather than a temporary one?"

**Imprisonment and repudiation of the contract**

Considerable doubt was cast upon the correctness of the decisions set out above by the Employment Appeal Tribunal in *Norris* v. *Southampton City Council.*[4] In March 1981 the applicant was committed in custody for sentence for two offences. An immediate sentence of imprisonment appeared to be very likely as he was awaiting sentence upon another matter, and was also in breach of a suspended sentence of imprisonment. The respondent employers were informed of the applicant's committal in custody by his girlfriend, who informed them that the applicant expected a sentence of at least six months' imprisonment. The following day they dismissed him. A month later he was granted bail. The Industrial Tribunal, held that the contract had been frustrated, but the Employment Appeal Tribunal allowed Mr. Norris's appeal and remitted the case to the Industrial Tribunal.

Kilner Brown J., giving the judgment of the Employment Appeal Tribunal, held that the Industrial Tribunal had erred in failing to follow the majority decision of the Court of Appeal in *London Transport Executive* v. *Clarke,*[5] decided the previous year, in which Dunn and Templeman L.JJ.

> "had clearly indicated that on the state of the law in the light of existing authorities, where a man by his own conduct made it impossible to perform the contract it is not frustration, it is not discharge, it is not a dismissal of himself by himself but is repudiatory conduct which entitles the employer to treat it as a repudiation and to dismiss him."

The judge drew a distinction between cases where there was no fault by the employee and those in which deliberate conduct led to the impossibility of performance:

> "We believe that in a case where the employee's conduct leads to impossibility of performance it has to be treated as

[4] [1982] I.R.L.R. 141; [1982] I.C.R. 177.
[5] [1981] I.C.R. 355; [1981] I.R.L.R. 166.

repudiatory, giving to the employer the option of whether or not to treat the contract as repudiated and, if yes, to dismiss him."

In the case of a man sentenced to a term of imprisonment this conduct was the commission of the offence which led to the sentence.

**Resolution of the conflict**

The above conflict was resolved by the Court of Appeal in an important judgment in *F.C. Shepherd & Co.* v. *Jerrom*,[6] which, whilst not expressly disapproving *Norris*, re-established the place of the doctrine of frustration in the case of employees who became incarcerated. The employers in the case employed an apprentice under a four-year training service agreement, which incorporated the terms of a joint industry board, providing for termination of the apprenticeship in cases of "serious misconduct warranting dismissal." The apprentice was convicted of affray and conspiracy to assault, and was sentenced to Borstal training. He was released after six months. His employers refused to take him back. Both the Industrial Tribunal and the Employment Appeal Tribunal held that the contract was not frustrated by the Borstal sentence, and that the employers had repudiated the contract by refusing to take the apprentice back into their employ. This amounted to a constructive dismissal, which was held to be unfair. The apprentice was awarded the maximum amount of compensation available.

The employers appealed successfully to the Court of Appeal which held that no such repudiation had occured. The actions of the apprentice in becoming involved in an affray and being sent to Borstal had nothing to do with his work or training and so could not be "serious misconduct warranting dismissal." The difficulty in holding that the doctrine of frustration could apply was the oft-quoted principle that frustration cannot be self-induced. As for this, Lawton and Mustill L.JJ. held that a party to a contract could not plead his own default in order to improve his position by asserting that an event, which would otherwise bring about a discharge by frustration, was caused by his own fault. Balcombe L.J. adopted what he described as a simplistic approach to a difficult jurisprudential problem, and, persuaded by the reasoning of Lord Denning M.R. in *Hare* v. *Murphy Bros.*,[7]

[6] [1987] Q.B. 301; [1986] 3 W.L.R. 801; [1986] 3 All E.R. 589.
[7] [1974] 3 A11 E.R. 940.

agreed that a custodial sentence imposed on an employee was capable of frustrating a contract of employment. He felt that in the context of employment (as opposed to commercial) law, it was irrelevant whether imprisonment amounted to "self-induced" frustration.

The decision in *F.C. Shepherd and Co.* v. *Jerrom* has much to commend it, restoring common sense and flexibility to a difficult area of employment law. *Norris* v. *Southampton City Council* can no longer be regarded as good law. Although the question of what length of sentence will be sufficient to frustrate a contract of employment is incapable of precise answer, depending as it always will upon the terms of the contract and the length of sentence, the courts are likelier now to favour the proposition that the contract has been frustrated.

## BUSINESS ACTIVITY

The standing orders provide that a prisoner (no distinction being made between those convicted and unconvicted) may not be permitted to conduct business activities from prison, but should be allowed reasonable facilities for arranging such conduct on his behalf. Governors are given discretion to allow the prisoner to deal with a limited range of business matters, such as the disposal of property, making a will, or signing cheques. The principle is that whilst the prisoner should not be allowed to conduct business activities *per se*, he should be able to arrange to protect the value of his property and business interests.

## POLITICAL ACTIVITY

By section 4(1) of the Representation of the People Act 1949. "a convicted person during the time that he shall be detained in a penal institution in pursuance of his sentence shall be legally incapable of voting at any parliamentary or local government election." The definition of convicted person extends to include those found guilty at courts martial, but does not include those dealt with by way of committal for contempt.

Until 1981, the fact that a person was serving a term of imprisonment did not generally prevent him from standing for election to Parliament. Indeed it was the sucessful candidature of an Irish prisoner in a parliamentary by-election which led to the enactment of the Representation of the People Act 1981. By section 1 of that Act, a sentence of imprisonment of one year or more in the United Kingdom or the Republic of Ireland disqualifies a person from membership of the House of Commons during the course of that sentence. Both the nomination for election and the election itself would be void in law, and if a sitting member of the House of Commons were to be sentenced to a term of imprisonment of one year or more, his seat would automatically fall vacant. Likewise those convicted of corrupt electoral practice are disenfranchised and disqualified from membership of the House of Commons for a period of five years by virtue of section 140(3) and (5) of the Representation of the People Act 1949.

Once imprisoned, a Member of Parliament has no special rights or privileges within the prison system.

## Marriage

Article 12 of the European Convention declares that "men and women of marriageable age have the right to marry and to found a family according to the national laws governing the exercise of this right." In *Hamer* v. *United Kingdom*,[8] the applicant was refused permission to marry in prison. The Commission found that this constituted a violation of Article 12. Personal liberty was not a precondition of the right to marry, and the exercise of the right did not involve the prisoner escaping the supervision of the prison authorities. To accord prisoners the right to marry would involve no threat to prison security and was not contrary to the public interest. The Commission regarded it as irrelevant that the prisoner would be unable to cohabit, or to consummate his marriage:

> "The essence of the right to marry, in the Commission's opinion, is the formation of a legally binding association between a man and a woman. It is for them to decide whether or not they wish to enter such an association in circumstances where they cannot cohabit."[9]

## Disqualifications Following a Sentence of Imprisonment

There are many activities which may be affected by a criminal conviction. An offender may be disqualified from driving, from

[8] (1982) 4 E.H.R.R. 139.
[9] *Ibid.*, at p. 143.

holding various kinds of licence, or from holding certain positions in a company. A sentence of imprisonment *per se* however, is the cause of disqualification only in the following circumstances:

(i) *Firearms*

By section 21(1) of the Firearms Act 1968,[10] a person who has been sentenced to a term of imprisonment or youth custody for three years or more (including life sentences) is permanently prohibited from having a firearm or ammunition in his possession. The same applies to those released on licence under section 53 of the Children and Young Persons Act 1933.

By section 21(2) of the Act, a person who has been sentenced to imprisonment, youth custody, or detention centre for a term of three months or more, but less than three years, is prohibited from having a firearm or ammunition in his possession for a period of five years from the date of his release.[11]

It is a criminal offence to contravene the above provisions, but a person so prohibited may apply to the Crown Court for removal of the prohibition.[12]

(ii) *Jury service*

By Part II Schedule I to the Juries Act 1974 as amended by the Juries (Disqualification) Act 1984, two categories of ex-prisoner are disqualified from jury service:

Any person who has at any time been sentenced in the United Kingdom, the Channel Islands or the Isle of Man to imprisonment or youth custody for a term of five years or more (including life), or to detention at Her Majesty's pleasure.

Any person who has at any time in the last ten years in the United Kingdom, the Channel Islands or the Isle of Man served any part of a sentence of imprisonment, youth custody, or detention, or been detained in a Borstal institution, or been the subject of a suspended sentence.

## REHABILITATION

In one important respect Parliament has assisted many who have been convicted of criminal offences, including most prisoners, to

[10] As amended by Schedule 14 to the Criminal Justice Act 1982.
[11] This does not extend to suspended sentences: *R.* v. *Fordham* [1970] 1 Q.B. 77.
[12] Section 21(6) of the 1968 Act.

put the past behind them. The Rehabilitation of Offenders Act 1974 introduced provisions under which the vast majority of criminal convictions would become "spent" after a given period. The Act suffered from poor drafting, so that the comparatively simple system which it sought to introduce became obscured by impenetrable language.

The rehabilitation period applicable before a conviction can become spent within the meaning of the Act varies according to the severity of the sentence imposed upon conviction. If an offender has been sentenced to a term of imprisonment which exceeds two-and-a-half years (including life sentences, detention at Her Majesty's pleasure, and preventive detention), the conviction is excluded from the provision and can never become spent. For sentences of between six months and two-and-a-half years, the rehabilitation period is 10 years, whereas for sentences of six months or less, the period is seven years: at the end of those periods, the conviction is deemed to be spent. Where more than one sentence is imposed in respect of a conviction, the longest rehabilitation period attaching to those sentences applies. Where an offender is convicted of a further offence during the rehabilitation period, that will be extended by the effect of the sentence imposed for the further conviction.

The effect of the Act's provisions is that a person who has become a rehabilitated person in respect of a spent conviction is treated for most purposes as a person who "has not committed or been charged with or prosecuted for or convicted of or sentenced for the offence or offences which were the subject of that conviction." (section 4(1)). Restrictions are placed upon the admissibility of evidence designed to prove the contrary. Of primary importance to the person rehabilitated within the meaning of the Act is that he need not disclose the existence of spent convictions in his past when applying for most jobs. The Act provides that any question relating to a person's previous convictions, offences, conduct or circumstances shall be treated as not relating to spent convictions, and that such a person shall not be prejudiced by reason of his failure to acknowledge or disclose the existence of spent convictions. In particular, a spent conviction, or a failure to disclose its existence, cannot justify dismissal. There are a variety of occupations and professions to which the above provisions do not apply. These are set out in the Rehabilitation of Offenders Act 1974 (Exceptions) Order 1975 and broadly extend to occupations in the legal, medical, accountancy, educational and military fields, as well as to occupations which might involve access to the young or the disabled. Finally, reference to spent convictions in subsequent criminal proceedings cannot generally be made without the prior authority of the judge in those proceedings. Some guidance is given by a Practice Direction issued by the Lord Chief Justice on June 30, 1975, and by *R.* v. *Nye.*[13]

[13] (1982) 75 Cr.App.Rep. 247.

APPENDIX 1

# PRISON RULES 1964

S.I. 1964 No. 388[1]

## PART I

## *Prisoners*

### Purpose of prison training and treatment

1. The purpose of the training and treatment of convicted prisoners shall be to encourage and assist them to lead a good and useful life.

### Maintenance of order and discipline

2. (1) Order and discipline shall be maintained with firmness, but with no more restriction than is required for safe custody and well ordered community life.

(2) In the control of prisoners, officers shall seek to influence them through their own example and leadership, and to enlist their willing cooperation.

(3) At all times the treatment of prisoners shall be such as to encourage their self-respect and a sense of personal responsibility, but a prisoner shall not be employed in any disciplinary capacity.

### Classification of prisoners

3. (1) Prisoners shall be classified, in accordance with any directions of the Secretary of State, having regard to their age, temperament and record and with a view to maintaining good order and facilitating training and, in the case of convicted prisoners, of furthering the purpose of their training and treatment as provided by Rule 1 of these Rules.

(2) Unconvicted prisoners shall be kept out of contact with convicted prisoners as far as this can reasonably be done.

(3) Nothing is this Rule shall require a prisoner to be deprived unduly of the society of other persons.

### Privileges

4. There shall be established at every prison systems of privileges approved by the Secretary of State and appropriate to the classes of prisoners there, which shall include arrangements under which money earned by prisoners in prison may be spent by them within the prison.

[1] As amended by: 1968 No. 440; 1971 No. 2019; 1972 No. 1860; 1974 No. 713; 1976 No. 503; 1981 No. 70; 1982 No. 260; 1987 No. 1256; 1988 No. 89; 1988 No. 747 (which extends the meaning of "prison officer" in the Rules to constables and members of the armed forces employed in emergency to assist the prison governor, by performing duties ordinarily performed by a prison officer); 1988 No. 1421.

**Remission of sentence**

5. (1) A prisoner serving a sentence of imprisonment for an actual term of more than five days may, on the ground of his industry and good conduct, be granted remission in accordance with the provisions of this Rule:
Provided that this Rule shall not permit the reduction of the actual term to less than five days, or in the case of a prisoner (other than a prisoner within paragraph (2)(b) of the Rule) who has been released on licence and recalled to prison, permit his release before the thirtieth day following his return to prison on recall.

(2) The remission granted under this rule shall not exceed—

(a) in the case of a sentence of more than 12 months, one third of the total of the actual term and any period taken into account under section 67 of the Criminal Justice Act 1967; and in the case of a sentence for a term not exceeding 12 months, one half of that total or

(b) in the case of a prisoner in respect of whom an extended sentence certificate was issued when sentence was passed on him and who has been released on licence and recalled to prison, one-third of that part of his sentence unexpired at the time of his recall.

(2A) In the case of a prisoner in respect of whom a sentence of imprisonment for an offence has been passed with an order under subsection (1) of section 47 of the Criminal Law Act—

(a) if he has not been released from prison since the sentence for the offence was passed, he shall be treated for the purposes of this Rule as if his only sentence for that offence were any portion of it that he is required to serve in prison under subsection (1) or (3) of the said section 47; and

(b) if he has been released from prison but part of his sentence for the offence has subsequently been restored under subsection (3) of that section, he shall be treated for the purposes of this Rule as if his only sentence for that offence were the part of the sentence so restored.

(3) For the purpose of this Rule—

(a) a person committed to prison in default of payment of a sum adjudged to be paid by a conviction or detained in prison by virtue of a sentence of detention in a young offender institution or an order committing him to be detained under section 9 of the Criminal Justice Act 1982 shall be treated as serving a sentence of imprisonment; and

(b) consecutive terms of imprisonment shall be treated as one term.

(4) This Rule shall have effect subject to any disciplinary award of

forfeiture of remission, and shall not apply to a prisoner serving a sentence of imprisonment for life.

(4A) In the case of a prisoner who is received into a prison from another institution (other than a prison) to which the Prison Act 1952 applies and who, immediately before his reception, was subject to a disciplinary award of forfeiture of remission imposed, or having effect as if imposed, under rules made under section 47 of that Act in relation to that other institution, the award shall have effect for the purposes of this Rule as if it has been imposed under these Rules.

(5) In this Rule—

(a) "actual term" means the term of a sentence of imprisonment as reduced by section 67 of the Criminal Justice Act 1967;

(b) "forfeiture of remission" includes, in the case of a disciplinary award made before April 1, 1968, postponement of eligibility for release on licence;

(c) a reference to a person being recalled to prison shall include a reference to the revocation of a licence by a court;

(d) a reference to the said section 67 shall, in the case of a sentence passed before October 1, 1967, include a reference to section 17(2) of the Criminal Justice Administration Act 1962(a).

**Temporary Release**

6. (1) A prisoner to whom this Rule applies may be temporarily released for any period or periods and subject to any conditions.

(2) A prisoner may be temporarily released under this Rule for any special purpose or to enable him to engage in employment, to receive instruction or training or to assist him in his transition from prison life to freedom.

(3) A prisoner released under this Rule may be recalled to prison at any time whether the conditions of his release have been broken or not.

(4) This Rule applies to prisoners other than persons committed in custody for trial or to be sentenced or otherwise dealt with before or by the Crown Court or remanded in custody by an court.

**Information to prisoners**

7. (1) Every prisoner shall be provided, as soon as possible after his reception into prison, and in any case within 24 hours, with information in writing about those provisions of these Rules and other matters which it is necessary that he should know, including earnings and privileges, and the proper method of making requests and complaints and of petitioning the Secretary of State.

(2) In the case of a prisoner aged less than 18, or a prisoner aged 18

or over who cannot read or appears to have difficulty in understanding the information so provided, the governor, or an officer deputed by him, shall so explain it to him that he can understand his rights and obligations.

(3) A copy of these Rules shall be made available to any prisoner who requests it.

## Applications

8. (1) Every request by a prisoner to see the governor, a visiting officer of the Secretary of State or a member of the board of visitors shall be recorded by the officer to whom it is made and promptly passed on to the governor.

(2) On every day, other than a Sunday or public holiday, the governor shall hear the applications of prisoners who have asked to see him.

(3) Where a prisoner has asked to see any other such person as aforesaid, the governor shall ensure that that person is told of the request on his next visit to the prison.

## Women prisoners

9. (1) Women prisoners shall be kept entirely separate from male prisoners.

(2) Repealed by S.I. 1976 No. 503

(3) The Secretary of State may, subject to any conditions he thinks fit, permit a woman prisoner to have her baby with her in prison, and everything necessary for the baby's maintenance and care may be provided there.

## Religious denominations

10. A prisoner shall be treated as being of the religious denomination stated in the record made in pursuance of section 10(5) of the Prison Act 1952 but the governor may, in a proper case and after due enquiry, direct that record to be amended.

## Special duties of chaplains and prison ministers

11. (1) The chaplain or prison minister of a prison shall—

(a) interview every prisoner of his denomination individually soon after the prisoner's reception into that prison and shortly before his release; and

(b) if no other arrangements are made, read the burial service at the funeral of any prisoners of his denomination who die in that prison.

(2) The chaplain shall visit daily all prisoners belonging to the Church of England who are sick, under restraint or undergoing

cellular confinement; and a prison minister shall do the same, as far as he reasonably can, for prisoners of his own denomination.

(3) If the prisoner is willing, the chaplain shall visit any prisoner not of the Church of England who is sick, under restraint or undergoing cellular confinement, and is not regularly visited by a minister of his own denomination.

## Regular visits by ministers of religion

12. (1) The chaplain shall visit the prisoners belonging to the Church of England.

(2) A prison minister shall visit the prisoners of his denomination as regularly as he reasonably can.

(3) Where a prisoner belongs to a denomination for which no prison minister has been appointed, the governor shall do what he reasonably can, if so requested by the prisoner, to arrange for him to be visited regularly by a minister of that denomination.

## Religious services

13. (1) The chaplain shall conduct Divine Service for prisoners belonging to the Church of England at least once every Sunday, Christmas Day and Good Friday, and such celebrations of Holy Communion and weekday services as may be arranged.

(2) Prison ministers shall conduct Divine Service for prisoners of their denominations at such times as may be arranged.

## Substitute for chaplain or prison minister

14. (1) A person approved by the Secretary of State may act for the chaplain in his absence.

(2) A prison minister may, with the leave of the Secretary of State, appoint a substitute to act for him in his absence.

## Sunday work

15. Arrangements shall be made so as not to require prisoners of the Christian religion to do any unnecessary work on Sunday, Christmas Day or Good Friday, or prisoners of other religions on their recognised days of religious observance.

## Religious books

16. There shall, so far as reasonably practicable, be available for the personal use of every prisoner such religious books recognised by his denomination as are approved by the Secretary of State for use in prisons.

## Medical attendance

17. (1) The medical officer of aprison shall have the care of the health, mental and physical, of the prisoners in that prison.

(2) Every request by a prisoner to see the medical officer shall be recorded by the officer to whom it is made and promptly passed on to the medical officer.

(3) The medical officer may call another medical practitioner into consultation at his discretion, and shall do so if time permits before performing any serious operation.

(4) If an unconvicted prisoner desires the attendance of a registered medical practitioner or dentist, and will pay any expense incurred, the governor shall, if he is satisfied that there are reasonable grounds for the request and unless the Secretary of State otherwise directs, allow him to be visited and treated by that practitioner or dentist in consultation with the medical officer.

## Special illnesses and conditions

18. (1) The medical officer shall report to the governor on the case of any prisoner whose health is likely to be injuriously affected by continued imprisonment or any conditions of imprisonment. The governor shall send the report to the Secretary of State without delay, together with his own recommendations.

(2) The medical officer shall pay special attention to any prisoner whose mental condition appears to require it, and make any special arrangements which appear necessary for his supervision or care.

(3) The medical officer shall inform the governor if he suspects any prisoner of having suicidal intentions, and the prisoner shall be placed under special observation.

## Notification of illness or death

19. (1) If a prisoner dies, becomes seriously ill, sustains any severe injury or is removed to hospital on account of mental disorder, the governor shall, if he knows his or her address, at once inform the prisoner's spouse or next of kin, and also any person who the prisoner may reasonably have asked should be informed.

(2) If a prisoner dies, the governor shall give notice immediately to the coroner having jurisdiction, to the board of visitors and to the Secretary of State.

## Clothing

20. (1) An unconvicted prisoner may wear clothing of his own if and in so far as it is suitable, tidy and clean, but, subject to that, the provisions of this Rule shall apply to him as to a convicted prisoner. An unconvicted prisoner shall be permitted to arrange for the supply to him from outside prison of sufficient clean clothing.

(2) A convicted prisoner shall be provided with clothing adequate for warmth and health in accordance with a scale approved by the Secretary of State.

(3) The clothing provided under this Rule shall include suitable protective clothing for use at work, where this is needed.

(4) Subject to the provisions of Rule 38(3) of these Rules, a convicted prisoner shall wear clothing provided under this Rule and no other, except on the directions of the Secretary of State.

(5) A prisoner may be provided, where necessary, with suitable and adequate clothing on his release.

## Food

21. (1) [*Repealed by S.I.* 1988 *No.* 89]

(2) Subject to any directions of the Secretary of State, no prisoner shall be allowed, except as authorised by the medical officer, to have any food other than that ordinarily provided.

(3) No prisoners shall be given less food than is ordinarily provided, except upon the written recommendation of the medical officer.

(4) The food provided shall be wholesome, nutritious, well prepared and served, reasonably varied and sufficient in quantity.

(5) The medical officer shall regularly inspect the food both before and after it is cooked and shall report any deficiency or defect to the governor.

(6) In this Rule "food" includes drink.

## Alcohol and tobacco

22. (1) No prisoner shall be allowed to have any intoxicating liquor except under a written order of the medical officer specifying the quantity and the name of the prisoner.

(2) No prisoner shall be allowed to smoke or to have any tobacco except as a privilege under Rule 4 of these Rules and in accordance with any orders of the governor.

## Sleeping accommodation

23. (1) No room or cell shall be used as sleeping accommodation for a prisoner unless it has been certified in the manner required by section 14 of the Prison Act 1952 in the case of a cell used for the confinement of a prisoner.

(2) A certificate given under that section or this Rule shall specify the maximum number of prisoners who may sleep or be confined at one time in a room or cell to which it relates, and the number so specified shall not be exceeded without the leave of the Secretary of State.

## Beds and bedding

24. Each prisoner shall be provided with a separate bed and with separate bedding adequate for warmth and health.

## Special accommodation

25. The governor or board of visitors may, on application by an unconvicted prisoner, permit him on payment of a sum fixed by the Secretary of State—

(a) to occupy a room or cell specially fitted for such prisoners and provided with suitable bedding and other articles in addition to, or different from, those ordinarily provided, and to have at his own expense the use of private furniture and utensils approved by the governor; and

(b) to be relieved of the duty of cleaning his room or cell and similar duties.

## Hygiene

26. (1) Every prisoner shall be provided with toilet articles necessary for his health and cleanliness, which shall be replaced as necessary.

(2) Every prisoner shall be required to wash at proper times, have a hot bath on reception and thereafter at least once a week and, in the case of a man not excused or excepted by the governor or medical officer, to shave or be shaved daily, and to have his hair cut as may be necessary for neatness: Provided that an unconvicted prisoner or a convicted prisoner who has not yet been sentenced shall not be required to have his hair cut or any beard or moustache usually worn by him shaved off except where the medical officer directs this to be done for the sake of health or cleanliness.

(3) A woman prisoner's hair shall not be cut without her consent except where the medical officer certifies in writing that this is necessary for the sake of health or cleanliness.

## Daily Exercise

27. (1) A prisoner not engaged in outdoor work, or detained in an open prison, shall be given exercise in the open air for not less than one hour in all, each day, if weather permits:
Provided that exercise consisting of physical training may be given indoors instead of in the open air.

(2) The Secretary of State may in special circumstances authorise the reduction of the period aforesaid to half an hour a day.

(3) The medical officer shall decide upon the fitness of every prisoner for exercise and physical training, and may excuse a prisoner from, or modify, any activity on medical grounds.

## Work

28. (1) A convicted prisoner shall be required to do useful work for not more than ten hours a day, and arrangements shall be made to allow prisoners to work, where possible, outside the cells and in association with one another.

(2) The medical officer may excuse a prisoner from work on medical grounds, and no prisoner shall be set to do work which is not of a class for which he has been passed by the medical officer as being fit.

(3) No prisoner shall be set to do work of a kind not authorised by the Secretary of State.

(4) No prisoner shall work in the service of another prisoner or an officer, or for the private benefit of any person, without the authority of the Secretary of State.

(5) An unconvicted prisoner shall be permitted, if he wishes, to work as if he were a convicted prisoner.

(6) Prisoners may be paid for their work at rates approved by the Secretary of State, either generally or in relation to particular cases.

**Education**

29. (1) Every prisoner able to profit from the education facilities provided at a prison shall be encouraged to do so.

(2) Programmes of evening educational classes shall be arranged at every prison and, subject to any directions of the Secretary of State, reasonable facilities shall be afforded to prisoners who wish to do so to improve their education by correspondence courses or private study, or to practise handicrafts, in their spare time.

(3) Special attention shall be paid to the education of illiterate prisoners, and if necessary they shall be taught within the hours normally allotted to work.

**Library books**

30. A library shall be provided in every prison, and subject to any directions of the Secretary of State, every prisoner shall be allowed to have library books and to exchange them.

**Outside contacts**

31. (1) Special attention shall be paid to the maintenance of such relations between a prisoner and his family as are desirable in the best interests of both.

(2) A prisoner shall be encouraged and assisted to establish and maintain such relations with persons and agencies outside prison as may, in the opinion of the governor, best promote the interests of his family and his own social rehabilitation.

**After-care**

32. From the beginning of a prisoner's sentence, consideration shall be given, in consultation with the appropriate aftercare organisation, to the prisoner's future and the assistance to be given him on and after his release.

**Letters and visits generally**

33. (1) The Secretary of State may, with a view to securing discipline and good order or the prevention of crime or in the interests of any persons, impose restrictions, either generally or in a particular case, upon the communications to be permitted between a prisoner and other persons.

(2) Except as provided by statute or these Rules, a prisoner shall not be permitted to communicate with any outside person, or that person with him, without the leave of the Secretary of State.

(3) Except as provided by these Rules, every letter or communication to or from a prisoner may be read or examined by the governor or an officer deputed by him, and the governor may, at his discretion, stop any letter or communication on the ground that its contents are objectionable or that it is of inordinate length.

(4) Every visit to a prisoner shall take place within the sight of an officer, unless the Secretary of State otherwise directs.

(5) Except as provided by these Rules, every visit to a prisoner shall take place within the hearing of an officer, unless the Secretary of State otherwise directs.

(6) The Secretary of State may give directions, generally or in relation to any visit or class of visits, concerning the days and time when prisoners may be visited.

## Personal letters and visits

34. (1) An unconvicted prisoner may send and receive as many letters and may receive as many visits as he wishes within such limits and subject to such conditions as the Secretary of State may direct, either generally or in a particular case.

(2) A convicted prisoner shall be entitled—

(a) to send and to receive a letter on his reception into a prison and thereafter once a week; and

(b) to receive a visit once in four weeks.

(3) The governor may allow a prisoner an additional letter or visit where necessary for his welfare or that of his family.

(4) The governor may allow a prisoner entitled to a visit to send and to receive a letter instead.

(5) The governor may defer the right of a prisoner to a visit until the expiration of any period of cellular confinement.

(6) The board of visitors may allow a prisoner an additional letter or visit in special circumstances, and may direct that a visit may extend beyond the normal duration.

(7) The Secretary of State may allow additional letters and visits in relation to any prisoner or class of prisoners.

(8) A prisoner shall not be entitled under this Rule to receive a visit from any person other than a relative or friend, except with the leave of the Secretary of State.

(9) Any letter or visit under the succeeding provisions of these Rules shall not be counted as a letter or visit for the purposes of this Rule.

**Police interviews**

35. A police officer may, on production of an order issued by or on behalf of a chief officer of police, interview any prisoner willing to see him.

**Securing release**

36. A person detained in prison in default of finding a surety, or of payment of a sum of money, may communicate with and be visited at any reasonable time on a weekday by, any relative or friend to arrange for a surety or payment in order to secure his release from prison.

**Legal advisers**

37. (1) The legal adviser of a prisoner in any legal proceedings, civil or criminal, to which the prisoner is a party shall be afforded reasonable facilities for interviewing him in connection with those proceedings, and may do so out of hearing but in the sight of an officer.

(2) A prisoner's legal adviser may, with the leave of the Secretary of State, interview the prisoner in connection with any other legal business in the sight and hearing of an officer.

**Further facilities in connection with legal proceedings**

37A. (1) A prisoner who is a party to any legal proceedings may correspond with his legal adviser in connection with the proceedings and unless the governor has reason to suppose that any such correspondence contains matter not relating to the proceedings it shall not be read or stopped under Rule 33(3) of these Rules.

(2) A prisoner shall on request be provided with any writing materials necessary for the purposes of paragraph (1) of this Rule.

(3) Subject to any directions given in the particular case by the Secretary of State, a registered medical practitioner selected by or on behalf of such a prisoner as aforesaid shall be afforded reasonable facilities for examining him in connection with the proceedings, and may do so out of hearing but in the sight of an officer.

(4) Subject to any directions of the Secretary of State, a prisoner may correspond with a solicitor for the purpose of obtaining legal advice concerning any cause of action in relation to which the prisoner may become a party to civil proceedings or for the purpose of instructing the solicitor to issue such proceedings.

**Custody outside prison**

38. (1) A person being taken to or from a prison in custody shall be exposed as little as possible to public observation, and proper care shall be taken to protect him from curiosity and insult.

(2) A prisoner required to be taken in custody anywhere outside a prison shall be kept in the custody of an officer appointed under section 3 of the Prison Act 1952 or a police officer.

(3) A prisoner required to be taken in custody to any court shall wear his own clothing or clothing different from the dress worn at any institution to which the Prison Act 1952 applies.

## Search

39. (1) Every prisoner shall be searched when taken into custody by an officer, on his reception into a prison and subsequently as the governor thinks necessary.

(2) A prisoner shall be searched in as seemly a manner as is consistent with discovering anything concealed.

(3) No prisoner shall be stripped and searched in the sight of another prisoner or in the sight or presence of an officer not of the same sex.

(4) A prisoner shall be searched only by an officer of the same sex.

## Record and photograph

40. (1) A personal record of each prisoner shall be prepared and maintained in such manner as the Secretary of State may direct.

(2) Every prisoner may be photographed on reception and subsequently, but no copy of the photograph shall be given to any person not authorised to receive it.

## Prisoners' Property

41. (1) Subject to any directions of the Secretary of State, an unconvicted prisoner may have supplied to him at his expense and retain for his own use books, newspapers, writing materials and other means of occupation, except any that appear objectionable to the board of visitors or, pending consideration by them, to the governor.

(2) Anything, other than cash, which a prisoner has at a prison and which he is not allowed to retain for his own use shall be taken into the governor's custody. An inventory of a prisoner's property shall be kept, and he shall be required to sign it, after having a proper opportunity to see that it is correct.

(3) Any cash which a prisoner has at a prison shall be paid into an account under the control of the governor and the prisoner shall be credited with the amount in the books of the prison.

(3A) Any article belonging to a prisoner which remains unclaimed for a period of more than 3 years after he leaves prison, or dies, may be sold or otherwise disposed of; and the net proceeds of any sale shall be paid to the National Association for the Care and Resettlement of Offenders, for its general purposes.

(4) The governor may confiscate any unauthorised article found in the possession of a prisoner after his reception into prison, or concealed or deposited anywhere within a prison.

**Money and articles received by post**

42. (1) Any money or other article (other than a letter or other communication) sent to a convicted prisoner through the post office shall be dealt with in accordance with the provisions of this Rule, and the prisoner shall be informed of the manner in which it is dealt with.

(2) Any cash shall, at the discretion of the governor be—

(a) dealt with in accordance with rule 41(3) of these Rules; or

(b) returned to the sender; or

(c) in a case where the sender's name and address are not known, paid to the National Association for the Care and Resettlement of Offenders, for its general purposes:

Provided that in relation to a prisoner committed to prison in default of payment of any sum of money, the prisoner shall be informed of the receipt of the cash and, unless he objects to its being so applied, it shall be applied in or towards the satisfaction of the amount due from him.

(3) Any security for money shall, at the discretion of the governor, be—

(a) delivered to the prisoner or placed with his property at the prison; or

(b) returned to the sender; or

(c) encashed and the cash dealt with in accordance with Paragraph (2) of this Rule.

(4) Any other article to which this Rule applies shall, at the discretion of the governor, be—

(a) delivered to the prisoner or placed with his property at the prison; or

(b) returned to the sender; or

(c) in the case where the sender's name and address are not known or the article is of such a nature that it would be unreasonable to return it, sold or otherwise disposed of, and the net proceeds of any sale applied in accordance with paragraph (2) of this Rule.

**Removal from association**

43. (1) Where it appears desirable, for the maintenance of good order or discipline or in his own interests, that a prisoner should not associate with other prisoners, either generally or for particular purposes the governor may arrange for the prisoner's removal from association accordingly.

(2) A prisoner shall not be removed under this Rule for a period of more than 24 hours without the authority of a member of the board

of visitors, or of the Secretary of State. An authority given under this paragraph shall be for a period not exceeding one month, but may be renewed from month to month except that, in the case of a person aged less than 21 years who is detained in prison by virtue of a sentence of detention in a young offender institution, such an authority shall be for a period not exceeding 14 days, but may be renewed from time to time for a like period.

(3) The governor may arrange at his discretion for such a prisoner as aforesaid to resume association with other prisoners, and shall do so if in any case the medical officer so advises on medical grounds.

**Use of force**

44. (1) An officer in dealing with a prisoner shall not use force unnecessarily and, when the application of force to a prisoner is necessary, no more force than is necessary shall be used.

(2) No officer shall act deliberately in a manner calculated to provoke a prisoner.

**Temporary confinement**

45. The governor may order a refractory or violent prisoner to be confined temporarily in a special cell, but a prisoner shall not be so confined as a punishment, or after he has ceased to be refractory or violent.

**Restraints**

46. (1) The governor may order a prisoner to be put under restraint where this is necessary to prevent the prisoner from injuring himself or others, damaging property or creating a disturbance.

(2) Notice of such an order shall be given without delay to a member of the board of visitors, and to the medical officer.

(3) On receipt of the notice the medical officer shall inform the governor whether he concurs in the order. The governor shall give effect to any recommendation which the medical officer may make.

(4) A prisoner shall not be kept under restraint longer than necessary, nor shall he be so kept for longer than 24 hours without a direction in writing given by a member of the board of visitors or by an officer of the Secretary of State (not being an officer of a prison). Such a direction shall state the grounds for the restraint and the time during which it may continue.

(5) Particulars of every case of restraint under the foregoing provisions of this Rule shall be forthwith recorded.

(6) Except as provided by this Rule no prisoner shall be put under restraint otherwise than for safe custody during removal, or on medical grounds by direction of the medical officer. No prisoner shall be put under restaint as a punishment.

(7) Any means of restraint shall be of a pattern authorised by the Secretary of State, and shall be used in such manner and under such conditions as the Secretary of State may direct.

## Offences against discipline

47. A prisoner shall be guilty of an offence against discipline if he—

(1) mutinies or incites another prisoner to mutiny;

(2) does gross personal violence to an officer;

(3) does gross personal violence to any person not being an officer;

(4) commits any assault;

(5) escapes from prison or from legal custody;

(6) absents himself without permission from any place where he is required to be, whether within or outside prison;

(7) has in his cell or room or in his possession any unauthorised article, or attempts to obtain such an article;

(8) delivers to or receives from any person any unauthorised article;

(9) sells or delivers to any other person, without permission, anything he is allowed to have only for his own use;

(10) takes improperly or is in unauthorised possession of any article belonging to another person or to a prison;

(11) wilfully damages or disfigures any part of the prison or any property not his own;

(12) makes any false and malicious allegation against an officer;

(13) treats with disrespect an officer or any person visiting a prison;

(14) uses any abusive, insolent, threatening or other improper language;

(15) is indecent in language, act or gesture;

(16) repeatedly makes groundless complaints;

(17) is idle, careless or negligent at work or, being required to work, refuses to do so;

(18) disobeys any lawful order or refuses or neglects to conform to any rule or regulation of the prison;

(19) attempts to do any of the foregoing things;

(20) in any way offends against good order and discipline; or

(21) does not return to prison when he should have returned after being temporarily released from prison under Rule 6 of these Rules, or does not comply with any condition upon which he was so released.

**Disciplinary charges**

48. (1) Where a prisoner is to be charged wi[illegible] cipline, the charge shall be laid as soon [illegible]

(2) A prisoner who is to be charged w[illegible] cipline may be kept apart from [illegible] adjudication.

(3) Every charge shall be inquired into, [illegible] governor.

(4) Every charge shall be first inquired in[illegible] tional circumstances, than the next da[illegible] public holiday, after it is laid.

**Rights of prisoners charged**

49. (1) Where a prisoner is charged with an [illegible] he shall be informed of the charge as so[illegible] case, before the time when it is inquired into by the governor.

(2) At any inquiry into a charge against a prisoner he shall be given a full opportunity of hearing what is alleged against him and of presenting his own case.

**Governor's awards**

50. Subject to Rules 51, 52 and 52A of these Rules, the governor may make any one or more of the following awards for an offence against discipline:—

(a) caution;

(b) forfeiture for a period not exceeding 28 days of any of the privileges under Rule 4 of these Rules;

(c) exclusion from associated work for a period not exceeding 14 days;

(d) stoppage of earnings for a period not exceeding 28 days;

(e) cellular confinement for a period not exceeding 3 days;

(f) forfeiture of remission, of a period not exceeding 28 days;

(g) forfeiture for any period, in the case of a prisoner otherwise entitled thereto, of the right under Rule 41(1) of these Rules to have the articles there mentioned;

(h) forfeiture for any period, in the case of a prisoner otherwise entitled thereto who is guilty of escaping or attempting to escape, of the right to wear clothing of his own under Rule 20(1) of these rules.

**Graver offences**

51. (1) Where a prisoner is charged with any of the following offences against discipline:—

(a) escaping or attempting to escape from prison or from legal custody.

(b) assaulting an officer, or

(c) doing gross personal violence to any person not being an officer.

the governor shall, unless he dismisses the charge, forthwith inform the Secretary of State and shall, unless otherwise directed by him, refer the charge to the board of visitors.

(2) Where a prisoner is charged with any serious or repeated offence against discipline (not being an offence to which Rule 52 of these Rules applies) for which the awards the governor can make seem insufficient, the governor may, after investigation, refer the charge to the board of visitors.

(3) Where a charge is referred to the board of visitors under this Rule, the chairman thereof shall summon a special meeting at which not more than five nor fewer than two members shall be present.

(4) The Board so constituted shall inquire into the charge and, if they find the offence proved, shall, subject to Rule 52A of these Rules, make one or more of the following awards:—

(a) caution;

(b) forfeiture for a period of any of the privileges under Rule 4 of these Rules;

(c) exclusion from associated work for a period not exceeding 56 days;

(d) stoppage of earnings for a period not exceeding 56 days;

(e) cellular confinement for a period not exceeding 56 days;

(f) forfeiture of remission, of a period not exceeding 180 days;

(g) forfeiture for any period, in the case of a prisoner otherwise entitled thereto, of the right under Rule 41(1) of these Rules to have the articles there mentioned;

(h) forfeiture for any period, in the case of a prisoner otherwise entitled thereto who is guilty of escaping or attempting to escape, of the right to wear clothing of his own under Rule 20(1) of these rules.

(5) The Secretary of State may require any charge to which this Rule applies to be referred to him, instead of to the board of visitors, and in that case an officer of the Secretary of State (not being an officer of a prison) shall inquire into the charge and, if he finds the offence proved, make one or more of the awards listed in paragraph (4) of this Rule.

**Especially grave offences**

52. (1) Where a prisoner is charged with one of the following offences:—

(a) mutiny or incitement to mutiny; or

(b) doing gross personal violence to an officer,

the governor shall forthwith inform the Secretary of State and shall, unless otherwise directed by him, refer the charge to the board of visitors.

(2) Where a charge is referred to the board of visitors under this Rule, the chairman thereof shall summon a special meeting at which not more than five nor fewer than three members, at least two being justices of the peace, shall be present.

(3) The board constituted as aforesaid shall inquire into the charge and, if they find the offence proved, shall, subject to Rule 52A of these Rules, make one or more of the awards listed in Rule 51(4) of these Rules, so however that, if they make an award of forfeiture of remission, the period forfeited may exceed 180 days.

**Offences committed by young persons**

52A. In the case of an offence against discipline committed by a person detained in a prison who was under the age of 21 when the offence was committed (other than an offender in relation to whom the Secretary of State has given a direction under section 13(1) of the Criminal Justice Act 1982 that he shall be treated as if he had been sentenced to imprisonment)—

(a) Rule 50 of these Rules shall have effect with the substitution in each of paragraphs (b) and (d) thereof of "14" for "28";

(b) paragraph (4) of Rule 51 of these Rules shall have effect as if—

(i) in sub-paragraph (b), there were substituted for the words "for any period" the words "for a period not exceeding 28 days";

(ii) in sub-paragraph (c) and (d) there were substituted "28" for "56";

(iii) in sub-paragraph (e) there were substituted "7" for "56"; and

(iv) in sub-paragraph (f) there were inserted after the words "180 days" the words "in the case of an offence of assaulting an officer or doing gross personal violence to any person not being an officer and 90 days in the case of any other offence"; and

(c) paragraph (3) of Rule 52 of these Rules shall have effect as if there were inserted after the word "exceed" the words "90 days but may not exceed".

**Provisions in relation to particular awards**

53. (1) An award of stoppage of earnings may, instead of forfeiting all a

prisoner's earnings for a specified period not exceeding 28 days or as the case may be 56 days, be expressed so as to forfeit a proportion (not being less than one half) of his earnings for a specified period not exceeding a correspondingly greater number of days.

(2) No award of cellular confinement shall be made unless the medical officer has certified that the prisoner is in a fit state of health to be so dealt with.

## Prospective forfeiture of remission

54. (1) In the case of an offence against discipline committed by a prisoner who is detained only on remand or to await trial or sentence, an award of forfeiture of remission may be made notwithstanding that the prisoner has not (or had not at the time of the offence) been sentenced.

(2) An award under paragraph (1) above shall have effect only in the case of a sentence of imprisonment or detention in a young offender institution being imposed which is reduced, by section 67 of the Criminal Justice Act 1967, by a period which includes the time when the offence against discipline was committed.

## Conversion of sentence of youth custody to sentence of imprisonment

54A. In the case of a prisoner who has been sentenced to a term of detention in a young offender institution and who, by virtue of a direction of the Secretary of State under section 13 of Criminal Justice Act 1982, is treated as if he had been sentenced to imprisonment for that term, any award made in respect of him for an offence against discipline before the said direction was given shall, if it has not been exhausted or remitted, continue to have effect as if made under Rule 50 or 51 of these Rules.

## Disciplinary awards: transitional

54B. (1) In the case of a person detained in a prison who, by virtue of paragraph 4 of Schedule 17 to the Criminal Justice Act 1982, on 24 May 1983 falls to be treated for purposes of detention, release and supervision as if his sentence had been a youth custody sentence, any award for an offence against discipline made in respect of him before that date under Rule 49 or 50 of the Borstal Rules 1964 shall, if it has not been exhausted or remitted, continue to have effect, subject to the provisions of paragraph (2) of this Rule, as if it had been made under Rule 50 or 51 respectively of these Rules.

(2) An award of reduction in grade, or postponement of promotion to a higher grade, for a specified period made under Rule 49(e) or 50(4)(e) of the Borstal Rules 1964 shall continue to have effect under this Rule as if it had been an award of loss of remission of a like period.

(3) In the case of a person detained in a prison who, by virtue of

paragraph 12 of Schedule 8 to the Criminal Justice Act 1988, on October 1, 1988, falls to be treated for all purposes of detention, release and supervision as if his sentence had been a sentence of detention in a young offender institution, any award for an offence against discipline made in respect of him before that date under Rule 50, 51 or 52 of these Rules or treated, by virtue of Rule 5(4A) thereof, as having been imposed under these Rules shall, if it has not been exhausted or remitted, continue to have effect as if it had been made under Rule 50, 51 or 52 of these Rules, as the case may be.

**Suspended awards**

55. (1) Subject to any direction of the Secretary of State, the power to make a disciplinary award (other than a caution) shall include power to direct that the award is not to take effect unless, during a period specified in the direction (not being more than 6 months from the date of the direction), the prisoner commits another offence against discipline and a direction is given under paragraph (2) below.

(2) Where a prisoner commits an offence against discipline during the period specified in a direction given under paragraph (1) above the person or board dealing with that offence may:—

(a) direct that the suspended award shall take effect; or

(b) reduce the period or amount of the suspended award and direct that it shall take effect as so reduced; or

(c) vary the original direction by substituting for the period specified therein a period expiring not later than 6 months from the date of variation; or

(d) give no direction with respect to the suspended award.

**Remission and mitigation of awards**

56. (1) The Secretary of State may remit a disciplinary award or mitigate it either by reducing it or by substituting another award which is, in his opinion, less severe.

(2) Subject to any directions of the Secretary of State, the governor may remit or mitigate any award made by a governor and the board of visitors may remit or mitigate any disciplinary award.

[*Rules* 57–62 *repealed by S.I.* 1972 *No.* 1860]

**Prisoners committed for contempt, &c**

63. (1) A prisoner committed or attached for contempt of court, or for failing to do or abstain from doing anything required to be done or left undone, shall have the same privileges as an unconvicted prison under Rules 20(1) and 34(1) of these Rules.

(2) Such prisoners shall be treated as a separate class for the purposes of Rule 3 of these Rules but, notwithstanding anything in that

Rule, such prisoners may be permitted to associate with any other class of prisoners if they are willing to do so.

(3) A prisoner detained in a prison for a stated term of time of more than 5 days on committal or attachment for contempt of court shall, for the purposes of Rule 5 of these Rules, be treated as serving a sentence of imprisonment for a like term.

[*Rule* 64 *repealed by S.I.* 1972 *No.* 1860]
[*Rules* 65–71 *repealed by S.I.* 1968 *No.* 440]

*Prisoners under sentence of death*

**Application of foregoing Rules**
72. The foregoing provisions of these Rules shall apply in relation to a prisoner under sentence of death only in so far as they are compatible with that sentence and with Rules 73 to 76 of these Rules.

**Search**
73. A prisoner under sentence of death shall be searched with special care and every article shall be taken from him which it might be dangerous or inexpedient to leave in his possession.

**Confinement**
74. (1) A prisoner under sentence of death shall be confined in a separate cell and shall be kept apart from all other prisoners.

(2) He shall be kept by day and night in the constant charge of two officers.

(3) He shall not be required to work, but shall, if he wishes, be given work to do in his cell.

(4) Subject to the provisions of Rule 75 of these Rules, no person other than a member of the board of visitors or an officer shall have access to a prisoner under sentence of death without the leave of the Secretary of State.

**Visits**
75. (1) Every visit to a prisoner under sentence of death, other than a visit by the chaplain or a prison minister, shall take place in the sight and hearing of an officer.

(2) Such a prisoner may be visited by any relation, friend or legal adviser whom he wishes to see, and who is authorised to visit him by an order in writing of a member of the board of visitors or the Secretary of State.

(3) The chaplain shall have free access to every such prisoner belonging to the Church of England, and to every other such prisoner who wishes to see him.

(4) Where such a prisoner belongs to a denomination other than the Church of England, a minister of that denomination shall have free access to him.

**Correspondence**
76. A prisoner under sentence of death shall be given all necessary facilities to enable him to correspond with his legal advisers, relatives and friends.

[*Rules 77–84, forming part II of the Rules, contain provisions relating solely to prison officers and are not reproduced here.*]

PART III

*Persons having access to a prison*

**Prohibited articles**
85. No person shall, without authority, convey into or throw into or deposit into a prison, or convey or throw out of a prison, or convey to a prisoner, or deposit in any place with intent that it shall come into the possession of a prisoner, any money, clothing, food, drink, tobacco, letter, paper, book, tool or other article whatever. Anything so conveyed, thrown or deposited may be confiscated by the governor.

**Control of persons and vehicles**
86. (1) Any person or vehicle entering or leaving a prison may be stopped, examined and searched.

(2) The governor may direct the removal from a prison of any person who does not leave on being required to do so.

**Viewing of prisons**
87. (1) No outside person shall be permitted to view a prison unless authorised by statute or the Secretary of State.

(2) No person viewing a prison shall be permitted to take a photograph, make a sketch or communication with a prisoner unless authorised by statute or the Secretary of State.

PART IV

*Boards of visitors*

**Disqualification for membership**
88. Any person interested in any contract for the supply of goods or

services to a prison shall not be a member of the board of visitors for that prison.

[*Rules* 89–91 *repealed by S.I.* 1971 *No.* 2019]

## Board of visitors

92. (1) A member of the board of visitors for a prison appointed by the Secretary of State under section 6(2) of the Prison Act 1952 shall hold office for three years, or such less period as the Secretary of State may appoint.

(2) When a board is first constituted, the Secretary of State shall appoint one of its members to be chairman for a period not exceeding twelve months.

(3) Subject to paragraph (2) of this Rule, at their first meeting in any year of office the board shall appoint one of their number to be chairman for that year, and thereafter shall fill any casual vacancy in that office promptly.

(4) The board may appoint one of their number to be vice-chairman to hold office for the remainder of the period for which the chairman was appointed.

## Proceedings of boards

93. (1) The boards of visitors for a prison shall meet at the prison once a month or, it they resolve for reasons specified in the resolution that less frequent meetings are sufficient, no fewer than eight times in twelve months.

(2) The board may fix a quorum of not fewer than three members for proceedings other than those under Rules 51 and 52 of these Rules.

(3) The board shall keep minutes of their proceedings.

(4) The proceedings of the board shall not be invalidated by any vacancy in the membership or any defect in the appointment of a member.

## General duties of boards

94. (1) The board of visitors for a prison shall satisfy themselves as to the state of the prison premises, the administration of the prison and the treatment of the prisoners.

(2) The board shall inquire into and report upon any matter in which the Secretary of State asks them to inquire.

(3) The board shall direct the attention of the governor to any matter which calls for his attention, and shall report to the Secretary of State any matter which they consider it expedient to report.

(4) The board shall inform the Secretary of State immediately of any abuse which comes to their knowledge, and shall have power in any case of urgent necessity to suspend any officer until the decision of the Secretary of State is known.

(5) Before exercising any power under these Rules (other than Rules 51, 52 and 56) the board and any member of the board shall consult the governor in relation to any matter which may affect discipline.

**Particular duties**

95. (1) The board of visitors for a prison and any member of the board shall hear any complaint or request which a prisoner wishes to make to them or him.

(2) The board shall arrange for the food of the prisoners to be inspected by a member of the board at frequent intervals.

(3) The board shall inquire into any report made to them, whether or not by a member of the board, that a prisoner's health, mental or physical, is likely to be injuriously affected by any conditions of his imprisonment.

**Members visiting prisons**

96. (1) The members of the board of visitors for a prison shall visit the prison frequently, and the board shall arrange a rota whereby at least one of its members visits the prison between meetings of the board.

(2) A member of the board shall have access at any time to every part of the prison and to every prisoner, and he may interview any prisoner out of the sight and hearing of officers.

(3) A member of the board shall have access to the records of the prison.

**Annual report**

97. The board of visitors for a prison shall make an annual report to the Secretary of State at the end of each year concerning the state of the prison and its administration, including in it any advice and suggestions they consider appropriate.

## PART V

*Supplemental*

**Delegation by governor**

98. The governor of a prison may, with the leave of the Secretary of State, delegate any of his powers and duties under these Rules to another officer of that prison.

**Interpretation**

99. (1) In these Rules, where the context so admits, the expression—
"convicted prisoner" means, subject to the provisions of Rules 63 of these Rules, a prisoner who has been convicted or found guilty of an offence or committed or attached for contempt of court or for failing

to do or abstain from doing anything required to be done or left undone, and the expression "unconvicted prisoner" shall be construed accordingly;
"governor" includes an officer for the time being in charge of a prison;
"legal adviser" means, in relation to a prisoner, his counsel or solicitor, and includes a clerk acting on behalf of his solicitor;
"officer" means an officer of a prison;
"prison minister" means, in relation to a prison, a minister appointed to that prison under section 10 of the Prison Act 1952.

(2) In these Rules a reference to the Church of England includes a reference to the Church of Wales.

(3) The Interpretation Act 1889 shall apply for the interpretation of these Rules as it applies for the interpretation of an Act of Parliament.

## Revocations and savings

100. (1) The Rules specified in the Schedule to these Rules are hereby revoked.

(2) For the purpose of these Rules any appointment, approval, authority, certificate, condition, direction or restriction made, given or imposed under any provision of any of the Rules revoked by this Rule shall be treated as having been made, given or imposed under the corresponding provision of these Rules.

Note:

By virtue of the Prison (Amendment) (No.2) Rules 1988 (S.I. 1988 No. 747), where any constable or member of the armed forces of the Crown is employed by reason of any emergency to assist the governor of a prison by performing duties ordinarily performed by an officer of the prison, any reference in Part I of the Prison Rules 1964 to such an officer (other than a governor), shall be construed as including a reference to a constable or a member of the armed forces of the Crown so employed.

# APPENDIX 2

## THE EUROPEAN PRISON RULES 1987

### Revised European version of the Standard Minimum Rules for the Treatment of Prisoners

*Preamble*

The purposes of these rules are:

a. to establish a range of minimum standards for all those aspects of prison administration that are essential to human conditions and positive treatment in modern and progressive systems;
*b.* to serve as a stimulus to prison administrations to develop policies and management style and practice based on good contemporary principles of purpose and equity;
*c.* to encourage in prison staffs professional attitudes that reflect the important social and moral qualities of their work and to create conditions in which they can optimise their own performance to the benefit of society in general, the prisoners in their care and their own vocational satisfaction;
*d.* to provide realistic basic criteria against which prison administrations and those responsible for inspecting the conditions and management of prisons can make valid judgments of performance and measure progress towards higher standards.

It is emphasised that the rules do not constitute a model system and that, in practice, many European prison services are already operating well above many of the standards set out in the rules and that others are striving, and will continue to strive, to do so. Wherever there are difficulties or practical problems to be overcome in the application of the rules, the Council of Europe has the machinery and the expertise available to assist with advice and the fruits of the experience of the various prison administrations within its sphere.

In these rules, renewed emphasis has been placed on the precepts of human dignity, the commitment of prison administrations to humane and positive treatment, the importance of staff roles and effective modern management approaches. They are set out to provide ready reference, encouragement and guidance to those who are working at all levels of prison administration. The explanatory memorandum that accompanies the rules is intended to ensure the understanding, acceptance and flexibility that are necessary to achieve the highest realistic level of implementation beyond the basic standards.

### Part I

### The Basic Principles

1. The deprivation of liberty shall be effected in material and moral conditions which ensure respect for human dignity and are in conformity with these rules.

2. The rules shall be applied impartially. There shall be no discrimination on grounds of race, colour, sex, language, religion, political or other opinion, national or social origin, birth, economic or other status. The religious beliefs and moral precepts of the group to which a prisoner belongs shall be respected.

3. The purposes of the treatment of persons in custody shall be such as to sustain their health and self-respect and, so far as the length of sentence permits, to develop their sense of responsibility and encourage those attitudes and skills that will assist them to return to society with the best chance of leading law-abiding and self-supporting lives after their release.

4. There shall be regular inspections of penal institutions and services by qualified and experienced inspectors appointed by a competent authority. Their task shall be, in particular, to monitor whether and to what extent these institutions are administered in accordance with existing laws and regulations, the objectives of the prison services and the requirements of these rules.

5. The protection of the individual rights of prisoners with special regard to the legality of the execution of detention measures shall be secured by means of a control carried out, according to national rules, by a judicial authority or other duly constituted body authorised to visit the prisoners and not belonging to the prison administration.

6. (1) These rules shall be made readily available to staff in the national languages;

(2) They shall also be available to prisoners in the same languages and in other languages so far as is reasonable and practicable.

PART II

THE MANAGEMENT OF PRISON SYSTEMS

## Reception and registration

7. (1) No person shall be received in an institution without a valid commitment order.

(2) The essential details of the commitment and reception shall immediately be recorded.

8. In every place where persons are imprisoned a complete and secure record of the following information shall be kept concerning each prisoner received:

(a) information concerning the identity of the prisoner;

(b) the reasons for commitment and the authority therefor;

(c) the day and hour of admission and release.

9. Reception arrangements shall conform with the basic principles of the rules and shall assist prisoners to resolve their urgent personal problems.

10. (1) As soon as possible after reception, full reports and relevant information about the personal situation and training programme of each prisoner with a sentence of suitable length in preparation for ultimate release shall be drawn up and submitted to the director for information or approval as appropriate.

(2) Such reports shall always include reports by a medical officer and the personnel in direct charge of the prisoner concerned.

(3) The reports and information concerning prisoners shall be maintained with due regard to confidentiality on an individual basis, regularly kept up to date and only accessible to authorised persons.

### The allocation and classification of prisoners

11. (1) In allocating prisoners to different institutions or régimes, due account shall be taken of their judicial and legal situation (untried or convicted prisoner, first offender or habitual offender, short sentence or long sentence), of the special requirements of their treatment, of their medical needs, their sex and age.

(2) Males and females shall in principle be detained separately, although they may participate together in organised activities as part of an established treatment programme.

(3) In principle, untried prisoners shall be detained separately from convicted prisoners unless they consent to being accommodated or involved together in organised activities beneficial to them.

(4) Young prisoners shall be detained under conditions which as far as possible protect them from harmful influences and which take account of the needs peculiar to their age.

12. The purposes of classification or re-classification of prisoners shall be:

(a) to separate from others those prisoners who, by reasons of their criminal records or their personality, are likely to benefit from that or who may exercise a bad influence; and

(b) to assist in allocating prisoners to facilitate their treatment and social resettlement taking into account the management and security requirements.

13. So far as possible separate institutions or separate sections of an institution shall be used to facilitate the management of different treatment régimes or the allocation of specific categories of prisoners.

### Accommodation

14. (1) Prisoners shall normally be lodged during the night in individual cells except in cases where it is considered that there are advantages in sharing accommodation with other prisoners.

(2) Where accommodation is shared it shall be occupied by prisoners suitable to associate with others in those conditions. There shall

be supervision by night, in keeping with the nature of the institution.

15. The accommodation provided for prisoners, and in particular all sleeping accommodation, shall meet the requirements of health and hygiene, due regard being paid to climatic conditions and especially the cubic content of air, a reasonable amount of space, lighting, heating and ventilation.

16. In all places where prisoners are required to live or work:

(a) the windows shall be large enough to enable the prisoners *inter alia*, to read or work by natural light in normal conditions. They shall be so constructed that they can allow the entrance of fresh air except where there is an adequate air conditioning system. Moreover, the windows shall, with due regard to security requirements, present in their size, location and construction as normal an appearance as possible;

(b) artificial light shall satisfy recognised technical standards.

17. The sanitary installations and arrangements for access shall be adequate to enable every prisoner to comply with the needs of nature when necessary and in clean and decent conditions.

18. Adequate bathing and showering installations shall be provided so that every prisoner may be enabled and required to have a bath or shower, at a temperature suitable to the climate, as frequently as necessary for general hygiene according to season and geographical region, but at least once a week. Wherever possible there should be free access at all reasonable times.

19. All parts of an institution shall be properly maintained and kept clean at all times.

## Personal hygiene

20. Prisoners shall be required to keep their persons clean, and to this end they shall be provided with water and with such toilet articles as are necessary for health and cleanliness.

21. For reasons of health and in order that prisoners may maintain a good appearance and preserve their self-respect, facilities shall be provided for the proper care of the hair and beard, and men shall be enabled to shave regularly.

## Clothing and bedding

22. (1) Prisoners who are not allowed to wear their own clothing shall be provided with an outfit of clothing suitable for the climate and adequate to keep them in good health. Such clothing shall in no manner be degrading or humiliating.

(2) All clothing shall be clean and kept in proper condition. Underclothing shall be changed and washed as often as necessary for the maintenance of hygiene.

(3) Whenever prisoners obtain permission to go outside the institution, they shall be allowed to wear their own clothing or other inconspicuous clothing.

23. On the admission of prisoners to an institution, adequate arrangements shall be made to ensure that their personal clothing is kept in good condition and fit for use.

24. Every prisoner shall be provided with a separate bed and separate and appropriate bedding which shall be kept in good order and changed often enough to ensure its cleanliness.

## Food

25. (1) In accordance with the standards laid down by the health authorities, the administration shall provide the prisoners at the normal times with food which is suitably prepared and presented, and which satifies in quality and quantity the standards of dietetics and modern hygiene and takes into account their age, health, the nature of their work, and so far as possible, religious or cultural requirements.

(2) Drinking water shall be available to every prisoner.

## Medical services

26. (1) At every institution there shall be available the services of at least one qualified general practitioner. The medical services should be organised in close relation with the general health administration of the community or nation. They shall include a psychiatric service for the diagnosis and, in proper cases, the treatment of states of mental abnormality.

(2) Sick prisoners who require specialist treatment shall be transferred to specialised institutions or to civil hospitals. Where hospital facilities are provided in an institution, their equipment, furnishings and pharmaceutical supplies shall be suitable for the medical care and treatment of sick prisoners, and there shall be a staff of suitably trained officers.

(3) The services of a qualified dental officer shall be available to every prisoner.

27. Prisoners may not be submitted to any experiments which may result in physical or moral injury.

28. (1) Arrangements shall be made wherever practicable for children to be born in a hospital outside the institution. However, unless special arrangements are made, there shall in penal institutions be the necessary staff and accommodation for the confinement and post-natal care of pregnant women. If a child is born in prison, this fact shall not be mentioned in the birth certificate.

(2) Where infants are allowed to remain in the institution with their mothers, special provision shall be made for a nursery staffed by

qualified persons, where the infants shall be placed when they are not in the care of their mothers.

29. The medical officer shall see and examine every prisoner as soon as possible after admission and thereafter as necessary, with a view particularly to the discovery of physical or mental illness and the taking of all measures necessary for medical treatment; the segregation of prisoners suspected of infectious or contagious conditions; the noting of physical or mental defects which might impede resettlement after release; and the determination of the fitness of every prisoner to work.

30. (1) The medical officer shall have the care of the physical and mental health of the prisoners and shall see, under the conditions and with a frequency consistent with hospital standards, all sick prisoners, all who report illness or injury and any prisoner to whom attention is specially directed.

(2) The medical officer shall report to the director whenever it is considered that a prisoner's physical or mental health has been or will be adversely affected by continued imprisonment or by any condition of imprisonment.

31. (1) The medical officer or a competent authority shall regularly inspect and advise the director upon:

(a) The quantity, quality, preparation and serving of food and water;

(b) the hygiene and cleanliness of the institution and prisoners;

(c) The sanitation, heating, lighting and ventilation of the institution;

(d) the suitability and cleanliness of the prisoners' clothing and bedding.

(2) The director shall consider the reports and advice that the medical officer submits according to Rules 30, paragraph 2, and 31, paragraph 1, and, when in concurrence with the recommendations made, shall take immediate steps to give effect to those recommendations; if they are not within the director's competence or if the director does not concur with them, the director shall immediately submit a personal report and the advice of the medical officer to higher authority.

32. The medical services of the institution shall seek to detect and shall treat any physical or mental illness or defects which may impede a prisoner's resettlement after release. All necessary medical, surgical and psychiatric services including those available in the community shall be provided to the prisoner to that end.

**Discipline and punishment**

33. Discipline and order shall be maintained in the interests of safe custody, ordered community life and the treatment objectives of the institution.

34. (1) No prisoner shall be employed, in the service of the institution, in any disciplinary capacity.

(2) This rule shall not, however, impede the proper functioning of arrangements under which specified social, educational or sports activities or responsibilities are entrusted under supervision to prisoners who are formed into groups for the purposes of their participation in régime programmes.

35. The following shall be provided for and determined by the law or by the regulation of the competent authority:

(a) conduct constituting a disciplinary offence;

(b) the types and duration of punishment which may be imposed;

(c) the authority competent to impose such punishment;

(d) access to, and the authority of, the appellate process.

36. (1) No prisoner shall be punished except in accordance with the terms of such law or regulation, and never twice for the same act.

(2) Reports of misconduct shall be presented promptly to the competent authority who shall decide on them without undue delay.

(3) No prisoner shall be punished unless informed of the alleged offence and given a proper opportunity of presenting a defence.

(4) Where necessary and practicable prisoners shall be allowed to make their defence through an interpreter.

37. Collective punishments, corporal punishment, punishment by placing in a dark cell, and all cruel, inhuman or degrading punishment shall be completely prohibited as punishments for disciplinary offences.

38. (1) Punishment by disciplinary confinement and any other punishment which might have an adverse effect on the physical or mental health of the prisoner shall only be imposed if the medical officer, after examination, certifies in writing that the prisoner is fit to sustain it.

(2) In no case may such punishment be contrary to, or depart from, the principles stated in Rule 37.

(3) The medical officer shall visit daily prisoners undergoing such punishment and shall advise the director if the termination or alteration of the punishment is considered necessary on grounds of physical or mental health.

**Instruments of restraint**

39. The use of chains and irons shall be prohibited. Handcuffs, restraint-jackets and other body restraints shall never be applied as a punishment. They shall not be used except in the following circumstances:

(a) if necessary, as a precaution against escape during a transfer, provided that they shall be removed when the prisoner appears before a judicial or administrative authority unless that authority decides otherwise;

(b) on medical grounds by direction and under the supervision of the medical officer;

(c) by order of the director, if other methods of control fail, in order to protect a prisoner from self-injury, injury to others or to prevent serious damage to property; in such instances the director shall at once consult the medical officer and report to the higher administrative authority.

40. The patterns and manner of use of the instruments of restraint authorised in the preceding paragraph shall be decided by law or regulation. Such instruments must not be applied for any longer time than is strictly necessary.

## Information to, and complaints by, prisoners

41. (1) Every prisoner shall on admission be provided with written information about the regulations governing the treatment of prisoners of the relevant category, the disciplinary requirements of the institution, the authorised methods of seeking information and making complaints, and all such other matters as are necessary to understand the rights and obligations of prisoners and to adapt to the life of the institution.

(2) If a prisoner cannot understand the written information provided, this information shall be explained orally.

42. (1) Every prisoner shall have the opportunity every day of making requests or complaints to the director of the institution or the officer authorised to act in that capacity.

(2) A prisoner shall have the opportunity to talk to, or to make requests or complaints to, an inspector of prisons or to any other duly constituted authority entitled to visit the prison without the director or other members of the staff being present. However, appeals against formal decisions may be restricted to the authorised procedures.

(3) Every prisoner shall be allowed to make a request or complaint, under confidential cover, to the central prison administration, the judicial authority or other proper authorities.

(4) Every request or complaint addressed or referred to a prison authority shall be promptly dealt with and replied to by this authority without undue delay.

## Contact with the outside world

43. (1) Prisoners shall be allowed to communicate with their families and, subject to the needs of treatment, security and good order, persons or representatives of outside organisations and to receive visits from these persons as often as possible.

(2) To encourage contact with the outside world there shall be a system of prison leave consistent with the treatment objectives in Part IV of these rules.

44. (1) Prisoners who are foreign nationals should be informed, without delay, of their right to request contact and be allowed reasonable facilities to communicate with the diplomatic or consular representative of the state to which they belong. The prison administration should co-operate fully with such representatives in the interests of foreign nationals in prison who may have special needs.

(2) Prisoners who are nationals of states without diplomatic or consular representation in the country and refugees or stateless persons shall be allowed similar facilities to communicate with the diplomatic representative of the state which takes charge of their interests or national or international authority whose task it is to serve the interests of such persons.

45. Prisoners shall be allowed to keep themselves informed regularly of the news by reading newspapers, periodicals and other publications, by radio or television transmissions, by lectures or by any similar means as authorised or controlled by the administration. Special arrangements should be made to meet the needs of foreign nationals with linguistic difficulties.

## Religious and moral assistance

46. So far as practicable, every prisoner shall be allowed to satisfy the needs of his religious, spiritual and moral life by attending the services or meetings provided in the institution and having in his posssession any necessary books or literature.

47. (1) If the institution contains a sufficient number of prisoners of the same religion, a qualified representative of that religion shall be appointed and approved. If the number of prisoners justifies it and conditions permit, the arrangement should be on a full-time basis.

(2) A qualified representative appointed or approved under paragraph 1 shall be allowed to hold regular services and activities and to pay pastoral visits in private to prisoners of his religion at proper times.

(3) Access to a qualified representative of any religion shall not be refused to any prisoner. If any prisoner should object to a visit of any religious representative, the prisoner shall be allowed to refuse it.

## Retention of prisoners' property

48. (1) All money, valuables, and other effects belonging to prisoners which under the regulations of the institution they are not allowed to retain shall on admission to the institution be placed in safe custody. An inventory thereof shall be signed by the prisoner. Steps shall be taken to keep them in good condition. If it has been found necessary to destroy any article, this shall be recorded and the prisoner informed.

(2) On the release of the prisoner, all such articles and money shall be returned except insofar as there have been authorised withdrawals of money or the authorised sending of any such property out of the institution, or it has been found necessary on hygienic grounds to destroy any article. The prisoner shall sign a receipt for the articles and money returned.

(3) As far as practicable, any money or effects received for a prisoner from outside shall be treated in the same way unless they are intended for and permitted for use during imprisonment.

(4) If a prisoner brings in any medicines, the medical officer shall decide what use shall be made of them.

## Notification of death, illness, transfer, etc.

49. (1) Upon the death or serious illness of or serious injury to a prisoner, or removal to an institution for the treatment of mental illness or abnormalities, the director shall at once inform the spouse, if the prisoner is married, or the nearest relative and shall in any event inform any other person previously designated by the prisoner.

(2) A prisoner shall be informed at once of the death or serious illness of any near relative. In these cases and wherever circumstances allow, the prisioner should be authorised to visit this sick relative or see the deceased either under escort or alone.

(3) All prisoners shall have the right to inform at once their families of imprisonment or transfer to another institution.

## Removal of prisoners

50. (1) When prisoners are being removed to or from an institution, they shall be exposed to public view as little as possible, and proper safeguards shall be adopted to protect them from insult, curiosity and publicity in any form.

(2) The transport of prisoners in conveyances with inadequate ventilation or light, or in any way which would subject them to unnecessary physical hardship or indignity shall be prohibited.

(3) The transport of prisioners shall be carried out at the expense of the administration and in accordance with duly authorised regulations.

## Part III

## Personnel

51. In view of the fundamental importance of the prison staff to the proper management of the institutions and the pursuit of their organisational and treatment objectives, prison administrations shall give high priority to the fulfilment of the rules concerning personnel.

52. Prison staff shall be continually encouraged through training, consultative procedures and a positive management style to aspire to

humane standards, higher efficiency and a committed approach to their duties.

53. The prison administration shall regard it as an important task continually to inform public opinion of the roles of the prison system and the work of the staff, so as to encourage public understanding of the importance of their contribution to society.

54. (1) The prison administration shall provide for the careful selection on recruitment or in subsequent appointments of all personnel. Special emphasis shall be given to their integrity, humanity, professional capacity and personal suitability for the work.

(2) Personnel shall normally be appointed on a permanent basis as professional prison staff and have civil service status with security of tenure subject only to good conduct, efficiency, good physical and mental health and an adequate standard of education. Salaries shall be adequate to attract and retain suitable men and women; employment benefits and conditions of service shall be favourable in view of the exacting nature of the work.

(3) Whenever it is necessary to employ part-time staff, these criteria should apply to them as far as that it is appropriate.

55. (1) On recruitment or after an appropriate period of practical experience, the personnel shall be given a course of training in their general and specific duties and be required to pass theoretical and practical tests unless their professional qualifications make that unnecessary.

(2) During their career, all personnel shall maintain and improve their knowledge and professional capacity by attending courses of in-service training to be organised by the administration at suitable intervals.

(3) Arrangements should be made for wider experience and training for personnel whose professional capacity would be improved by this.

(4) The training of all personnel should include instruction in the requirements and application of the European Prison Rules and the European Convention on Human Rights.

56. All members of the personnel shall be expected at all times so to conduct themselves and perform their duties as to influence the prisoners for good by their example and to command their respect.

57. (1) So far as possible the personnel shall include a sufficient number of specialists such as psychiatrists, psychologists, social workers, teachers, trade, physical education and sports instructors.

(2) These and other specialist staff shall normally be employed on a permanent basis. This shall not preclude part-time or voluntary workers when that is appropriate and beneficial to the level of support and training they can provide.

58. (1) The prison administration shall ensure that every institution is at all times in the full charge of the director, the deputy director or other authorised official.

(2) The director of an institution should be adequately qualified for that post by character, administrative ability, suitable professional training and experience.

(3) The director shall be appointed on a full-time basis and be available or accessible as required by the prison administration in its management instructions.

(4) When two or more institutions are under the authority of one director, each shall be visited at frequent intervals. A responsible official shall be in charge of each of these institutions.

59. The administration shall introduce forms of organisation and management systems to facilitate communication between the different categories of staff in an institution with a view to ensuring co-operation between the various services, in particular, with respect to the treatment and re-socialisation of prisoners.

60. (1) The director, deputy, and the majority of the other personnel of the institution shall be able to speak the language of the greatest number of prisoners, or a language understood by the greatest number of them.

(2) Whenever necessary and practicable the services of an interpreter shall be used.

61. (1) Arrangements shall be made to ensure at all times that a qualified and approved medical practitioner is able to attend without delay in cases of urgency.

(2) In institutions not staffed by one or more full-time medical officers, a part-time medical officer or authorised staff of a health service shall visit regularly.

62. The appointment of staff in institutions or parts of institutions housing prisoners of the opposite sex is to be encouraged.

63. (1) Staff of the institutions shall not use force against prisoners except in self-defence or in cases of attempted escape or active or passive physical resistance to an order based on law or regulations. Staff who have recourse to force must use no more than is strictly necessary and must report the incident immediately to the director of the institution.

(2) Staff shall as appropriate be given special technical training to enable them to restrain aggressive prisoners.

(3) Except in special circumstances, staff performing duties which bring them into direct contact with prisoners should not be armed. Furthermore, staff should in no circumstances be provided with arms unless they have been fully trained in their use.

## PART IV

### TREATMENT OBJECTIVES AND RÉGIME

64. Imprisonment is by the deprivation of liberty a punishment in itself. The conditions of imprisonment and the prison and the prison régimes shall not, therefore, except as incidental to justifiable segregation or the maintenance of discipline, aggravate the suffering inherent in this.

65. Every effort shall be made to ensure that the régimes of the institutions are designed and managed so as:

(a) to ensure that the conditions of life are compatible with human dignity and acceptable standards in the community;

(b) to minimise the detrimental effects of imprisonment and the differences between prison life and life at liberty which tend to diminish the self-respect or sense of personal responsibility of prisoners;

(c) to sustain and strengthen those links with relatives and the outside community that will promote the best interests of prisoners and their families;

(d) to provide opportunities for prisoners to develop skills and aptitudes that will improve their prospects of successful resettlement after release.

66. To these ends all the remedial, educational, moral, spiritual and other resources that are appropriate should be made available and utilised in accordance with the individual treatment needs of prisoners. Thus the régimes should include:

(a) spiritual support and guidance and opportunities for relevant work, vocational guidance and training, education, physical education, the development of social skills, counselling, group and recreational activities;

(b) arrangements to ensure that these acitivities are organised, so far as possible, to increase contacts with and opportunities within the outside community so as to enhance the prospects for social resettlement after release;

(c) procedures for establishing and reviewing individual treatment and training programmes for prisoners after full consultations among the relevant staff and with individual prisoners who should be involved in these as far as practicable;

(d) communications systems and a management style that will encourage appropriate and positive relationships between staff and prisoners that will improve the prospects for effective and supportive régimes and treatment programmes.

67. (1) Since the fulfilment of these objectives requires individualisation of treatment and, for this purpose, a flexible system of allocation, prisoners should be placed in separate institutions or units where each can receive the appropriate treatment and training.

(2) The type, size, organisation and capacity of these institutions or units should be determined essentially by the nature of the treatment to be provided.

(3) It is necessary to ensure that prisoners are located with due regard to security and control but such measures should be the minimum compatible with safety and comprehend the special needs of the prisoner. Every effort should be made to place prisoners in institutions that are open in character or provide ample opportunities for contacts with the outside community. In the case of foreign nationals, links with people of their own nationality in the outside community are to be regarded as especially important.

68. As soon as possible after admission and after a study of the personality of each prisoner with a sentence of a suitable length, a programme of treatment in a suitable institution shall be prepared in the light of the knowledge obtained about individual needs, capacities and dispositions, especially proximity to relatives.

69. (1) Within the régimes, prisoners shall be given the opportunity to participate in activities of the institution likely to develop their sense of responsibility, self-reliance and to stimulate interest in their own treatment.

(2) Efforts should be made to develop methods of encouraging co-operation with and the participation of the prisoners in their treatment. To this end prisoners shall be encouraged to assume, within the limits specified in Rule 34, responsibilities in certain sectors of the institution's activity.

70. (1) The preparation of prisoners for release should begin as soon as possible after reception in a penal institution. Thus, the treatment of prisoners should emphasise not their exclusion from the community but their continuing part in it. Community agencies and social workers should, therefore, be enlisted wherever possible to assist the staff of the institution in the task of social rehabilitation of the prisoners particularly maintaining and improving the relationships with their families, with other persons and with the social agencies. Steps should be taken to safeguard, to the maximum extent compatible with the law and the sentence, the rights and other social benefits of prisoners.

(2) Treatment programmes should include provision for prison leave which should also be granted to the greatest extent possible on medical, educational, occupational, family and other social grounds.

(3) Foreign nationals should not be excluded from arrangements for prison leave solely on account of their nationality. Furthermore, every effort should be made to enable them to participate in régime activities together so as to alleviate their feelings of isolation.

## Work

71. (1) Prison work should be seen as a positive element in treatment, training and institutional management.

(2) Prisoners under sentence may be required to work, subject to their physical and mental fitness as determined by the medical officer.

(3) Sufficient work of a useful nature, or if appropriate other purposeful activities shall be provided to keep prisoners actively employed for a normal working day.

(4) So far as possible the work provided shall be such as will maintain or increase the prisoner's ability to earn a normal living after release.

(5) Vocational training in useful trades shall be provided for prisoners able to profit thereby and especially for young prisoners.

(6) Within the limits compatible with proper vocational selection and with the requirements of institutional administration and discipline, the prisoners shall be able to choose the type of employment in which they wish to participate.

72. (1) The organisation and methods of work in the institutions shall resemble as closely as possible those of similar work in the community so as to prepare prisoners for the conditions of normal occupational life. It should thus be relevant to contemporary working standards and techniques and organised to function within modern management systems and production processes.

(2) Although the pursuit of financial profit from industries in the institutions can be valuable in raising standards and improving the quality and relevance of training, the interests of the prisoners and of their treatment must not be subordinated to that purpose.

73. Work for prisoners shall be assured by the prison administration:

(a) either on its own premises, workshops and farms; or

(b) in co-operation with private contractors inside or outside the institution in which case the full normal wages for such shall be paid by the persons to whom the labour is supplied, account being taken of the output of the prisoners.

74. (1) Safety and health precautions for prisoners shall be similar to those that apply to workers outside.

(2) Provision shall be made to indemnify prisoners against industrial injury, including occupational disease, on terms not less favourable than those extended by law to workers outside.

75. (1) The maximum daily and weekly working hours of the prisoners shall be fixed in conformity with local rules or custom in regard to the employment of free workmen.

(2) Prisoners should have at least one rest-day a week and sufficient time for education and other activities required as part of their treatment and training for social resettlement.

76. (1) There shall be a system of equitable remuneration of the work of prisoners.

(2) Under the system prisoners shall be allowed to spend at least a part of their earnings on approved articles for their own use and to allocate a part of their earnings to their family or for other approved purposes.

(3) The system may also provide that a part of the earnings be set aside by the administration so as to constitute a savings fund to be handed over to the prisoner on release.

## Education

77. A comprehensive education programme shall be arranged in every institution to provide opportunities for all prisoners to pursue at least some of their individual needs and aspirations. Such programmes should have as their objectives the improvement of the prospects for successful social resettlement, the morale and attitudes of prisoners and their self-respect.

78. Education should be regarded as a régime activity that attracts the same status and basic remuneration within the régime as work, provided that it takes place in normal working hours and is part of an authorised individual treatment programme.

79. Special attention should be given by prison administrations to the education of young prisoners, those of foreign origins or with particular cultural or ethnic needs.

80. Specific programmes of remedial education should be arranged for prisoners with special problems such as illiteracy or innumeracy.

81. So far as practicable, the education of prisoners shall:

(a) be integrated with the educational system of the country so that after their release they may continue their education without difficulty.

(b) take place in outside educational insititutions.

82. Every institution shall have a library for the use of all categories of prisoners, adequately stocked with a wide range of both recreational and instructional books, and prisoners shall be encouraged to make full use of it. Wherever possible the prison library should be organised in co-operation with community library services.

## Physical education, exercise, sport and recreation

83. The prison régimes shall recognise the importance to physical and

mental health of properly organised activities to ensure physical fitness, adequate exercise and recreational opportunities.

84. Thus a properly organised programme of physical education, sport and other recreational activity should be arranged within the framework and objectives of the treatment and training régime. To this end space, installations and equipment should be provided.

85. Prison administrations should ensure that prisoners who participate in these programmes are physically fit to do so. Special arrangements should be made, under medical direction, for remedial physical education and therapy for those prisoners who need it.

86. Every prisoner who is not employed in outdoor work, or located in an open institution, shall be allowed, if the weather permits, at least one hour of walking or suitable exercise in the open air daily, as far as possible, sheltered from inclement weather.

**Pre-release preparation**

87. All prisoners should have the benefit of arrangements designed to assist them in returning to society, family life and employment after release. Procedures and special courses should be devised to this end.

88. In the case of those prisoners with longer sentences, steps should be taken to ensure a gradual return to life in society. This aim may be achieved, in particular, by a pre-release régime organised in the same institution or in another appropriate institution, or by conditional release under some kind of supervision combined with effective social support.

89. (1) Prison administration should work closely with the social services and agencies that assist released prisoners to reestablish themselves in society, in particular with regard to family life and employment.

(2) Steps must be taken to ensure that on release prisoners are provided, as necessary, with appropriate documents and identification papers and assisted in finding suitable homes and work to go to. They should also be provided with immediate means of subsistence, be suitably and adequately clothed having regard to the climate and season, and have sufficient means to reach their destination.

(3) The approved representatives of the social agencies or services should be afforded all necessary access to the institution and to prisoners with a view to making a full contribution to the preparation for release and after-care programme of the prisoner.

## PART V

### ADDITIONAL RULES FOR SPECIAL CATEGORIES

90. Prison administration should be guided by the provisions of the rules as a whole so far as they can appropriately and in practice be applied for

the benefit of those special categories of prisoners for which additional rules are provided hereafter.

**Untried prisoners**

91. Without prejudice to legal rules for the protection of individual liberty or prescribing the procedure to be observed in respect of untried prisoners, these prisoners, who are presumed to be innocent until they are found guilty, shall be afforded the benefits that may derive from Rule 90 and treated without restrictions other than those necessary for the penal procedure and the security of the institution.

92. (1) Untried prisoners should be allowed to inform their families of their detention immediately and given all reasonable facilities for communication with family and friends and persons with whom it is in their legitimate interest to enter into contact.

(2) They shall also be allowed to receive visits from them under humane conditions subject only to such restrictions and supervision as are necessary in the interests of the administration of justice and of the security and good order of the institution.

(3) If an untried prisoner does not wish to inform any of these persons, the prison administration should not do so on its own initiative unless there are good overriding reasons as, for instance, the age, state of mind or any other incapacity of the prisoner.

93. Untried prisoners shall be entitled, as soon as imprisoned, to choose a legal representative, or shall be allowed to apply for free legal aid where such aid is available and to receive visits from that legal adviser with a view to their defence and to prepare and hand to the legal adviser, and to receive, confidential instructions. On request they shall be given the free assistance of an interpreter for all essential contacts with the administration and for their defence. Interviews between prisoners and their legal advisers may be within sight but not within hearing, either direct or indirect, of the police or institution staff. The allocation of untried prisoners shall be in comformity with the provisions of Rule 11, paragraph 3.

94. Except where there are circumstances that make it undesirable, untried prisoners shall be given the opportunity of having separate rooms.

95. (1) Untried prisoners shall be given the opportunity of wearing their own clothing if it is clean and suitable.

(2) Prisoners who do not avail themselves of this opportunity, shall be supplied with suitable dress.

(3) If they have no suitable clothing of their own, untried prisoners shall be provided with civilian clothing in good condition in which to appear in court or on authorised outings.

96. Untried prisoners shall, whenever possible, be offered the opportunity to work but shall not be required to work. Those who choose to work shall be paid as other prisoners. If educational or trade training is

available, untried prisoners shall be encouraged to avail themselves of these opportunities.

97. Untried prisoners shall be allowed to procure at their own expense or at the expense of a third party such books, newspapers, writing materials and other means of occupation as are compatible with the interests of the administration of justice and the security and good order of the institution.

98. Untried prisoners shall be given the opportunity of being visited and treated by their own doctor or dentist if there is reasonable ground for the application. Reasons should be given if the application is refused. Such costs as are incurred shall not be the responsibility of the prison administration.

## Civil prisoners

99. In countries where the law permits imprisonment by order of a court under any non-criminal process, persons so imprisoned shall not be subjected to any greater restriction or severity than is necessary to ensure safe custody and good order. Their treatment shall not be less favourable than that of untried prisoners, with the reservation, however, that they may be required to work.

## Insane and mentally abnormal prisoners

100. (1) Persons who are found to be insane should not be detained in prisons and arrangements shall be made to remove them to appropriate establishments for the mentally ill as soon as possible.

(2) Specialised institutions or sections under medical management should be available for the observation and treatment of prisoners suffering gravely from other mental disease or abnormality.

(3) The medical or psychiatric service of the penal institutions shall provide for the psychiatric treatment of all prisoners who are in need of such treatment.

(4) Action should be taken, by arrangement with the appropriate community agencies, to ensure where necessary the continuation of psychiatric treatment after release and the provision of social psychiatric after-care.

# INDEX